Inside the Common Core Classroom

Practical ELA Strategies for Grades 3–5

Brenda J. Overturf

PEARSON

Boston • Columbus • Indianapolis • New York • San Francisco • Upper Saddle River
Amsterdam • Cape Town • Dubai • London • Madrid • Milan • Munich • Paris • Montréal • Toronto
Delhi • Mexico City • São Paulo • Sydney • Hong Kong • Seoul • Singapore • Taipei • Tokyo

Vice President and Editorial Director: Jeffery Johnston
Acquisitions Editor: Kathryn Boice
Editorial Assistant: Carolyn Schweitzer
Executive Field Marketing Manager: Krista Clark
Senior Product Marketing Manger: Christopher Barry
Program Manager: Karen Mason
Project Manager: Barbara Strickland
Editorial Production Service: Electronic Publishing Services Inc., NYC
Manufacturing Buyer: Linda Sager
Electronic Composition: Jouve
Project Coordination & Interior Design: Electronic Publishing Services Inc., NYC
Photo Researcher: Jorgensen Fernandez
Cover Designer: Central Covers

Credits and acknowledgments borrowed from other sources and reproduced, with permission, in this textbook appear on page 199 or on the appropriate page within text.

Cover Image Credit: Monkey Business Images/Shutterstock

Many of the designations by manufacturers and sellers to distinguish their products are claimed as trademarks. Where those designations appear in this book, and the publisher was aware of a trademark claim, the designations have been printed in initial caps or all caps.

Note: Every effort has been made to provide accurate and current Internet information in this book. However, the Internet and information on it are constantly changing, so it is inevitable that some of the Internet addresses listed in this textbook will change.

Library of Congress Cataloging-in-Publication Data

Overturf, Brenda J.
  Inside the common core classroom: practical ELA strategies for grades 3-5 / Brenda J. Overturf.
      pages cm
  Includes bibliographical references and index.
  ISBN 978-0-13-336297-8
  1. Language arts (Elementary)—United States.   2. Language arts (Elementary)—Standards—United
      States.   3. Language arts—Correlation with content subjects—United States.   I. Title.
LB1576.M29 2013
372.6'044—dc23
                                                                          2013045955

10 9 8 7 6 5 4 3 2 1

ISBN 10:   0-13-336297-3
ISBN 13: 978-0-13-336297-8

Dedication

- *To all teachers who are working together to implement the ELA Standards*

Contents

Preface

WELCOME TO THE AGE OF THE COMMON CORE! Thank you for joining us in our quest to teach students to meet the Common Core English Language Arts (ELA) Standards.

This volume, *Inside the Common Core Classroom: Practical ELA Strategies for Grades 3–5*, is part of Pearson's *College and Career Readiness Series*. The books in this series have been written for in-service teachers to support their implementation of the Common Core State Standards for English language arts in K–12 classrooms. The four volumes in the series address the standards in grades K–2, 3–5, 6–8, and 9–12, respectively.

The purpose of the series is to help teachers create connections between the Common Core and their school curriculums. Each book provides in-depth information about the standards at a particular grade-level band and offers examples of a variety of teaching ideas to support students' meeting the expectations of the ELA Standards.

About This Book

The Common Core State Standards have ushered in a new era in education. For the first time, schools across the nation are working to achieve the same goals. However, as you will see in this book, a common set of standards does not mean one size fits all. The English Language Arts Standards are open-ended, simply listing a set of skills that students should be able to do. It is up to educators to implement the Standards in ways that respect the unique literacy needs of students.

From the beginning of third grade to the end of fifth grade, students develop from primary children to early adolescents. They also move from learning to read to being readers who are able to comprehend complex and challenging text independently. Many creative, thoughtful, and dedicated teachers are working hard to plan instruction and assessment so students at this age meet the ELA Standards. Is it difficult sometimes? Of course! But it is also exciting to see kids connect new ideas, find answers by doing research, write about and discuss their opinions using academic vocabulary, and develop and share creative presentations—even though they are often still learning to read different types of texts.

This volume was written with a focus on the particular needs of students in grades 3–5. Authentic voices of teachers and kids provide insight on ways to implement standards-based literacy instruction so it makes sense for students in these grades. You will find an abundance of information about the Standards themselves, exciting ideas for classroom practice, and glimpses into real classrooms where the Standards are being successfully implemented with a variety of student populations. Teachers of grades 3–5 who are working with the Standards have also shared some realizations as they embarked upon this journey.

Chapter 1 considers typical literacy development of students in these grades and provides a preview of the expectations of the Standards for these students. There is a new way of thinking about literacy education that accompanies the Standards. This chapter describes the instructional shifts that teachers and students must make to meet the English Language Arts Standards.

Chapter 2 explores how the Standards align with what we know about comprehension. Students in grades 3–5 are at a critical age for comprehension development. As you will see, classroom teachers have found ways to blend new expectations for deep comprehension of more complex texts with research-based comprehension practices. Because deep comprehension requires students to read, write, discuss, and think about text, there are references to comprehension also woven within other chapters.

Vocabulary expectations are the focus of Chapter 3. An emphasis on academic vocabulary is one of the instructional shifts, and this chapter explains the references to vocabulary peppered throughout the Standards. A staircase of text complexity is another instructional shift. Chapter 4 examines the concept of text complexity, the types of texts suggested, and the practice of close reading with students in grades 3–5.

There are many existing resources about developing expressive writers at the elementary level. Chapter 5 describes how writing nurtures comprehension. It then hones in on academic writing and helping students learn to summarize, support opinions, and inform an audience. Suggestions for using technology for research and publication round out this chapter.

One of the exciting ideas in the ELA Standards is the encouragement of instructional talk in the classroom. Chapter 6 is about speaking and listening, from students contributing to literature discussions to preparing and participating in debates to creating and sharing multimedia presentations.

Chapter 7 describes curriculum implications when planning to implement the Standards. There are many decisions to be made when implementing the ELA Standards. Teachers will need to work together to make these decisions and learn from each other. A variety of resources are included in this chapter.

Finally, students learn best when they can connect ideas to build knowledge. Chapter 8 demonstrates how to integrate strategies in a standards-based thematic unit about mythology that incorporates science and social studies concepts as well as Common Core expectations in literature, informational text, foundational skills, writing, speaking and listening, and language.

Acknowledgments

NO AUTHOR PRODUCES A BOOK WITHOUT THE EXTENSIVE help of others. I am grateful to my colleagues in this series: Donna Ogle, Lesley Mandel Morrow, Erin Kramer, Amy Monaco, Maureen McLaughlin, and Katherine McKnight. I would also like to thank Barbara Strickland, Kathryn Boice, and Aurora Martínez at Pearson Education, as well as Carrie Fox at Electronic Publishing Services for making this book a reality.

Writing would be impossible without the loving support of friends and family, especially Jim, Whitney, and Drew.

Special thanks go to the following excellent teachers of the third, fourth, and fifth grades for generously sharing their classroom insights and expertise as they implement the CCSS:

Melissa Durham
Taylor Haydock
Melissa Logsdon
Leslie Montgomery
Margot Holmes Smith
Kelly Sraj Toms
Laura Szabo
Lonydea Todd
Cassaundra Watkins

Finally, I would like to thank the reviewers for this first edition: Janine A. Jackson of Lafayette Elementary School (Washington, DC) and Ryan Murray of Greenbrier Elementary (Illinois).

Introduction

Donna Ogle

THE COMMON CORE STATE STANDARDS (CCSS) provide a challenging set of expectations that public schools must meet to ensure that all students can be successful in meeting the literacy demands of the twenty-first century. The CCSS also make clear that developing literacy is a shared responsibility and challenge educators to think and work together to meet these expectations. As part of the extended reach of the CCSS, the English Language Arts (ELA) standards include literacy in science, social studies, and technical subjects as integral to this process. These standards underscore the reality that skills in reading, writing, and oral language are needed across the content areas. The ELA CCSS invite teachers to work together within and across grade levels and content areas to ensure that students will meet these expectations.

Across the United States, the national, state, and local organizations that have taken this challenge seriously are in the process of analyzing current curricula and adjusting the foci of instruction and expected student outcomes according to these new needs and demands. The two national assessment consortia—the Partnership for Assessment of Readiness for College and Career (PARCC, n.d.) and Smarter Balanced (n.d.)—are in the process of designing new assessment systems, which will be administered for the first time during the 2014–2015 school year. These consortia have suggested how school curricula should be organized to encompass the broad-reaching outcomes elaborated in the CCSS. Taking the CCSS seriously means making some significant adjustments in how our schools have focused on literacy and the kinds of literacy-related opportunities they provide. Our students deserve this support. They want to be successful both within and beyond schooling, and we want them to have this success.

Defining the Need for the Change

THE CCSS DESCRIBE IN GRADE-BY-GRADE DETAIL THE WIDE range of competencies that literacy entails and that teachers need to develop in their students. The starting point for this effort is central to the standards' importance: What is required of students to be college and career ready?

Several research reports over the last decade have alerted interested educators to the decline in difficulty of many school texts and to the challenge faced by students with low reading proficiency when they take college-level tests. In fact, Appendix A of the CCSS cites a 2006 ACT report, *Reading Between the Lines,* to illustrate this two-part problem (NGA & CCSSO, 2010b, Appendix A, p. 2). Recognizing this problem led the developers of the CCSS to collect texts being used by students in freshmen-level college/university courses and by individuals entering the workforce after high school. These texts were compared with high school texts and the types and difficulty levels of assigned student work.

In this analysis, the CCSS developers identified a significant gap between the work required of upper-level high school students and the expectations for success in college and career. (See Appendix A of the CCSS for elaboration on this issue [NGA & CCSSO, 2010b].) The CCSS were then developed with this end point in mind: to determine the level of language arts development needed at each grade level for students to be prepared for these greater literacy demands and thus ready for college and career.

After the CCSS had been written, they were reviewed by college faculty who teach freshman- and sophomore-level courses, who gave the standards high marks. Interestingly, in addition to the need for students to read informational texts critically and to write effective analytical essays (not personal reflection pieces), these faculty rated the oral communication skills identified in the CCSS as particularly important.

The fact that perspectives from higher education and the workforce were included in developing the CCSS is important. The standards make this connection very clear: Students need to be college and career ready.

The CCSS are significant in another way, too. Since the first round of standards was developed in the late 1990s, individual states have crafted their own standards and measured achievement with their own state-specific assessments. The only comparison of achievement across states has been made by the National Assessment of Educational Progress (NAEP), and these evaluations have regularly revealed huge state-by-state differences in literacy achievement. Now, with the CCSS, we have, for the first time, a set of standards that has been adopted by most states across the country.

This high level of adoption will help all educators evaluate their success and feel confident that their students are receiving a high-quality education that will serve them beyond public school. Both the standards and the assessments being developed can help all educators engage in a shared conversation and commitment to excellence. Rather than relying on the current patchwork of state standards, the CCSS bring together a common set of standards and permit the development of more common assessments.

Expectations for Literacy Achievement

AS THE UNITED STATES MOVES FORWARD WITH the new standards, all educators need to be involved and take seriously new expectations for the future. The CCSS raise the bar for student literacy achievement in several ways:

- Reading comprehension is at the heart of the new standards. To be college and career ready, students must understand challenging texts and attend to authors' ideas and ways of presenting information. In the CCSS Reading standards, three clusters identify these foci: Key Ideas and Details, Craft and Structure, and Integration of Knowledge and Ideas. For both literature and informational texts, readers are expected to engage in careful reading of the ideas presented, to recall main ideas and details, to recognize the organization of information and author's craft, and to synthesize and critically respond to what they have read.

- This expectation for greater understanding is heightened by the expectation that students will read texts at a more accelerated level of difficulty than currently designated for grade levels by readability formulas and reading anthologies. For twelfth-grade texts, the expected level will be about 200 Lexile points higher than the current level.

- The CCSS also devote greater attention to reading informational text, so it receives equal coverage as reading fictional literature. Most elementary programs and secondary language arts courses have been developed primarily around fictional/narrative literature. The CCSS create a broader framework for literacy development that includes the content areas, especially social studies, science, and technical subjects. With two sets of standards for reading—one for literature and one for informational text—this shift in foci to informational texts and to the importance of using reading to build knowledge is clear. At the secondary level, the CCSS differentiate expectations for literacy development in social studies, science, and technical subjects. The curriculum design from PARCC (n.d.), which establishes four basic modules, includes a balance of informational and literary texts across the modules.

- The CCSS emphasize not only the understanding of individual texts but also the importance of reading across texts to look for different authors' purposes and the evidence authors provide in support of their ideas. Students who read only one text on a topic or theme have little opportunity to learn about how authors can vary in terms of purpose and presentation of ideas. The CCSS clearly advocate that students should read several texts on the same topic or theme. In addition, completing quarterly research projects provides individuals with opportunities to search for information across multiple texts and media sources and to use that information critically in their reporting.

- The shift in how information is communicated in the twenty-first century is also recognized in the CCSS. We live in a visual society: All sorts of images try to inform us and persuade us. The ability to use visual and graphic information thoughtfully is expected of students. In fact, visual images can be powerful motivators to engage students in thoughtful analyses of how ideas are communicated to us and influence us. Across the content areas, readers are also expected to use electronic sources in building their knowledge in presenting information and completing research projects.

- There is also a shift in focus in the writing standards from writing personal narratives to writing expository and argumentative texts. Students need to be able to use evidence to support their arguments, as well as to recognize possible alternative points of view. In addition, writing is now being used as a way of measuring students' reading comprehension. Students need to think about the meanings of the texts they read, how authors present and support ideas, and what counter-arguments and evidence are provided.

- Although speaking and listening have always been part of the language arts, the CCSS recognize the importance of these communication tools. This priority is evident in the Speaking and Listening Standards and also embedded in the expectations that students discuss what they read at every grade level and learn to report to classmates what they learn from individual research projects. The preliminary assessment design from PARCC (n.d.) includes a school-based assessment of oral skills midway through the year. Even though these skills are difficult to measure using large-scale assessments, they are important. The value of speaking and listening skills has been well established by the university and workplace communities.

- The CCSS also include expectations for vocabulary. Specifically, students should learn and use standard forms of English and appropriate general academic and domain-specific vocabulary in both writing and oral language. Vocabulary and word-learning strategies need to be developed concurrently with the knowledge and content literacy standards, especially as related to the domain-specific terms students need to know to understand the content of science, social studies, and technical subjects.

Implementing the CCSS

IMPLEMENTING THE CCSS REPRESENTS A SIGNIFICANT CHALLENGE TO teachers and schools. To address the difficulty of this task, many states have put together teams to guide their thinking about what is already being done and what needs to be adjusted in the current curriculum to meet expectations for literacy in the twenty-first century. Other educational organizations have also made significant efforts to help in the development of curriculum and instructional frameworks—for example, the Lucas Foundation, Annenberg Foundation, Alliance for Effective Education, AchieveNY, Gates Foundation, International Reading Association, and National Council of Teachers of English.

Publishers have responded, as well, by reorienting materials to reflect the broader expectation for responding to texts and by including more academic writing and attention to content. An interesting publisher's initiative has brought together teacher teams from school districts and used their materials to reorganize the content and rewrite the questions in the published programs to align more closely with the CCSS.

The major goal of all of these efforts is to better prepare students for college and careers. Doing so requires addressing the range of texts students read, the depth of thinking they do, and the styles of writing they perform. Given these new and challenging expectations, professionals across the educational system need to collaborate in helping students from preschool through grade 12 develop the competencies, commitment, and confidence needed for life beyond high school.

Rethinking the Complexity of the Texts Students Read

The issue of text complexity is central to the CCSS and one that deserves study by teachers and school teams. Students need to engage in more challenging texts at each grade level, at least beyond the primary grades, and they need to read more informational texts, which are rich in content.

The authors of the CCSS have tried to move away from a single, numerically derived formula for determining the appropriate reading levels of texts of all kinds. According to the CCSS, three criteria should be considered when determining the level of any text:

1. **Qualitative evaluation of the text:** levels of meaning, structure, language conventionality and clarity, and knowledge demands

2. **Quantitative evaluation of the text:** readability measures and other scores of text complexity

3. **Matching the reader to the text and the task:** reader variables (e.g., motivation, knowledge, and experiences) and task variables (e.g., the purpose and complexity of the task assigned and the questions posed) (NGA & CCSSO, 2010b, p. 4).

Appendix B of the CCSS (NGA & CCSSO, 2010c) provides lists of illustrative books that have been "leveled." The purpose of these lists is not to imply that these books should be used in the schools, but rather to identify books that are familiar to the educational community. However, teachers who want simply to select books from these lists need to remember the third criterion: matching the reader to the text and the task.

Given the variety of interests, experiences, and needs of students across the United States, many teachers will want to use contemporary, high-interest materials to motivate students to think and reflect deeply about important issues. Moreover, instead of permitting students to read only books at their designated levels (based on Lexiles or Fountas & Pinnell scores), teachers will ask students in the intermediate grades and higher to read several books or articles on the same topic, beginning with a comfortable-level book/article and then using the knowledge they have developed to read more difficult texts on the same topic.

Using this strategy is certainly one way to help students increase their reading power. The CCSS guidelines also provide models of how teachers can engage groups of students in close readings of anchor texts or targeted short texts. When teachers regularly model an analytical and questioning approach to reading, students will likely follow the same approach. It is also important that students engage with a large quantity of texts, finding their own favorite authors and experiencing the joy of being real readers.

Organizing Instruction into Content-Rich Units

The range and complexity of literacy standards included in the CCSS has prompted many organizations (e.g., PARCC and Smarter Balanced), as well as school districts and state education departments (e.g., Wisconsin Department of Public Instruction), to reorganize their literacy priorities to align with the CCSS by designing units with content-related themes and topics. Using this approach, instruction in literacy is combined with instruction in social studies and science. Many school districts have asked teams of teachers to develop one unit as a starting point with plans to expand this effort over time.

A clear message from the developers of the CCSS is that students need to be engaged in learning content in social studies, science, and technical subjects at a deeper level than is now often the case. In the CCSS guidelines, the final section about the elementary standards is entitled "Staying on Topic Within a Grade and Across Grades: How to Build Knowledge Systematically in English Language Arts K–5" (NGA & CCSSO, 2010a, p. 33). Included in this section is a matrix illustrating how students should encounter the same topic (in this example, the human body) at increasingly deeper levels across all of the grades. This shift in combining attention to content knowledge with literacy development is one of the hallmarks of the CCSS.

While combining these purposes makes good sense, it means that schools must expand efforts at integrating reading and writing with content area instruction. Classroom and school libraries should contain ample amounts of informational books and magazines at a variety of levels of complexity so that all students have access to the materials needed to develop deep knowledge. As the CCSS authors explain in the section "Staying on Topic Within a Grade and Across Grades":

> Building knowledge systematically in English language arts is like giving children various pieces of a puzzle in each grade that, over time, will form one big picture. At a curricular or instructional level, texts—within and across grade levels—need to be selected around topics or themes that systematically develop the knowledge base of students. Within a grade level, there should be an adequate number of titles on a single topic that would allow children to study that topic for a sustained period. The knowledge children have learned about particular topics in early grade levels should then be expanded and developed in subsequent grade levels to ensure an increasingly deeper understanding of these topics. Children in the upper elementary grades will generally be expected to read these texts independently and reflect on them in writing. However, children in the early grades (particularly K–2) should participate in rich, structured conversations with an adult in response to the written texts that are read aloud, orally comparing and contrasting as well as analyzing and synthesizing, in the manner called for by the *Standards*. (NGA & CCSSO, 2010a, p.33)

At the secondary level, there is an even greater expectation for students to develop the strategies necessary for reading the varied texts and materials that contain the key content of disciplinary study. Reading primary source documents in history and science is a central part of students' literacy engagement. Also, the texts used in math and science require students to analyze a variety of visual displays, including equations, tables, diagrams, and graphs. As noted in the Carnegie Report *Writing to Read* (Graham & Hebert, 2010), for students to comprehend and produce these types of texts, they must be immersed in the language and thinking processes of these disciplines and they must be supported by an expert guide: their teacher.

Given the expectation for students to develop the competence needed to comprehend the wide variety of texts that is required for success in and beyond schooling, it is clear that the responsibility for literacy development cannot reside solely with English language arts teachers. Meeting this expectation requires both the development of foundational knowledge that makes deep learning possible and the skills needed to read a wide variety of text types and formats across the disciplines. The CCSS challenge all content area teachers to accept their part in developing the literacy skills, dispositions, discipline-specific discourse, and academic vocabulary requisite for students to become independent learners. The more often that elementary and secondary reading/literacy coaches team up with their content area colleagues, the more likely that CCSS goals will be met by providing interesting and positive instructional experiences for students.

more time, more knowledge

The thematic-unit framework provides students with the opportunity to read several texts on the same theme or topic and build their background knowledge of a specific topic. Spending more time on a specific topic also helps students to deepen their knowledge of the content and become familiar with the academic and domain-specific vocabulary central to that learning. In addition, by reading across several texts, students can develop their understanding of the ways different authors select materials to include in particular texts and then organize that information, as well as the value of reading deeply to build clear understanding of complex ideas.

Having these commitments to reading makes students' written and oral communications much stronger. Students know what they are explaining and have options to represent their ideas, including visual, graphic, and oral formats. This ability to develop one's own understanding based on research and then to present one's ideas is woven into the four research projects students are expected to do each year. In addition, the CCSS directive to engage in a deeper study of topics encourages teachers to vary the kinds of learning experiences they provide for their students—differentiating texts/materials, activities, products, and assessments (Tomlinson's framework).

Engaging in Schoolwide Collaboration for Change

The challenges and cross-content literacy expectations of the CCSS can be achieved within a long-range timeframe and with the understanding that they will develop over the course of students' schooling. Realizing these requisites for achievement can unite teachers. The CCSS underscore the importance of involving teams of educators representing all grade levels, special services (e.g., English language learning, special education, library and media), and content areas in studying the CCSS, analyzing their implications, and designing ways to implement them over time.

Discussing the CCSS across grade levels is a good way to start. Providing visual displays that trace the same standard across different grades will help teachers to understand the structure and rationale that underlie the CCSS. An example follows using Standard 2 of the elementary Anchor Standards for Reading, which appears in the cluster Key Ideas and Details:

Standard 2: Determine central ideas or themes of a text and analyze their development; summarize the key supporting details and ideas.

Table I.1 shows the grade-level expectations for Standard 2 for reading both literature and informational text for kindergarten through fifth grade, allowing examination of the expectations across grades.

TABLE I.1 ● *Anchor Standards for Reading, Key Ideas and Details, Standard 2:* K–Grade 5

Kindergarten	Grade 1	Grade 2
Literature	**Literature**	**Literature**
2. With prompting and support, retell familiar stories, including key details	2. Retell stories, including key details, and demonstrate understanding of their central message or lesson	2. Recount stories, including fables and folktales from diverse cultures, and determine their central message, lesson, or moral.
Informational Text	**Informational Text**	**Informational Text**
2. With prompting and support, identify the main topic and retell key details of a text.	2. Identify the main topic and retell key details of a text.	2. Identify the main topic of a multiparagraph text as well as the focus of specific paragraphs within the text.
Grade 3	**Grade 4**	**Grade 5**
Literature	**Literature**	**Literature**
2. Recount stories, including fables, folktales, and myths from diverse cultures; determine the central message, lesson, or moral and explain how it is conveyed through key details in the text	2. Determine a theme of a story, drama, or poem from details in the text; summarize the text.	2. Determine a theme of a story, drama, or poem from details in the text, including how characters in a story or drama respond to challenges or how the speaker in a poem reflects upon a topic; summarize the text.
Informational Text	**Informational Text**	**Informational Text**
2. Determine the main idea of a text; recount the key details and explain how they support the main idea.	2. Determine the main idea of a text and explain how it is supported by key details; summarize the text.	2. Determine two or more main ideas of a text and explain how they are supported by key details; summarize the text.

Source: NGA & CCSSO (2010).

Clearly, within Standard 2, there is a gradual progression of difficulty from kindergarten through fifth grade. At each grade level, there is the same basic expectation—that students learn to retell stories and identify main ideas—but the level of the expectation varies. In kindergarten, the teacher is clearly involved with the students, providing prompting and support. By first grade, students are expected to retell independently, and by second grade, they are expected to do so for a wider range of materials. By fifth grade, students are expected to apply this skill with drama, and in reading informational text, they are expected to identify two main ideas.

While the spiraling nature of these expectations may seem somewhat arbitrary, looking across grade levels and text types should indicate the sense of shared effort that is needed among teachers. In addition, it should provide a starting point for conversations about what students are able to do and what they need to learn to ensure ongoing development in reading comprehension. No one grade level of teachers is responsible for students' mastery of any standard, but across the grades, teachers should guide students in using reading skills in increasingly challenging and varied materials. Teachers should think together to find ways to help students apply their abilities to retell stories and identify main ideas/supporting details in the texts they read each year.

Just as it is important for teams of teachers to look at the standards' expectations for skill development across the grades, it is important for them to read across the areas within the CCSS. In contrast to the orientation in some districts and schools, in which teaching focuses on one standard at a time, the areas within the CCSS are interrelated and build on each other. Not only are standards provided for both literature and informational text, but in addition, many key expectations are scattered across the reading, writing, and language standards. For example, a cluster called Integration of Knowledge and Ideas is included in the standards for Reading Literature, Reading Informational Text, Writing, and Speaking and Listening. The cluster Integration of Knowledge and Ideas appears in the two groups of Reading standards. However, the research standards are an important place where integration occurs and where students are held accountable for using this ability.

The Speaking and Listening Standards address the importance of students creating visual and media displays—both skills that are often overlooked in contemporary literacy instruction in the elementary grades. In the past, visual and media literacy seem to have been the purview of secondary instruction, but in the CCSS, they are introduced in the early elementary grades. Highlighting this aspect of integration will likely prompt some important reflection among teachers: Just how are students encouraged to interpret visuals and to use media displays to augment their presentations?

Some important instructional areas that teachers are accustomed to seeing as parts of reading development are embedded elsewhere in the CCSS. Vocabulary, for example, does not have a separate set of standards, as do reading literature and writing, yet developing vocabulary skills is very important and is addressed in several sections of the CCSS. Teacher teams might begin by studying the Language Standards section, Vocabulary Acquisition and Use, with its focus on learning academic and domain-specific vocabulary, and then locate other places in the standards where vocabulary skills are addressed.

In addition, teacher teams need to consider carefully the expectation to include science, social studies, and technical subjects that is part of their responsibility in implementing these new more content-focused standards. Some states, such as Wisconsin, have developed their own extensions of the CCSS (Wisconsin Department of Public Instruction, n.d.), and these models can provide valuable resources as school teams examine their curriculum options and make decisions about how to move forward.

Figure I.1 provides several illustrations of how the standards in various sections and clusters are connected. In each example, the Anchor Standard is provided first, followed by the grade-level expectations for one or more grades (as noted in parentheses at the end of each description).

Assessment in the CCSS

IN RECOGNIZING THE DEPTH OF THE CCSS and the high level of expectations for students' literacy development, teachers need to monitor the pace of their instruction carefully, challenging students on a regular basis but not overwhelming them. Similarly, assessment must be ongoing without overwhelming instruction.

Assessment should be formative, thus helping teachers modify their instruction. The best formative assessment is rooted in instruction and depends on teachers being adept at gathering information from students' classroom engagement and work. Throughout this series of books,

---

FIGURE I.1 ● Examples of Connections Across the CCSS

Anchor Standards for Reading

Integration of Knowledge and Ideas

Standard 7: Integrate and evaluate content presented in diverse media and formats, including visually and quantitatively, as well as in words.

- *Literature:* Analyze how visual and multimedia elements contribute to the meaning, tone, or beauty of a text (e.g., graphic novel, multimedia presentation of fiction, folktale, myth, poem) (grade 5).
- *Informational Text:* Explain how specific images (e.g., a diagram showing how a machine works) contribute to and clarify a text (grade 2).

Anchor Standards for Writing

Research to Build and Present Knowledge

Standard 8: Gather relevant information from multiple print and digital sources, assess the credibility and accuracy of each source, and integrate the information while avoiding plagiarism.

Text Types and Purposes

Standard 2: Write informative/explanatory texts to examine a topic and convey ideas and information clearly and accurately through the effective selection, organization, and analysis of content.

a. Introduce a topic clearly, provide a general observation and focus, and group related information logically; include formatting (e.g., headings), illustrations, and multimedia when useful to aiding comprehension (grade 5).

Anchor Standards for Speaking and Listening

Presentation of Knowledge and Ideas

Standard 5: Make strategic use of digital media and visual displays of data to express information and enhance understanding of presentations.

- Create audio recordings of stories or poems; add drawings or other visual displays to stories or recounts of experiences when appropriate to clarify ideas, thoughts, and feelings (grade 2).

Source: NGA & CCSSO (2010).

the authors provide examples of ways to assess students' readiness and learning of key content and strategies. Assessment is an area in which teacher/administrative discussions and decisions are critically important.

In addition, the requirements of the CCSS include large-scale comparative assessments to ensure that schools across the country have the same expectations of students. These assessments involve students in responding to a variety of texts and in formulating some of their responses in writing. In fact, one of the most important changes in assessment prompted by the CCSS is the use of students' written responses to measure their reading comprehension. Achieving this deeper look at students' comprehension is complicated by several pragmatic issues, such as the time and cost involved in scoring students' writing. Regardless, this approach is certainly a major part of the assessment systems being designed. Assessment systems for research (using technology) and speaking and listening are also still being developed, so these are other areas in which teachers and informal classroom assessments will continue to be important.

Using These Books to Enhance Study of the CCSS

THIS SERIES OF TEACHER RESOURCE BOOKS WAS CREATED in response to the invitation issued by the CCSS for literacy educators to refocus the instruction they provide to help prepare students for college and career. These books are intended to support teachers, administrators, and teacher teams as they look across grade levels while designing CCSS-responsive instruction.

As noted earlier, the CCSS expect teachers to think broadly about the impact of their instruction and the foundation they lay for students' future literacy development. For many teachers, meeting this expectation will be a challenge, and these books can provide guidance in several areas: adjusting instruction, adding reading and writing of informational text, creating content-rich instructional units, and assessing students in different ways.

In writing the four books in this series, the authors have been conscious of the importance of helping teachers build across grade levels. These books can be used together to support a rich discussion and analysis. When possible, the authors have included the same major chapters on comprehension, writing, vocabulary, language, and other areas of the CCSS. Teachers at different grade levels can read about the particular expectations for their levels and consider appropriate examples and instructional suggestions. Then, in discussions with teachers of other grade levels, they can learn from others and think through how to create the most supportive instructional sequence and organization using themes and content units. The books are very practical and include activities and frameworks that teachers can use to help students become competent in using literacy for pleasure and for learning.

These books are not intended to be used alone; rather, teachers should read them while studying the CCSS. To begin, all teachers should download the CCSS and appendices so they are accessible and can be referred to regularly (see URLs for these materials in the References). In addition, the standards and related tools are available on several useful apps from organizations such as Mastery Connect and Learning Unlimited (again, see the References). It is also helpful to bookmark the websites for PARCC (n.d.) and Smarter Balanced (n.d.) and then check with them periodically. In fact, so many resource sites are coming online that it is worth checking from time to time to see what might be worth reviewing. School districts, educational organizations, and state departments of education are developing instructional units and often make them available (or at least provide some of the structural components).

Much within the CCSS themselves also deserves careful analysis, study, and discussion among teachers of all grades. These efforts should lead to an identification of what is already in the curriculum and where instruction is currently aligned versus misaligned with the CCSS. Teachers must bear in mind that with the central focus on understanding texts, assessments need to be refocused, too. Specifically, schools should ask students to respond in writing to the content of the stories and articles they read so that a baseline can be developed to guide instructional decisions and the time allotted to each aspect of engagement with texts. Many states and districts have developed pilot assessments to ascertain how well their students do on tasks similar to those proposed by the two large consortia: PARCC and Smarter Balanced. All teachers will find it useful to review the development of the assessments periodically and to compare them to the tools they use to assess their own students.

In designing this series of books, we have attempted to focus on the most important aspects of the CCSS and to provide a set of instructional strategies and tools that will help teachers adjust their instruction as needed to address these standards. Most of these strategies and tools have been tested by teachers and research studies and can therefore be used reliably, and others are variations of good instructional practices that reflect particular emphases of the CCSS. Some of these strategies and tools may seem familiar to teachers and have perhaps already been incorporated into their instructional routines. Regardless, these measures now take on added importance, because they can help align instruction with the expectations of the CCSS and the requirements of the assessments currently being developed.

It is important for teachers to develop a few strong instructional routines that allow them to observe and monitor students' growth over time. These routines should underscore the components of good reading comprehension, thereby helping students adopt them as regular reading practices. It is also important for teachers to keep students central in planning. Students should be able to see the purpose in whatever they are asked to do, and they should be involved in the assessment of their learning needs and achievements. Moreover, students' particular interests and experiences should be honored in classroom activities and other forms of engagement.

The CCSS provide an opportunity for teachers and districts to rethink the priorities, emphases, and assessments that are currently in place and to review how students are already engaged. The CCSS also challenge schools to look at the materials being used and the collaboration taking place across disciplines in the development of students' literacy. As stated in the beginning of this Introduction, the CCSS present both an opportunity and a challenge. It is up to educators to respond thoughtfully and with vision and commitment to all students.

REFERENCES

American College Testing (ACT). (2006). *Reading between the lines: What the ACT reveals about college readiness in reading.* Iowa City, IA: Author.

Graham, S., & Hebert, M. (2010). *Writing to read: Evidence for how writing can improve reading. A Carnegie Corporation Time to Act Report.* Washington, DC: Alliance for Excellent Education. Retrieved from http://carnegie.org/fileadmin/Media/Publications/WritingToRead_01.pdf.

Learning Unlimited. (n.d.). Learning Unlimited Common Core resources. *Learning Unlimited.* Retrieved from www.learningunlimitedllc.com/common-core.

Mastery Connect. (n.d.). Goodies. *Mastery Connect.* Retrieved from www.masteryconnect.com/learn-more/goodies.html.

National Assessment Governing Board. (2008). Reading framework for the 2009 National Assessment of Educational Progress. Washington, DC: U.S. Government Printing Office.

National Governors Association Center for Best Practices & Council of Chief State School Officers (NGA & CCSSO). (2010a). *Common Core State Standards.* Washington, DC: Authors. Retrieved from www.corestandards.org/assets/CCSSI_ELA%20Standards.pdf.

National Governors Association Center for Best Practices & Council of Chief State School Officers (NGA & CCSSO). (2010b). Appendix A, *Common Core State Standards.* Washington, DC: Authors. Retrieved from www.corestandards.org/assets/Appendix_A.pdf.

National Governors Association Center for Best Practices & Council of Chief State School Officers (NGA & CCSSO). (2010c). Appendix B, *Common Core State Standards.* Washington, DC: Authors. Retrieved from www.corestandards.org/assets/Appendix_B.pdf.

Partnership for Assessment of Readiness for College and Careers (PARCC). (n.d.). *PARCC.* Retrieved from www.parcconline.org.

SMARTER Balanced Assessment Consortium. (n.d.). Common Core State Standards Tools & Resources. *SMARTER Balanced.* Retrieved from www.smarterbalanced.org/k-12-education/common-core-state-standards-tools-resources.

Wisconsin Department of Public Instruction. (n.d.) Common Core State Standards. *Wisconsin Department of Public Instruction.* Retrieved from http://standards.dpi.wi.gov/stn_ccss.

chapter 1

The Common Core State Standards in Grades 3–5

IN THE STORY OF *SEVEN BLIND MICE* (YOUNG, 1992/2002), each of seven different-colored mice explores a separate part of an elephant using only the sense of touch and comes to an individual conclusion about what an elephant might be. "An elephant is like a spear," muses the yellow mouse, who has felt only the elephant's tusk. "No, no, an elephant is like a rope!" argues the blue mouse, who has considered only the elephant's tail. It is not until the mice put together all of their observations of separate parts that they understand the whole concept of an elephant.

Leslie Montgomery

Sometimes, we may feel like one of the "blind mice" as we work to understand the CCSS and best practices for implementation. Each of us may best understand the CCSS initiative from his or her own perspective—as a third-grade, fourth-grade, or fifth-grade teacher in a particular state, district, and school. It is challenging to understand the whole picture of the U.S. "elephant" of implementation, and as educators across the country work to carry out the CCSS initiative, fresh information becomes available almost every day.

Knowing that there is always something new to learn, we work with our colleagues to comprehend the CCSS and what they mean for us and for our students. We read the Standards closely, interpret the expectations, follow the guidelines of our states and districts, and decide the best instruction and assessment strategies to help our students meet the expectations. We want our students to achieve, and we want to plan for what they need. We do not teach standards—we teach kids!

The Literate Natures of Students in Grades 3–5

STUDENTS IN GRADES 3, 4, AND 5 ARE at a critical transition in their education, which makes effective implementation of the CCSS even more crucial. In grade 3, children are still at the primary level. In grade 5, students are thought of as young adolescents. In grade 4, they are in between these stages.

What happens during these three years is vitally important to our students' future success in school, and it certainly affects how we approach classroom instruction based on the Standards. How might the literate natures of third-, fourth-, and fifth-graders affect how we plan for literacy achievement in a Common Core classroom? What do third-, fourth-, and fifth-graders already know? What do students in these grades need to learn?

Literacy in Third Grade

Tiana is a third grade student in Ms. Embry's class. When Ms. Embry assesses Tiana to note her progress in literacy, she sees that Tiana can make analogies to known words to recognize unknown words, can break apart larger words into smaller chunks, and can figure out longer words by looking at syllables and affixes. Tiana can already read 92 words per minute with expression, and is well on her way to reach the third grade fluency goal of 107 wpm by the end of the year. She is able to read and comprehend both fiction and nonfiction that is written for third-grade level, summarize major points in a text, and ask questions about the text. When reading nonfiction, Tiana can distinguish cause and effect, fact and opinion, and main idea and supporting details. Tiana still needs to work on vocabulary development, and to develop the ability to write different types of text for extended periods of time. Ms. Embry notes that Tiana exhibits the characteristics of a typical third grade reader. (Almasi, Garas-York, & Hildreth, 2007).

Third grade is a turning point for many students. They are typically in the last year of the primary grades and continuing to learn the basics of reading. As noted by the National Reading Panel, many third-graders still need explicit instruction in phonics, fluency, vocabulary, and comprehension to learn to read well (NRP, 2000).

We have known for some time that third-grade reading achievement is a predictor of future academic success (Lloyd, 1978). We now know that reading achievement at the third-grade year can predict academic attainment in middle school and beyond. Third-grade reading achievement is a predictor for eighth-grade reading scores, and students who are above grade level for reading in grade 3 graduate from high school and enroll in college at higher rates than children who are at or below grade level (Lesnick et al., 2010). Children who live in poverty and belong to diverse populations are at even more risk of not achieving in school. Hernandez (2012) has reported the following trends:

- Sixteen percent of third grade children who are not reading on grade level do not graduate from high school on time. The graduation rate is four times higher for children who did read proficiently in third grade.
- Poverty makes a difference. Children who live in poverty and do not read on grade level in third grade have a three times higher likelihood of dropping out or not graduating from high school than more affluent children.
- Race and ethnicity also matter. Children who are African American or Hispanic and are not reading on grade level by the end of third grade are twice as likely as white children to be high school dropouts.

Students like Tiana are probably on the pathway to academic success. To help her continue to succeed, it is particularly important that we continue to teach basic reading skills and strategies in word recognition, fluency, vocabulary, and comprehension, as well as work on the rigorous expectations of the ELA Standards. All indicators suggest that students who are readers in third grade become high school graduates. Mastering the expectations of the ELA Standards will also help these students become prepared for college.

Literacy in Fourth Grade

Ms. Diaz teaches fourth grade. She observes that her student Caleb has mastered basic reading skills, and the majority of his instructional time is spent learning new concepts using reading and writing as tools for learning. Ms. Diaz sees that Caleb can understand and appreciate more complex storylines and sophisticated humor, but he still needs instruction in reading comprehension with more complex materials. Caleb has met the fourth-grade fluency goal, reading 123 words per minute with expression and comprehension. However, he needs to develop academic vocabulary and strategies for content area literacy. He also needs to build stamina to read and write for longer periods of time. Ms. Diaz records that Caleb displays the characteristics of a typical fourth-grade reader (Johnson, 2008).

Fourth-graders are the "tweens" in most elementary schools. They are no longer in the primary grades, and academic expectations are much more rigorous. Texts become harder and provide fewer supports, such as pictures, larger fonts, and white space. By the time students are in fourth grade, only 29% choose to read daily (Johnson, 2008). These and other factors may explain the unfortunate "fourth-grade slump."

Much has been written about the fourth-grade slump. Sanacore and Palumbo (2009) have hypothesized that in fourth grade, children are expected to perform tasks that are traditionally much different than those in the primary grades, such as the following:

- comprehend large amounts of expository text
- understand related vocabulary

- gain information from text features such as graphics, charts, and tables
- comprehend text with varied text structures, such as comparison–contrast, problem–solution, and cause–effect

Sanacore and Palumbo also cited inadequate access to interesting texts, less school time for actual reading, and less reading instruction as factors in the fourth-grade slump.

Poverty seems to be a factor for many children. Chall and Jacobs (2003) found that even when low-income students in grades 2 and 3 achieved as well as more affluent children, their achievement began to decelerate at grade 4 when they were living in poverty. These children lacked adequate fluency and vocabulary development, which affected their reading achievement. According to Chall and Jacobs, "Those who have reading difficulties in the intermediate grades will, most likely, have serious trouble with the study of science, social studies, literature, mathematics, and other content study that depend, in great part, on printed text" (p. 15).

For students like Caleb to avoid the fourth-grade slump, they need quality instruction to learn how to read and comprehend the harder materials they are expected to use. It is not enough for teachers to plan for instruction to help meet the CCSS; we must also plan quality instruction in comprehension processes. Fourth-graders also need access to a wide variety of texts at different levels and time to read independently while they take on the new expectations of the ELA Standards.

Literacy in Fifth Grade

Mariah and Jasmine are best friends in Mr. Freeman's fifth-grade language arts class. Mr. Freeman perceives that the girls have different literacy abilities. Both girls can decode unfamiliar words, have developed a sizeable vocabulary, and choose to read to some extent outside school. However, Mariah can adequately monitor her comprehension to ensure that she understands what she reads, while Jasmine is still working on this skill. This difference means that Mariah is able to comprehend more difficult text independently, while Jasmine still needs support. Mariah and Jasmine both need to learn content vocabulary, multisyllabic words, and words that have multiple meanings. Mariah has already reached the fifth-grade fluency goal of reading at 139 words per minute, while Jasmine, at 127 wpm, is continuing to develop fluency skills. Mr. Freeman understands that both girls can be considered typical fifth-grade readers (McMahon & Wells, 2006).

Fifth-graders are on the verge of adolescence. The Association for Middle Level Education considers middle-grade students to be those ages 10 to 15 and typically in grades 5–9 (AMLE, 2012). Fifth-graders, most of whom begin the school year as 10-year-olds, often have many of the physical, intellectual, emotional/psychological, moral/ethical, and social characteristics of young adolescents (Caskey & Anfara, 2007). Whereas some fifth-graders are still concrete thinkers, others are moving into the stage of formal operations, in which they begin to reason in more abstract and logical ways, become more idealistic, and can think more about the future (McMahon & Wells, 2006). Students in fifth grade come in all shapes and sizes and have varied levels of maturity. They can be found organized into a variety of groups, from being the "big kids" at the elementary level to the "babies" in a middle school setting. This variety of characteristics makes it difficult to describe a typical fifth-grade student.

Fifth-grade students and their literacy competencies are as varied as snowflakes, but they have common literacy needs. Students like Mariah and Jasmine have increasing competence in reading comprehension but still need instruction focused on helping them become strategic readers of both literary and informational texts. They need instruction in vocabulary and reading strategies, along with opportunities to develop fluency. They also need motivation to tackle varied types of challenging reading materials and resources as they work to master the ELA Standards.

The ELA Standards

THE K–12 CCSS FOR ENGLISH LANGUAGE ARTS and Literacy in History/Social Studies, Science, and Technical Subjects are based on a set of College and Career Readiness (CCR) Anchor Standards (NGA & CCSSO, 2010). The CCR Anchor Standards outline what students should know and be able to do when they graduate from high school to be successful individuals who can thrive in a college or employment setting.

There are 10 CCR Reading standards, 10 Writing standards, 6 Speaking and Listening Standards, and 6 Language standards. These Anchor Standards are the basis for the K–12 English Language Arts Common Core State Standards. The ELA CCSS, which are the focus of this book, are a set of skills that students need to know and be able to do to be prepared for college in the areas of reading, writing, speaking and listening, and language. The CCSS were designed by mapping backward from the CCR Standards. The CCSS begin at kindergarten and climb a staircase of complexity to the end of grade 12.

It is always helpful to begin with the end in mind. Let us take a minute and examine the CCR Anchor Standards for each area to get a better idea of where we want our students to be at the end of high school.

Anchor Standards for Reading

The CCR Anchor Standards for Reading are grouped into clusters: Key Ideas and Details, Craft and Structure, Integration of Knowledge and Ideas, and Range of Reading and Level of Text Complexity. When students leave the K–12 setting and enter college and careers, they will need to have mastered the 10 reading skills outlined in these clusters to be able to read all types of complex texts independently. Students will be expected to read closely to analyze a text, use a variety of high-level skills that demonstrate comprehension, and integrate knowledge from written texts. There is a particular expectation that students will be able to read complex texts independently and proficiently. The CCR Anchor Standards for Reading, as displayed in Table 1.1, demonstrate the level of skill that will be expected of students by the end of high school.

The K–12 CCSS include Reading standards for Literature, Informational Text, and Foundational Skills (K–5 only) that lead students to develop the skills needed to meet the CCR Anchor Standards. Students in grades 3–5 are expected to build the foundation necessary for acquiring these CCR Anchor Standards. To build toward college and career readiness in reading, students in grades 3–5 are expected to read and comprehend a variety of genres, read more complex texts than they have in the past, and analyze the texts they read.

Anchor Standards for Writing

The 10 CCR Anchor Standards for Writing form the basis for the types and intensity of writing expected of college students. These students will be expected to skillfully write arguments supported with reasons and evidence, as well as informative/explanatory pieces and narratives.

TABLE 1.1 ● *CCR Anchor Standards for Reading*

The K–5 Standards on the following pages define what students should understand and be able to do by the end of each grade. They correspond to the College and Career Readiness (CCR) Anchor Standards below by number. The CCR and grade-specific standards are necessary complements—the former providing broad standards, the latter providing additional specificity—that together define the skills and understandings that all students must demonstrate.

Key Ideas and Details

1. Read closely to determine what the text says explicitly and to make logical inferences from it; cite specific textual evidence when writing or speaking to support conclusions drawn from the text.

2. Determine central ideas or themes of a text and analyze their development; summarize the key supporting details and ideas.

3. Analyze how and why individuals, events, and ideas develop and interact over the course of a text.

Craft and Structure

4. Interpret words and phrases as they are used in a text, including determining technical, connotative, and figurative meanings, and analyze how specific word choices shape meaning or tone.

5. Analyze the structure of texts, including how specific sentences, paragraphs, and larger portions of the text (e.g., a section, chapter, scene, or stanza) relate to each other and the whole.

6. Assess how point of view or purpose shapes the content and style of a text.

Integration of Knowledge and Ideas

7. Integrate and evaluate content presented in diverse media and formats, including visually and quantitatively, as well as in words.*

8. Delineate and evaluate the argument and specific claims in a text, including the validity of the reasoning as well as the relevance and sufficiency of the evidence.

9. Analyze how two or more texts address similar themes or topics in order to build knowledge or to compare the approaches the authors take.

Range of Reading and Level of Text Complexity

10. Read and comprehend complex literary and informational texts independently and proficiently.

---

*Please see "Research to Build and Present Knowledge" in Writing and "Comprehension and Collaboration" in Speaking and Listening for additional standards relevant to gathering, assessing, and applying information from print and digital sources.
Source: NGA & CCSSO (2010).

They will be expected to use a process to plan, revise, edit, and publish their writing. College students will also be expected to complete research and integrate reading and writing thoroughly. The K–12 CCSS outline expectations at each grade level for students to become excellent writers by the time they leave high school. The CCR Anchor Standards for Writing are presented in Table 1.2.

To build toward college and career readiness in writing, the CCSS Writing Standards for grades 3–5 recommend that students learn to write opinions about texts and topics supported with reasons and evidence and to write informative/explanatory and narrative texts

TABLE 1.2 • *CCR Anchor Standards for Writing*

The K–5 Standards on the following pages define what students should understand and be able to do by the end of each grade. They correspond to the College and Career Readiness (CCR) Anchor Standards below by number. The CCR and grade-specific standards are necessary complements—the former providing broad standards, the latter providing additional specificity—that together define the skills and understandings that all students must demonstrate.

Text Types and Purposes*

1. Write arguments to support claims in an analysis of substantive topics or texts, using valid reasoning and relevant and sufficient evidence.

2. Write informative/explanatory texts to examine and convey complex ideas and information clearly and accurately through the effective selection, organization, and analysis of content.

3. Write narratives to develop real or imagined experiences or events using effective technique, well-chosen details, and well-structured event sequences.

Production and Distribution of Writing

4. Produce clear and coherent writing in which the development, organization, and style are appropriate to task, purpose, and audience.

5. Develop and strengthen writing as needed by planning, revising, editing, rewriting, or trying a new approach.

6. Use technology, including the Internet, to produce and publish writing and to interact and collaborate with others.

Research to Build and Present Knowledge

7. Conduct short as well as more sustained research projects based on focused questions, demonstrating understanding of the subject under investigation.

8. Gather relevant information from multiple print and digital sources, assess the credibility and accuracy of each source, and integrate the information while avoiding plagiarism.

9. Draw evidence from literary or informational texts to support analysis, reflection, and research.

Range of Writing

10. Write routinely over extended time frames (time for research, reflection, and revision) and shorter time frames (a single sitting or a day or two) for a range of tasks, purposes, and audiences.

*These broad types of writing include many subgenres. See Appendix A for definitions of key writing types.
Source: NGA & CCSSO (2010).

following grade-level guidelines. Students are to engage in a writing process and conduct short collaborative or individual research projects. They should also begin to write responses to the ideas in texts.

Anchor Standards for Speaking and Listening

The CCR Anchor Standards for Speaking and Listening indicate that college students must be prepared to participate in a number of different types of academic conversations. Students will be asked to participate in whole-class discussions about texts and topics and engage in small-group work to complete projects and discuss texts. Students in college classes must be able to analyze information presented by speakers and in multimedia formats and to make presentations and use multimedia themselves. The K–12 CCSS are designed to help students develop the skills needed to participate in group conversations, speak with purpose, and present information from K–12. Table 1.3 identifies the CCR Anchor Standards for Speaking and Listening.

To build the skills for college and career readiness in Speaking and Listening, the CCSS Speaking and Listening Standards for grades 3–5 suggest that students should engage in a range of collaborative discussions and follow a format for speaking and listening that will help them better learn content. By the end of grade 5, students should be able to report on a topic or text, retell a story, conduct an oral presentation for an audience, and create a multimedia presentation that aligns with assigned content.

Anchor Standards for Language

The CCR Anchor Standards for Language are divided into three categories. The first category demonstrates the expectation that students entering college have mastered standard English grammar and usage and standard English capitalization, punctuation, and spelling. The second category of the Standards is about understanding and using language in reading, writing, and speaking, and the third category provides specific vocabulary standards. The expectation for the Anchor Standards for Language is that they will be integrated across all of the other standards. Table 1.4 describes the CCR Anchor Standards for Language.

To build toward college and career readiness in language, the CCSS Anchor Standards for grades 3–5 recommend that students know and be able to use specific indicators for English

TABLE 1.3 ● *CCR Anchor Standards for Speaking and Listening*

The K–5 Standards on the following pages define what students should understand and be able to do by the end of each grade. They correspond to the College and Career Readiness (CCR) Anchor Standards below by number. The CCR and grade-specific standards are necessary complements—the former providing broad standards, the latter providing additional specificity—that together define the skills and understandings that all students must demonstrate.

Comprehension and Collaboration

1. Prepare for and participate effectively in a range of conversations and collaborations with diverse partners, building on others' ideas, and expressing their own clearly and persuasively.

2. Integrate and evaluate information presented in diverse media and formats, including visually, quantitatively, and orally.

3. Evaluate a speaker's point of view, reasoning, and use of evidence and rhetoric.

Presentation of Knowledge and Ideas

4. Present information, findings, and supporting evidence such that listeners can follow the line of reasoning and the organization, development, and style are appropriate to task, purpose, and audience.

5. Make strategic use of digital media and visual displays of data to express information and enhance understanding of presentations.

6. Adapt speech to a variety of contexts and communicative tasks, demonstrating command of formal English when indicated or appropriate.

Source: NGA & CCSSO (2010).

TABLE 1.4 ● *CCR Anchor Standards for Language*

The K–5 Standards on the following pages define what students should understand and be able to do by the end of each grade. They correspond to the College and Career Readiness (CCR) Anchor Standards below by number. The CCR and grade-specific standards are necessary complements—the former providing broad standards, the latter providing additional specificity—that together define the skills and understandings that all students must demonstrate.

Conventions of Standard English

1. Demonstrate command of the conventions of standard English grammar and usage when writing or speaking.
2. Demonstrate command of the conventions of standard English capitalization, punctuation, and spelling when writing.

Knowledge of Language

3. Apply knowledge of language to understand how language functions in different contexts, to make effective choices for meaning or style, and to comprehend more fully when reading or listening.

Vocabulary Acquisition and Use

4. Determine or clarify the meaning of unknown and multiple-meaning words and phrases by using context clues, analyzing meaningful word parts, and consulting general and specialized reference materials, as appropriate.
5. Demonstrate understanding of figurative language, word relationships, and nuances in word meanings.
6. Acquire and use accurately a range of general academic and domain-specific words and phrases sufficient for reading, writing, speaking, and listening at the college and career readiness level; demonstrate independence in gathering vocabulary knowledge when encountering an unknown term important to comprehension or expression.

Source: NGA & CCSSO (2010).

grammar, usage, capitalization, punctuation, and spelling. Students are expected to apply knowledge of language and its conventions when writing, speaking, reading, and listening. Students should be able to choose words and phrases for effect, differentiate between contexts that call for formal versus informal English, and expand, combine, and reduce sentences for interest and style when writing. A section of the Standards devoted to vocabulary outlines expectations for students to determine the meanings of unknown and multiple words and phrases. Students should also demonstrate understanding of figurative language, word relationships, and nuances in word meanings and acquire and use grade-appropriate academic and domain-specific words and phrases.

What Do the Standards Mean for Grades 3–5?

EACH OF THE CCSS BUILDS TO THE NEXT GRADE LEVEL, and each grade level is responsible for a step up the ladder to reach the CCR Anchor Standards. For example, CCR Reading Anchor Standard 6 for informational text is "Assess how point of view or purpose shapes the content and style of a text" (NGA & CCSSO, 2010). Here are the expectations outlined in the CCSS for grades 3, 4, and 5 to help students build to mastery of CCR Reading Anchor Standard 6 for informational text:

- **Grade 3:** Distinguish their own point of view from that of the author of the text. (RI.3.6)
- **Grade 4:** Compare and contrast a firsthand and secondhand account of the same event or topic; describe the differences in focus and the information provided. (RI.4.6)
- **Grade 5:** Analyze multiple accounts of the same event or topic; noting important similarities and differences in the point of view they represent. (RI.5.6)

> ## Tips for the Teacher
>
> "THE STANDARDS ARE THE END-OF-YEAR GOALS. The conversation we as teachers need to be having is about the skills and strategies we need to teach to get our students to meet these goals. I would say I didn't even realize this until I had worked with the Standards for a while. It was a huge insight for me, and it changes everything about the way I teach."
>
> —Leslie, grade 5 teacher

Those who have studied the elementary ELA CCSS have likely noticed that between grades 3 and 4 (depending on the standard), there is often a "cognitive leap" in student expectations. The demands become greater, and in many cases, students are expected to demonstrate dramatically increased competencies in all strands of the Standards. For example, consider Reading Anchor Standard 6. There is quite an increase in skill from distinguishing the reader's own point of view to comparing and contrasting firsthand and secondhand accounts of the same event or topic and describing the differences in focus and information provided. This sort of cognitive leap is found in varying degrees throughout the Standards at these grades.

Students in grades 3–5 are expected to build a strong foundation of skills for middle school, and the Standards in grades 6–12 are both broad and intense. It is the responsibility of end-of-primary and intermediate teachers to prepare students to meet the even higher demands of the middle school ELA Standards. Doing so may not be easy. As teachers of grades 3–5, we may have some students who are still reading and writing at an early primary level, some students who are learning English, and others who are reading at a level far beyond the elementary grades. As we discuss the ELA CCSS, we need to consider how to meet the needs of English learners, struggling readers, students with disabilities, and readers who are above level or considered gifted and talented readers. We must be careful and inclusive classroom planners to meet the needs of all our students and the expectations of the CCSS.

Instructional Shifts in Teaching and Learning

THE COMMON CORE INITIATIVE IS UNIQUE in several ways. One unique quality is the CCSS emphasis on a number of "instructional shifts" for the English language arts. Instructional shifts represent changes in the ways we must think about planning, teaching, and assessing in the language arts. These shifts include balancing the use of literary and informational texts, engaging students with increasingly complex texts, asking and answering text-based answers, writing from sources, and learning academic vocabulary. By emphasizing these instructional shifts, we will help our students build knowledge across subject areas.

Balance of Literary and Informational Texts

In the elementary grades, we have traditionally relied heavily on narrative texts in teaching reading. As a result, our intermediate students have not always been prepared for the demands of reading informational texts. By fourth grade, the CCSS expectation is that students will be engaged in reading 50% literary and 50% informational texts. Literary texts include stories, plays, and poems. Informational texts include literary nonfiction; texts in social studies, science, and technical subjects (such as math); and "how-to" books. We should plan for a balance of narrative and informational texts so that our students can build knowledge through reading a variety of content-rich texts.

Staircase of Text Complexity

Over the years, classroom texts have become easier as reading demands have increased. The Common Core initiative requires that students advance up a staircase of text complexity to be prepared for college and careers. Rather than focus only on the skills of reading and writing, students are expected to read and interpret challenging texts. Students should be engaged in lessons in which they must work to figure out the author's intended meaning. Although we should continue to teach reading and writing skills, we should also plan lessons that engage students in delving into more complex texts to try to interpret the author's meaning. Students should also write to support their thoughts about the text.

Text-Based Answers

Many students have come to rely on discussing personal experiences in connection to a text, rather than reading the text carefully. One of the major instructional shifts in the ELA Standards is that students are expected to provide text-based answers to text-dependent questions. This means that the questions we ask must be based on the text, not on students' personal experiences. Moreover, the answers must be logically inferred from the text, not from students' imaginations.

In this instructional shift, students have "rich and rigorous conversations which are dependent on a common text" and they write from sources "using evidence to inform or make an argument" (New York State Education Department, 2011). As students participate in lessons based on reading a complex text, they should learn to answer text-based questions, which require them to read the text closely and carefully to infer the author's meaning. Learning this skill is best accomplished by engaging students in lively, collaborative conversations about the meaning of the text.

Writing from Sources

To meet the ELA CCSS, students are expected to read to understand how an author supports a claim and determine the reasons and evidence that support it. Similarly, students are expected to use evidence from a text to support their own opinions and analyses and the information they gain from the text. We should plan lessons in which we teach students to write well-constructed opinions. We should also invite them to write in response to varied texts.

Academic Vocabulary

It is a well-known fact that vocabulary knowledge is a gatekeeper to academic success. The CCSS highlight the importance of learning and using academic vocabulary, and this expectation is connected to text complexity and comprehension in social studies, science, and technical subjects. To help our students achieve, we should plan for intentional and interesting vocabulary instruction across all subject areas.

The expectation is that this and the other instructional shifts will help students to engage with complex texts, extract and employ evidence, and build knowledge across the curriculum. Each of these instructional shifts will be explored as this book unfolds.

Instruction and Assessment Strategies and the CCSS

THE ELA CCSS ARE BASED ON AN INTEGRATED model of literacy. This means that they need to be intertwined in the instruction and assessment of our students. An appropriate Common Core assignment will be a rich instructional task, one that incorporates several reading, writing, speaking and listening, and language standards that build on each other to help students develop competence in literacy. The CCSS do not outline specific teaching strategies or instructional methods. In fact, they leave it to teachers to design instruction that will help their students achieve the expectations of the Standards. The writers of the CCSS document state, "Teachers are . . . free to provide students with whatever tools and knowledge their professional judgment and experience identify as most helpful for meeting the goals set out in the Standards" (NGA & CCSSO, 2010b, p. 4). Having this freedom provides us with the opportunity to be thoughtful and creative in our thinking as we plan for addressing the CCSS.

Teachers have freedom to plan how they want

So, what instructional strategies are best suited to help students meet the expectations of the CCSS? Of course, planning for instruction and assessment will depend on the needs of specific students. Even so, in this book, we will present some strategies for instruction and assessment that are appropriate in classroom planning for grades 3–5. As we proceed, we will address five areas of the CCSS that seem particularly important as we plan for instruction and assessment: comprehension, vocabulary, text complexity, writing, and speaking and listening. We will also explore curriculum implications as we plan for implementation of the CCSS in intermediate-grade classrooms, and examine a sample thematic unit of study that integrates a number of ELA standards as well as literacy in social studies and science.

Thinking about the Needs of Students in Grades 3–5

AS TEACHERS OF GRADES 3–5, WE KNOW THAT our students are expected to meet higher standards in English language arts and literacy than ever before. In addition, we want our students to achieve and become college and career ready. For this to happen, we must plan so that the CCSS are woven seamlessly into our instruction and curriculums in engaging ways that meet the needs of all our students. Our Common Core classrooms should be places where the Standards are living and breathing and where students are learning—every day.

REFERENCES

Alley, R. A. (1992). The forgotten fifth: Fifth grade in the middle school? Yes! *Middle School Journal, 23*(4), 26–29.

Allington, R. L., & Johnston, P. H. (2002). *Reading to learn: Lessons from exemplary fourth-grade classrooms.* New York, NY: Guilford Press.

Almasi, J. F., Garas-York, K., & Hildreth, L. (2007). *Teaching literacy in third grade.* New York, NY: Guilford Press.

Armbruster, B. B., Lehr, F., & Osborn, J. (2006). *Put reading first: Kindergarten through grade 3: The research blocks for teaching children to read, third edition.* Washington, DC: National Institute for Literacy. Retrieved from http://lincs.ed.gov/publications/pdf/PRFbooklet.pdf.

Association for Middle Level Education (AMLE). (2012). *About AMLE.* Retrieved from http://www.amle.org/AboutAMLE/tabid/76/Default.aspx.

Caskey, M. M., & Anfara, V. A., Jr. (2007). *Research summary: Young adolescents' developmental characteristics.* Retrieved from http://www.amle.org/portals/0/pdf/research/Research_Summaries/Developmental_Characteristics.pdf.

Chall, J. S., & Jacobs, V. A. (2003). The classic study on poor children's fourth-grade slump. *American Educator, 27*(1), 14–15.

Epstein, J. L., & MacIver, D. J. (1990). National practices and trends in the middle grades. *Middle School Journal, 22*(2), 36–40.

Hernandez, D. (2012). *The double jeopardy: How third-grade reading skills and poverty influence high school graduation.* Baltimore, MD: Annie E. Casey Foundation.

Johnson, D. (2008). *Teaching literacy in fourth grade.* New York, NY: Guilford Press.

Lesnick, J., Goerge, R. M., Smithgall, C., & Gwynne, J. (2010). *Reading on grade level in third grade: How is it related to high school performance and college enrollment?* Chicago, IL: Chapin Hall, University of Chicago.

Lloyd, D. N. (1978). Prediction of school failure from third-grade data. *Educational and Psychological Measurement, 38*(4), 1193–1200.

McMahon, S. I., & Wells, J. (2006). *Teaching literacy in fifth grade.* New York, NY: Guilford Press.

National Governors Association Center for Best Practices & Council of Chief State School Officers (NGA & CCSSO). (2010). *Common Core State Standards: English language arts and literacy in history/social studies, science, and technical subjects.* Washington, DC: Authors. Retrieved from http://www.corestandards.org/assets/CCSSI_ELA%20Standards.pdf.

National Reading Panel (NRP). (2000). *Teaching children to read: An evidence-based assessment of the scientific research literature on reading and its implications for reading instruction* (NIH Publication 00-4769). Washington, DC: National Institute of Child Health and Human Development.

New York State Education Department. (2012, October 30). Common Core shifts. EngageNY.org. Retrieved from http://www.engageny.org/resource/common-core-shifts.

Sanacore, J., & Palumbo, A. (2009). Understanding the fourth-grade slump: Our point of view. *The Educational Forum, 73,* 67–74.

Zygouris-Coe, V. (2001). *Balanced reading instruction in K–3 classrooms.* Orlando, FL: Florida Literacy and Reading Excellence Center. Retrieved from http://education.ucf.edu/mirc/Research/Balanced%20Reading.pdf.

LITERATURE CITED

Young, E. (2002). *Seven blind mice.* New York, NY: Puffin Books. (Original work published 1992)

Reading Comprehension

YOU HAVE PROBABLY HEARD A LOT ABOUT THE INCREASED expectations of the Common Core State Standards (CCSS) in the area of reading instruction. One of the instructional shifts is that students will engage in lessons with complex texts. This expectation presents a number of challenges for both students and educators. The challenge for intermediate students is to move from being primary readers at the beginning of grade 3 to being experienced readers of complex, nuanced text by the end of grade 5. The challenge for us, as teachers, is to help students develop a variety of strategies and skills they can rely on to become confident and independent readers of challenging text.

Leslie Montgomery

Achieving these goals leaves us with a number of questions: How can our students learn to become strong, independent readers who can comprehend complex text? What is the best way to teach comprehension in a CCSS classroom for grades 3–5?

Exploring the Reading Standards

IT WOULD SEEM LOGICAL FOR THE READING STANDARDS to include all of the components to foster reading comprehension. However, given what we know about comprehension processes and how they develop, the Reading Standards address only part of the pathway to comprehension in the CCSS. The Writing, Speaking and Listening, and Language Standards all play parts as well. Moreover, the CCSS do not include everything that students should know and be able to do. There are gaps that must be filled as we teach our students to be excellent readers.

In the English Language Arts (ELA) Standards, there are three strands for Reading: Literature, Informational Text, and Foundational Skills. (Foundational Skills is included only for grades K–5.) The Literature strand includes stories, dramas, and poetry. Table 2.1 presents the Reading Standards for Literature for grades 3–5.

The Informational Text strand includes literary nonfiction (i.e., works of nonfiction told like stories) and historical, scientific, and technical texts (NGA & CCSSO, 2010, p. 31). Table 2.2 presents the grades 3–5 Reading Standards for Informational Text.

There should be an equal balance of literary and informational texts in elementary instruction. According to the writers of the CCSS, reading instruction should comprise 50% literature and 50% informational text by fourth grade (NGA & CCSSO, 2010, p. 5).

equal balance of literacy and inform. and text.

TABLE 2.1 ● *Reading Standards for Literature, Grades 3–5*

Common Core State Standards for English Language Arts & Literacy in History/Social Studies, Science, and Technical Subjects

Grade 3 Students:	Grade 4 Students:	Grade 5 Students:
Key Ideas and Details		
1. Ask and answer questions to demonstrate understanding of a text, referring explicitly to the text as the basis for the answers.	1. Refer to details and examples in a text when explaining what the text says explicitly and when drawing inferences from the text.	1. Quote accurately from a text when explaining what the text says explicitly and when drawing inferences from the text.
2. Recount stories, including fables, folktales, and myths from diverse cultures; determine the central message, lesson, or moral and explain how it is conveyed through key details in the text.	2. Determine a theme of a story, drama, or poem from details in the text; summarize the text.	2. Determine a theme of a story, drama, or poem from details in the text, including how characters in a story or drama respond to challenges or how the speaker in a poem reflects upon a topic; summarize the text.
3. Describe characters in a story (e.g., their traits, motivations, or feelings) and explain how their actions contribute to the sequence of events.	3. Describe in depth a character, setting, or event in a story or drama, drawing on specific details in the text (e.g., a character's thoughts, words, or actions).	3. Compare and contrast two or more characters, settings, or events in a story or drama, drawing on specific details in the text (e.g., how characters interact).

(continued)

TABLE 2.1 ● *(continued)*

Craft and Structure

4. Determine the meaning of words and phrases as they are used in a text, distinguishing literal from nonliteral language.	4. Determine the meaning of words and phrases as they are used in a text, including those that allude to significant characters found in mythology (e.g., Herculean).	4. Determine the meaning of words and phrases as they are used in a text, including figurative language such as metaphors and similes.
5. Refer to parts of stories, dramas, and poems when writing or speaking about a text, using terms such as chapter, scene, and stanza; describe how each successive part builds on earlier sections.	5. Explain major differences between poems, drama, and prose, and refer to the structural elements of poems (e.g., verse, rhythm, meter) and drama (e.g., casts of characters, settings, descriptions, dialogue, stage directions) when writing or speaking about a text.	5. Explain how a series of chapters, scenes, or stanzas fits together to provide the overall structure of a particular story, drama, or poem.
6. Distinguish their own point of view from that of the narrator or those of the characters.	6. Compare and contrast the point of view from which different stories are narrated, including the difference between first- and third-person narrations.	6. Describe how a narrator's or speaker's point of view influences how events are described.

Integration of Knowledge and Ideas

7. Explain how specific aspects of a text's illustrations contribute to what is conveyed by the words in a story (e.g., create mood, emphasize aspects of a character or setting).	7. Make connections between the text of a story or drama and a visual or oral presentation of the text, identifying where each version reflects specific descriptions and directions in the text.	7. Analyze how visual and multimedia elements contribute to the meaning, tone, or beauty of a text (e.g., graphic novel, multimedia presentation of fiction, folktale, myth, poem).
8. (Not applicable to literature)	8. (Not applicable to literature)	8. (Not applicable to literature)
9. Compare and contrast the themes, settings, and plots of stories written by the same author about the same or similar characters (e.g., in books from a series).	9. Compare and contrast the treatment of similar themes and topics (e.g., opposition of good and evil) and patterns of events (e.g., the quest) in stories, myths, and traditional literature from different cultures.	9. Compare and contrast stories in the same genre (e.g., mysteries and adventure stories) on their approaches to similar themes and topics.

Range of Reading and Level of Text Complexity

10. By the end of the year, read and comprehend literature, including stories, dramas, and poetry, at the high end of the grades 2-3 text complexity band independently and proficiently.	10. By the end of the year, read and comprehend literature, including stories, dramas, and poetry, in the grades 4-5 text complexity band proficiently, with scaffolding as needed at the high end of the range.	10. By the end of the year, read and comprehend literature, including stories, dramas, and poetry, at the high end of the grades 4-5 text complexity band independently and proficiently.

Source: NGA & CCSSO (2010).

TABLE 2.2 ● *Reading Standards for Informational Text, Grades 3–5*

Common Core State Standards for English Language Arts & Literacy in History/Social Studies, Science, and Technical Subjects

Grade 3 Students:	Grade 4 Students:	Grade 5 Students:
Key Ideas and Details		
1. Ask and answer questions to demonstrate understanding of a text, referring explicitly to the text as the basis for the answers.	1. Refer to details and examples in a text when explaining what the text says explicitly and when drawing inferences from the text.	1. Quote accurately from a text when explaining what the text says explicitly and when drawing inferences from the text.
2. Determine the main idea of a text; recount the key details and explain how they support the main idea.	2. Determine the main idea of a text and explain how it is supported by key details; summarize the text.	2. Determine two or more main ideas of a text and explain how they are supported by key details; summarize the text.
3 Describe the relationship between a series of historical events, scientific ideas or concepts, or steps in technical procedures in a text, using language that pertains to time, sequence, and cause/effect.	3. Explain events, procedures, ideas, or concepts in a historical, scientific, or technical text, including what happened and why, based on specific information in the text.	3. Explain the relationships or interactions between two or more individuals, events, ideas, or concepts in a historical, scientific, or technical text based on specific information in the text.
Craft and Structure		
4. Determine the meaning of general academic and domain-specific words and phrases in a text relevant to a *grade 3 topic or subject area.*	4. Determine the meaning of general academic and domain-specific words or phrases in a text relevant to a *grade 4 topic or subject area.*	4. Determine the meaning of general academic and domain-specific words and phrases in a text relevant to a *grade 5 topic or subject area.*
5. Use text features and search tools (e.g., key words, sidebars, hyperlinks) to locate information relevant to a given topic efficiently.	5. Describe the overall structure (e.g., chronology, comparison, cause/effect, problem/solution) of events, ideas, concepts, or information in a text or part of a text.	5. Compare and contrast the overall structure (e.g., chronology, comparison, cause/effect, problem/solution) of events, ideas, concepts, or information in two or more texts.
6. Distinguish their own point of view from that of the author of a text.	6. Compare and contrast a firsthand and secondhand account of the same event or topic; describe the differences in focus and the information provided.	6. Analyze multiple accounts of the same event or topic, noting important similarities and differences in the point of view they represent.
Integration of Knowledge and Ideas		
7. Use information gained from illustrations (e.g., maps, photographs) and the words in a text to demonstrate understanding of the text (e.g., where, when, why, and how key events occur).	7. Interpret information presented visually, orally, or quantitatively (e.g., in charts, graphs, diagrams, time lines, animations, or interactive elements on Web pages) and explain how the information contributes to an understanding of the text in which it appears.	7. Draw on information from multiple print or digital sources, demonstrating the ability to locate an answer to a question quickly or to solve a problem efficiently.

(continued)

TABLE 2.2 ● *(continued)*

Integration of Knowledge and Ideas

8. Describe the logical connection between particular sentences and paragraphs in a text (e.g., comparison, cause/effect, first/second/third in a sequence).	8. Explain how an author uses reasons and evidence to support particular points in a text.	8. Explain how an author uses reasons and evidence to support particular points in a text, identifying which reasons and evidence support which point(s).
9. Compare and contrast the most important points and key details presented in two texts on the same topic.	9. Integrate information from two texts on the same topic in order to write or speak about the subject knowledgeably.	9. Integrate information from several texts on the same topic in order to write or speak about the subject knowledgeably.

Range of Reading and Level of Text Complexity

10. By the end of the year, read and comprehend informational texts, including history/social studies, science, and technical texts, at the high end of the grades 2–3 text complexity band independently and proficiently.	10. By the end of year, read and comprehend informational texts, including history/social studies, science, and technical texts, in the grades 4–5 text complexity band proficiently, with scaffolding as needed at the high end of the range.	10. By the end of the year, read and comprehend informational texts, including history/social studies, science, and technical texts, at the high end of the grades 4–5 text complexity band independently and proficiently.

Source: NGA & CCSSO (2010).

There is also a set of standards for Foundational Skills in reading, which describe expectations for important skills that support basic comprehension for students in grades K–5. The Reading Standards for Foundational Skills for grades 3–5 are shown in Table 2.3.

TABLE 2.3 ● *Reading Standards: Foundational Skills, Grades 3–5*

Common Core State Standards for English Language Arts & Literacy in History/Social Studies, Science, and Technical Subjects

Grade 3 Students:	Grade 4 Students:	Grade 5 Students:
Phonics and Word Recognition		
3. Know and apply grade-level phonics and word analysis skills in decoding words.	3. Know and apply grade-level phonics and word analysis skills in decoding words.	3. Know and apply grade-level phonics and word analysis skills in decoding words.
a. Identify and know the meaning of the most common prefixes and derivational suffixes.	a. Use combined knowledge of all letter-sound correspondences, syllabication patterns, and morphology (e.g., roots and affixes) to read accurately unfamiliar multisyllabic words in context and out of context.	a. Use combined knowledge of all letter-sound correspondences, syllabication patterns, and morphology (e.g., roots and affixes) to read accurately unfamiliar multisyllabic words in context and out of context.
b. Decode words with common Latin suffixes.		
c. Decode multisyllable words.		
d. Read grade-appropriate irregularly spelled words.		

(continued)

TABLE 2.3 ● *(continued)*

Fluency		
4. Read with sufficient accuracy and fluency to support comprehension.	4. Read with sufficient accuracy and fluency to support comprehension.	4. Read with sufficient accuracy and fluency to support comprehension.
a. Read on-level text with purpose and understanding.	a. Read on-level text with purpose and understanding.	a. Read on-level text with purpose and understanding.
b. Read on-level prose and poetry orally with accuracy, appropriate rate, and expression on successive readings	b. Read on-level prose and poetry orally with accuracy, appropriate rate, and expression on successive readings	b. Read on-level prose and poetry orally with accuracy, appropriate rate, and expression on successive readings
c. Use context to confirm or self-correct word recognition and understanding, rereading as necessary.	c. Use context to confirm or self-correct word recognition and understanding, rereading as necessary.	c. Use context to confirm or self-correct word recognition and understanding, rereading as necessary.

Source: NGA & CCSSO (2010).

Within the ELA Standards, the standards for Literature and Informational Text can be found before the standards for Foundational Skills. However, we will begin our exploration of the Reading standards with the Foundational Skills for grades 3–5.

Foundational Skills for Reading

IN GRADES 3, 4, AND 5, THE FOUNDATIONAL SKILLS standards focus on word recognition and phonics skills for decoding multisyllabic words, as well as fluency development. At first, these standards may look like they concentrate on isolated skills. However, word recognition and fluency development are actually part of comprehension development.

The ability to decode and determine the meanings of unfamiliar words and phrases in and out of context is a necessary skill that good readers possess. Proficient readers can decode and know strategies to figure out the meanings of hard words. Proficient readers can also read fluently with expression and understand what they read. In grades 3–5, students develop more complex word recognition skills and are able to read grade-level texts fluently to promote better comprehension.

Phonics and Word Recognition

Foundational Skill Standard 3 is included in the Phonics and Word Recognition cluster of standards. Word recognition is a key to comprehension. In grades 3–5, word recognition and phonics skills are not limited to matching letters with sounds. Students on track for grade-level reading at these grades should have already acquired basic phonemic awareness and phonics skills, such as letter–sound correspondence and knowledge of common high-frequency words. Students should be able to decode regularly spelled one- and two-syllable words and to recognize and read grade-appropriate, irregularly spelled words. (Teachers should keep in mind, however, that some students, including struggling readers and English language learners, may not have acquired these skills and may need instruction in these areas.) Instead, word recognition and phonics skills at this level include the ability to use earlier phonics skills plus additional knowledge of syllabication patterns and morphology (i.e., the study of the meanings of parts of words).

In grades 3–5, students should learn word-solving strategies to determine unfamiliar words in context. They should also learn to figure out the meanings of multisyllabic words by using the meanings of common prefixes, suffixes, and Greek and Latin roots (Bear et al., 2011; Goodwin, Lipsky, & Ahn, 2012; Kieffer & Lesaux, 2007; Rasinski et al., 2011). Foundational Skills Standard 3—"Know and apply grade-level phonics and word-analysis skills in decoding words" (NGA & CCSSO, 2010, p. 16)—is aligned with Vocabulary Acquisition and Use in the Language standards. (Details about determining words in context and the teaching of morphology are found in Chapter 3 on vocabulary development.)

Fluency

The ability to read fluently is also a skill that supports comprehension. LaBerge and Samuels (1974) define *fluency* as the ability to read accurately while also comprehending what is read. The CCSS seem to support this definition. Foundational Skills Standard 4 is focused on fluency, and it is the same for grades 3, 4, and 5: "Read with sufficient accuracy and fluency to support comprehension" (NGA & CCSSO, 2010, p. 16). Three indicators follow that support the fluency standard (RF.3.4a–c; RF.4.4a–c; RF.5.4a–c):

a. Read on-level text with purpose and understanding.
b. Read on-level prose and poetry orally with accuracy, appropriate rate, and expression on successive readings.
c. Use context to confirm or self-correct word recognition and understanding, rereading as necessary. (NGO & CCSSO, 2010, p. 16)

We know quite a bit about fluency development and its relationship to comprehension. LaBerge and Samuels (1974) have shown that fluent readers recognize most words automatically and do not have to stop to decode words as they read. Stopping to decode words requires cognitive attention, and comprehension is compromised when the reader continually stops to makes sense of individual words. Fluent readers possess automaticity; that is, they recognize words automatically and comprehend what they are reading.

In 2000, the National Reading Panel (NICHD, 2000) identified fluency as one of the five essential pillars of reading instruction, along with phonemic awareness, phonics, vocabulary, and comprehension. An efficient reader is a fluent reader.

Strategies for Teaching Fluency   Rasinski (2003) suggests several ways to support students to become fluent readers:

- teacher read-aloud
- supported oral reading
- repeated reading
- performance reading
- oral reading across the curriculum

Teacher Read-Alouds   When we read aloud to students, we model fluent reading, and students subsequently are better able to read with expression and enthusiasm. (Specific information about teacher read-alouds can be found in Chapter 6 on Speaking and Listening.)

Supported Oral Reading   Supported oral reading includes activities such as choral reading, paired reading, recorded reading, and echo reading (Rasinski, 2003). For example, in choral reading, we read aloud poems or stories expressively with our students as a group, so they practice fluent reading. In paired reading, students practice reading fluently to each other and keep track of their progress. Recorded reading involves students listening to a recording of an expressive reader and following along. In echo reading, we read a line aloud and the class repeats the line aloud together. In each of these methods, students listen to an expressive reader and practice reading aloud themselves so they can read more fluently.

Repeated Reading   Repeated reading is another method of developing fluency which is based on the theory of automaticity (LaBerge & Samuels, 1974; Rasinski, 2003). In repeated reading, a student reads a short passage orally several times. Research suggests that the student increases in accuracy, number of words per minute, and comprehension each time he or she reads the passage aloud. The student is then able to read subsequent passages of equal difficulty more fluently. The use of repeated reading is especially appropriate as one part of reading instruction for struggling readers.

Performance Reading   Performance reading includes Reader's Theater, in which students practice and read aloud parts from a script. Students enjoy practicing their parts to perform for an audience. Free Reader's Theater scripts for use in class are available on websites such as Author Online! (www.aaronshep.com).

Another type of performance reading is the poetry "coffeehouse" (sometimes called a poetry "slam"), in which students practice reading poems for an audience (Rasinski, 2003). In fact, participation in a Poetry Academy has been shown to help struggling readers build fluency, word recognition skills, and confidence (Wilfong, 2008).

In all of these methods, the student practices reading aloud to prepare for a performance. Each time the student reads aloud, he or she engages in repeated reading, which in turn improves fluency. Students in grades 3–5 usually like to do performance reading and so are especially motivated to participate in these types of activities.

Students read their parts to prepare for Reader's Theater.

Leslie Montgomery

Oral Reading Across the Curriculum
Oral reading across the curriculum includes embedding opportunities for fluency development throughout content area instruction. Many teachers use performance reading, such as Reader's Theater and radio reading, in science, social studies, and math lessons. For example, Putnam and Kingsley (2009) taught fifth-graders to write scripts that contained science vocabulary. The students then made weekly podcasts, which were put online and could be downloaded on iPods for them

to listen at home or on the go (for examples, go to www.podomatic.com). As a result, students were motivated to read and write, and their knowledge of content vocabulary increased as they practiced fluent reading for an authentic audience.

Assessing Fluency   We can use an oral reading fluency norms chart to draw conclusions and make decisions about a student's fluency. This chart is based on the number of words an average student can read aloud per minute in a timed test. Figure 2.1 shows the general guidelines for word counts per minute (wcpm) in grades 3–5.

However, fluency is not just about how many words per minute a student can read. We also want to consider the reader's expression and volume, phrasing, smoothness, and pace. These factors provide a window into comprehension development. The Multidimensional Fluency Rubric, developed by Rasinski (2012) for assessing fluent reading, is available online.

Allington (2009) reminds us that for students to develop fluency, they must hear fluent models, have opportunities for independent and repeated reading, read a large volume of materials, and read easier texts. The use of easier texts to develop fluency may seem to be at odds with the CCSS expectation to use more challenging texts in instruction. However, we should remember that when teaching reading in the elementary grades, we need to have a collection of various levels of texts to use for different purposes. Easier texts should be available for fluency practice and independent reading. More complex texts should be used in lessons in which all students are learning to comprehend at higher levels.

FIGURE 2.1 ● Norms Chart for Oral Reading Fluency: Grades 3–5

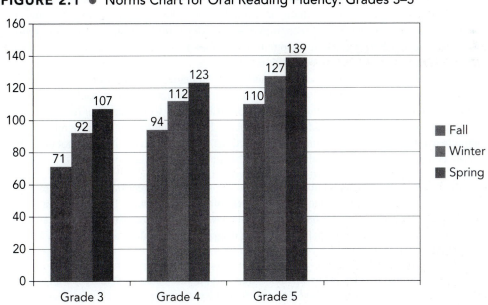

Source: Adapted from Hasbrouck & Tindal (2006).

Understanding Comprehension in the ELA Standards

SINCE THE MID-1970S, QUITE A BIT HAS BEEN published about the nature of comprehension and recommendations for teaching comprehension processes. We know that effective readers can comprehend various types of texts and that comprehension should be the goal of all reading instruction. It doesn't matter if students can pronounce every word on the page—if they don't understand the author's message, they are not effective readers. Even so, there is evidence that many intermediate teachers need to plan for comprehension instruction at a deeper level.

Studies have found that teachers of grades 3–6 often say they are teaching comprehension when they were actually only assessing it (Durkin 1978/79; Pressley et al., 1998). They assign reading and ask questions afterward, never really teaching comprehension strategies. Studies of comprehension instruction using intermediate basal reading materials have come to the same conclusion: that many of the comprehension activities in the materials are not based on what is known about effective comprehension instruction (Dewitz, Jones, & Leahy, 2009).

As Allington and Johnston (2002) remind us about the characteristics of exemplary fourth-grade classrooms, it is the teacher that makes the difference. We must make sure that effective instruction in comprehension strategies is a key part of the literacy curriculum in grades 3–5, as we teach students to meet the expectations of the ELA Standards.

Instruction in Metacognitive Strategies and the CCSS

For students to comprehend more challenging texts and meet the expectations of the CCSS, they need varied types of reading instruction. We need to make sure our students have the strategies they need to be able to comprehend as they learn to analyze and evaluate text.

One type of instruction should be focused on the use of metacognitive comprehension strategies. Proficient readers are metacognitive. As Pressley (2002) has stated, "Metacognition is knowledge about thinking, and metacognition about reading is specifically knowledge about reading and how reading is accomplished" (p. 304).

Proficient readers use a number of metacognitive strategies to construct meaning as they read. We can teach these strategies, and students can become proficient readers by learning to be metacognitive about comprehension strategy use. Components of deeper reading comprehension are embedded throughout the ELA Standards, but metacognitive comprehension strategies are not included. In fact, the Standards intentionally do not describe specific comprehension strategies that teachers should use in their classrooms:

> The Standards do not mandate such things as . . . the full range of metacognitive strategies that students may need to monitor and direct their thinking and learning. Teachers are thus free to provide students with whatever tools and knowledge their professional judgment and experience identify as most helpful for meeting the goals set out in the Standards. (NGA & CCSSO, 2010, p. 4)

As teachers and literacy professionals, we know that as texts become more complex after second grade, it becomes even more important for students to learn skills, strategies, and ways to comprehend varied types of texts. We want our students to avoid the "fourth-grade slump" and must work to prepare them for the types of challenging texts they will encounter in middle school and beyond. While the CCSS "focus on what is most essential, they do not describe all that can or should be taught" (NGA & CCSSO, 2010, p. 6).

What metacognitive strategies will help students comprehend at higher levels? A discussion of the metacognitive strategies that enhance comprehension follows.

Activating and Connecting to Background Knowledge   As readers, when we encounter text, we bring our own prior knowledge to bear. We all comprehend according to our individual frameworks for understanding the world (i.e., *schemata*) based on the experiences we have had. Activating background knowledge about the topic of a text can help the reader comprehend it (Anderson & Pearson, 1984). Prereading strategies, such as group discussions and graphic organizers, help students make text-to-self, text-to-text, and text-to-world connections to the text. Teaching a student to activate schema before and during reading will help him better comprehend the text. (The role of prereading strategy instruction in close reading lessons will be addressed more in Chapter 4.)

Monitoring Comprehension   Learning to monitor comprehension and to redirect when the text doesn't make sense is a lifelong reading skill that should be developed in grades 3–5. Harvey and Goudvis (2007) refer to monitoring comprehension as the reader's "inner conversation." Proficient readers carry on conversations about the text in their minds when they read, and they know whether they understand what they are reading. Good readers also have strategies at their disposal to help their comprehension.

We need to engage students in comprehension instruction that makes them aware of their own understanding and how they can help themselves understand the text. Students monitor their own comprehension when they identify where the difficulty lies in comprehending a certain passage, reread to clarify the author's meaning, and look back or ahead in the text (i.e., using context clues) to resolve the problem. The ability to monitor comprehension is vital for readers who are attempting to read complex texts.

Questioning   Proficient readers ask questions of themselves, the authors, and the texts they read (Palincsar & Brown, 1984). Good readers then read to answer their own questions. While they are reading, they may have new questions, which they then read to answer. Asking and answering questions is a key skill in the CCSS Reading Standards. Teaching students to ask and answer questions leads to higher comprehension of a text.

Visualizing and Inferring   Proficient readers create visual and other sensory images from the text during and after reading (Pressley, 1976). When readers visualize, they make inferences and construct meaning (Harvey & Goudvis, 2007). Teaching students to visualize helps their memory and comprehension of text improve (Pressley, 2002). We can teach students to visualize the text by creating a "movie in the mind" (Wilhelm, 1997).

Making inferences is a necessary part of the reading process. No text includes every word or idea that a reader must know to make sense of it, so readers must fill in the gaps by inferring what the author meant. Harvey and Goudvis (2007) link making inferences with visualizing, because students must visualize a character, setting, or concept to make an inference about the author's meaning.

Determining Importance   Readers who are proficient know how to determine the most important ideas and themes in a text (Palincsar & Brown, 1984). Most texts contain much more information than the reader can remember. While reading any piece of text, a proficient reader decides what is and isn't important to remember. We can teach students to decide which ideas and details are the most important, and this in turn enhances comprehension.

Summarizing and Synthesizing   Good readers continually summarize information as they read and add new information to what they have already read (Duke & Pearson, 2002). Proficient readers also synthesize the information in a passage to come up with a new idea about the text (Brown, Day, & Jones, 1983). For example, when reading a story, the reader has to synthesize the information in the story to determine the theme. We can teach students how to summarize text to understand the main ideas and how to synthesize those ideas for deeper comprehension.

Evaluating   *Evaluating* is making judgments about text and involves critical thinking. Readers analyze the author's craft, such as the aesthetic qualities of the text, choice of illustration and style, use of text structure, completeness of the text, power of the storytelling, evidence of style and voice, and use of interesting vocabulary and language structures. Readers also evaluate the authenticity, accuracy, or reliability of the content and the validity of the perspectives presented (Ontario Ministry of Education, n.d.). The ability to evaluate a text is at the heart of comprehension in the CCSS.

Teaching Metacognitive Comprehension Strategies

We teach comprehension strategies using the gradual release of responsibility model (Pearson & Gallagher, 1983), in which we scaffold instruction. Doing so means providing a lot of support at the beginning of instruction and gradually releasing responsibility to the students.

In the gradual release of responsibility model, we first demonstrate how to engage in the strategy, often thinking aloud (Davey, 1983) about our own thought processes while attempting to comprehend a text passage. Next, we have the students engage in the strategy with our support or support from peers. Finally, we ask students to engage in the strategy independently.

Fisher and Frey (2008) suggest using a gradual release of responsibility model to help middle-grades students understand comprehension processes, as well as vocabulary, text structures, and text features. Figure 2.2 provides a list of resources for comprehension strategy instruction.

Tips for the Teacher

"I THINK THESE STANDARDS GET US AWAY from a list of things to teach. With our previous state standards, many teachers thought of them as a checklist. For example, I taught main idea, details, text features . . . check. The Common Core Standards don't allow you that opportunity. The focus is the big picture."

—Melissa, grade 3 teacher

An additional concept that is important to teach students at grades 3, 4, and 5 is the use of visual representations of texts, often called *graphic organizers*. Using graphic organizers can help all students understand the structure of a text, thereby having better comprehension (Fountas & Pinnell, 2001; Marzano et al., 2001; McLaughlin & Overturf, 2013a). Many ideas for metacognitive strategy instruction make good use of graphic organizers.

Although strategies can be introduced individually, readers rarely use one strategy at a time. When we teach comprehension

FIGURE 2.2 ● Resources for Comprehension Strategy Instruction

Blachowicz, C., & Ogle, D. (2008). *Reading comprehension: Strategies for independent learners* (2nd ed.). New York, NY: Guilford Press.

Harvey, S., & Goudvis, A. (2007). *Strategies that work: Teaching comprehension for understanding and engagement* (2nd ed.). Portland, ME: Stenhouse.

McLaughlin, M. (2012). *Guided comprehension for English learners*. Newark, DE: International Reading Association.

McLaughlin, M., & Allen, M. B. (2009). *Guided comprehension in grades 3–8* (2nd ed.). Newark, DE: International Reading Association.

Oczkus, L. D. (2003). *Reciprocal teaching at work: Strategies for improving reading comprehension*. Newark, DE: International Reading Association.

Robb, L. (2003). *Teaching reading in social studies, science, and math: Practical ways to weave comprehension strategies in your content area teaching*. New York, NY: Scholastic.

strategies, we usually teach students that comprehension requires applying a combination of strategies (Pressley, 1976). A number of research-based comprehension routines based on collaborative text discussion have the potential for helping students meet the CCSS. (Comprehension routines are included in Chapter 6, where we discuss the role of speaking and listening in developing literacy.)

Comprehension Development in a CCSS Classroom

IN THE THIRD, FOURTH, AND FIFTH GRADES, we assume that students are already able to comprehend at a basic level. In these grades, we expect students to learn skills to analyze the text, which will lead to higher-level comprehension. Given this expectation, verbs such as *explain, analyze, interpret,* and *compare and contrast* are interspersed throughout the Reading Standards for grades 3–5.

Reading Standard 1: The Overarching Reading Standard

There is a difference between teaching metacognitive strategies to improve comprehension and teaching the skills and strategies needed for analyzing text. When we teach our students what *inference* means and how to make a *logical inference* when reading, we are teaching them metacognitive strategies for comprehension. Teaching these strategies is very different from meeting the expectations stated in the Reading Standards, which are skills that lead to text analysis for deeper comprehension.

Consider the language in Reading Standard 1 (which is the same for both Literature and Informational Text) for grades 3–5, which refers to the concept of inference:

- **Grade 3:** Ask and answer questions to demonstrate understanding of a text, referring explicitly to the text as the basis for the answers.

- **Grade 4:** Refer to details and examples in a text when explaining what the text says explicitly and when drawing inferences from the text.

- **Grade 5:** Quote accurately from a text when explaining what the text says explicitly and when drawing inferences from the text. (NGA & CCSSO, 2010, p. 12)

Note that the skill expectations build across the grades, from asking and answering questions to referring to details and examples to quoting accurately. The expectation that students are able to infer is implicit in these standards.

Reading Standard 1 is the bedrock of CCSS reading lessons. All of the other Reading standards (except for Standard 10, which focuses on text complexity) support students' abilities to meet Reading Standard 1. Let's examine Reading Standard 1 a bit more closely.

Asking Questions about Text   One expectation of Reading Standard 1 (which is stated explicitly in grade 3 and then expected in grades 4–12) is that students can ask questions about a text. Quite a bit of evidence indicates that teaching students to ask questions helps them learn to comprehend the text at a much higher level. Ciardiello (1998) reported that reading comprehension can be improved by teaching students as young as third grade to generate their own authentic questions about a text. Rothstein and Santana (2011) had similar findings and noted that "when students know how to ask their own questions, they take greater ownership of their learning, deepen comprehension, and make new connections and discoveries on their own" (p. 1). Peterson and Taylor (2012) observed that when they taught diverse middle-grades students to ask higher-order questions focused on theme, character interpretation, and making connections to students' lives, students' writing, and talking about books became much richer and their comprehension increased. To help students to learn to ask good questions, we need to plan opportunities for them to ask a lot of questions about texts, in both writing and discussion.

Answering Questions about Text   Another expectation of Reading Standard 1 (again, stated explicitly in the third grade) is the skill of answering questions. Answering questions while reading a text can increase comprehension. Raphael and Au (2005) found that both comprehension of content area texts and test-taking skills were enhanced when students learned where to locate answers to different types of questions—either "In the Book" or "In My Head." Students were taught to think about question–answer relationships (QARs), in which they identified the type of question to decide where the answer might be located: "Right There," "Think & Search," "Author & Me," or "On My Own." When students learned to use the QAR strategy, their skill at answering questions and their comprehension both increased.

We foster comprehension when we ask open, meaning-based questions about the text throughout the reading experience. McKeown, Beck, and Blake (2009) taught students a comprehension routine called Questioning the Author (QtA), in which students use the text as the basis for answers and inferences about informational text. (More information about QtA can be found in Chapter 6 on speaking and listening. Focusing on text-dependent questions helps students understand the text at a deeper level. (Chapter 4 of this book includes more information on the role of text-dependent questions in developing the ability to read complex texts.)

Quoting Accurately   One of the expectations of Reading Standard 1 for fifth-graders is for them to learn to quote accurately when explaining a text. The ability to extract a quote from a text to support thinking is a skill that takes practice. We should plan regular opportunities for students to read and highlight quotes that support their thinking.

Since intermediate students often have difficulty identifying the most important information and instead highlight everything on the page, another idea is to use removable highlighter tape. We can give students a limited amount of highlighter tape so that they can highlight only a small amount of text. As students revise their thinking, they can move the tape to another sentence or phrase. After discussion, invite students to write a summary or analysis of the text and include the phrases or sentences they have highlighted. In addition, remind students that using direct quotes requires quotation marks.

In the Common Core Classroom

Asking "Thick" and "Thin" Questions to Make Logical Inferences

Margot is a fifth-grade reading intervention teacher in a small urban school, and she is teaching her students to ask "thick" questions (those requiring more depth of thinking) versus "thin" questions (those at a more literal level) about a text (Lewin & Shoemaker, 1998). Although being able to "ask and answer questions" is an explicit expectation of Reading Standard 1 for grade 3 (NGA & CCSSO, 2010, p. 12), Margot realizes that asking and answering in-depth questions is a vital skill for comprehension and text analysis beyond this grade. She also knows that one of the major instructional shifts in the CCSS for Reading, beginning in third grade, is the emphasis on text-based evidence. Reading Standard 1 for fifth-grade students is "Quote accurately from a text when explaining what the text says explicitly and when drawing inferences from the text" (NGA & CCSSO, 2010, p. 12) The focus of Reading Standard 1 is being able to support an answer or opinion by referring to a text. Students should be able to make logical inferences and talk or write about the words in the text that helped them make those inferences.

Margot has evidence that her students need more time with these concepts. During a previous lesson on inference, Margot's students struggled. When she asked them to think of questions they could ask that would help them better understand the text, she realized that her students had not had much experience with asking higher-level questions. All of their questions were literal; that is, the questions could be answered in one or two words from the text. This brief formative assessment demonstrated that Margot's students needed more instruction on how to ask higher-level questions to make inferences. Margot planned three lessons to teach students how to ask "thicker" questions to infer as well as quote accurately from the text.

In the first lesson, Margot showed students a picture and provided examples of thick and thin questions that could be asked about the image. As students sorted the questions into "Thick" and "Thin" categories, they explained what made each question thick or thin. Margot and the class created an anchor chart that contained the definitions of thick and thin questions and question stems that students could use to help ask thicker questions—for example, "In what ways did . . .?" and "How did . . . affect . . .?" Margot discussed how students needed to use their inference skills to be able to create questions such as these.

In the second lesson, Margot encouraged her students to focus on the actual text by pulling quotes from a text selection and carefully enclosing each quote in quotation marks. She then invited students to ask thick and thin questions based on the quotes and the information in the text. During this lesson, Margot modeled less and encouraged students to practice the strategy more independently. Although she selected the first four quotes, she gradually released the responsibility to the students. Each student found two quotes on his or her own, enclosed them in quotation marks, and wrote a reflection about how asking questions improved his or her comprehension of the text.

For the third lesson, Margot selected a text excerpt about Christopher Columbus from *History Alive! America's Past* (Bower & Lobdell, 2001), which connected with the fifth-grade social studies unit. After briefly reviewing thick and thin questions and the anchor chart of question stems, Margot stated the purpose of the lesson: "We are learning how to ask thick versus thin questions to help us gain a better understanding of the text." She asked students to read the passage as a whole class first, so they had a general idea of what the passage was about. Next, she pulled four specific quotes from the text and modeled how to ask thick versus thin questions for the first two quotes. She modeled how to justify whether a question was thick or thin by thinking aloud about where she could find the information to answer the question. She also demonstrated how to complete a graphic organizer as she modeled her thinking.

For the third and fourth quotes, Margot invited students to turn and talk with partners about thick and thin questions they could ask based on the information from the text. The students also discussed their justifications for their questions. Margot asked each student to find two more quotes independently, write them on the graphic organizer (with quotation marks), and develop one thick and one thin question for a quote he or she had chosen. Margot asked probing questions to help guide some students who were struggling to create a thick question. Finally, she invited each student to write a short reflection at the bottom of the graphic organizer to explain how asking thicker questions help him or her understand the text better.

In the first two lessons, Margot had observed that students were just asking the first question that came to mind without referencing the text first to see if their questions could be answered. During the third lesson, Margot assessed her students through questioning and observation. As students worked together in small groups, they had great discussions about the questions. They often offered their partners suggestions on how to make a thin question into a thick question. Students also justified to one another why questions were thick or thin.

As students discussed their questions, Margot circulated around the room to help clarify any misconceptions and to informally assess which students were on target. Doing this also gave her the opportunity to ask students what new information they were learning based on their questions. Margot observed that some students still struggled a bit with how to word some of their thick questions, but they did a much better job of asking why for every question. She also observed that students were beginning to combine multiple strategies, such as making inferences and synthesizing information. Applying this combination of strategies really helped them begin to understand information that was not supplied by the author.

At the end of the third lesson, Margot collected each student's graphic organizer and assessed it on an individual basis. Doing this helped her get a sense of the ways in which individual students could infer by quickly analyzing how they used thick questions to make inferences about Christopher Columbus. She also noted that, based on the graphic organizers, all of the students were able to ask appropriate thin questions from both of

FIGURE 2.3 • Student's Completed Graphic Organizer on Questioning

Asking Questions Organizer

"Christopher Columbus"

Quote from text	Question	Justification (Thick vs. Thin)
"As a child, Columbus had read about the travels of Marco Polo."	• Why did columbus choose Marco polo to read about?	• This is a thick question because columbus could have chosen to read about someone else.
"Columbus named the island San Salvador, which means "Holy Savior" in Spanish. He claimed it for Spain."	• How did columbus claim san salvador for spain?	- This is a thick question because the text does not tell us how explorers marked or claimed territory for their country.
"In fact, when he died in 1506, he didn't know that he had reached the New World. Other Spanish and Portuguese explorers did find gold."	• What influences did he have on other explorers? • How were the spanish and portuguese explorers inspired by columbus?	• These are thick questions because the author does not tell us how columbus influenced other explorers, but we know he did because they continued to explore after his death.
"Columbus was also interested in finding these faraway lands."	• Was columbus interested in exploring these faraway lands?	• This is a thin question because the text tells us the answer.
"So, around the age 15, Columbus became a sailor."	• Did columbus become a sailor around the age 15?	• This is a thin question because the text tells me the answer.
"The portuguese were trying to get to asia by sailing south around the southern tip of Africa."	• What harsh conditions kept the portuguese from getting to Asia quickly?	• This is a thick question because the author does not tell me the things that the portuguese might have experienced on their voyage.

Reflection: Asking thicker questions helped me learn that columbus was an inspiration to other explorers even though he died without knowing that he had actually reached the new world.

the quotes Margot had selected and from their own quotes. Only three students were unsuccessful in asking appropriate thick questions from the quotes they selected. These students were in the same guided reading group, so Margot has decided to continue to practice with them in their reading group.

Most of Margot's students still need additional support with justifying why their question is a thick question. Many of them said their question was thick because the answer was not in the text. While that statement is true, Margot will need to go back and model how students can piece together information from the text and from thick questions to develop new ideas about a topic.

Students also practiced quoting accurately while supporting their inferences as they created questions about text. Figure 2.3 illustrates a fifth-grader's graphic organizer on asking and answering questions to support inferences.

Overview of the Reading Standards

THERE ARE FOUR CLUSTERS OF READING STANDARDS (for both Literature and Informational Text):

1. Key Ideas and Details
2. Craft and Structure

3. Integration of Knowledge and Ideas

4. Range of Reading and Level of Text Complexity (NGA & CCSSO, 2010)

Reading Standards 1–3 are in the category Key Ideas and Details cluster. These standards are focused on determining what the text says. In this cluster of standards, students are expected to determine the author's message. Besides learning the skills in Reading Standard 1, in Literature, students explore the theme, moral, or lesson that can be derived from the text and determine details about the characters, settings, and events. In the Informational Text standards, students learn to determine main ideas and details and identify relationships among concepts.

Reading Standards 4–6 are grouped under the cluster heading Craft and Structure. These standards are focused on the way the author wrote the text. Students are expected to think about the author's craft and the text structures the author used. In Literature, students analyze the author's choices of words and phrases, text structures, and point of view. In Informational Text, students emphasize domain-specific words and phrases, text structures for these kinds of texts, and point of view and author's purpose.

Reading Standards 7–9 (there is no Standard 8 for Literature) are grouped into the cluster Integration of Knowledge and Ideas. These standards are focused on the meaning of the text, its value, and how it connects to other texts. In this cluster of standards, students think about visual and multimedia elements of a text and compare and contrast texts.

Reading Standard 10 is the sole standard in the cluster for Range of Reading and Level of Text Complexity. This standard is focused on the expectation that students will move up the staircase of text complexity. Third-grade students are expected to read stories, poems, dramas, and informational texts in the grades 2–3 text complexity band. Fourth- and fifth-grade students are expected to read stories, poems, dramas, and informational texts in the grades 4–5 text complexity band. (See Chapter 4 for more information about text complexity expectations.)

The ELA Standards were designed to be an integrated model of literacy. Therefore, each Reading standard is tightly interwoven with the other Reading standards, as well as the standards in Writing, Speaking and Listening, and Language. We will rarely plan and teach a lesson that focuses on skills in a Reading standard that does not connect with the other ELA standards.

Reading Standards 2–9 for Literature and Informational Text

AS DISCUSSED EARLIER, READING STANDARD 1 is the overarching Reading standard. Reading Standard 1 is the expectation that students will read text closely to comprehend, analyze, and interpret. Reading Standard 10 is the standard that sets the expectation for text complexity. The skills that students must develop to read and comprehend such complex texts are included in Reading Standards 2–9.

Teaching Reading Standards 2–9 for Literature

Students will be able to read literary text with deeper comprehension if they learn particular concepts emphasized in grades 3–5. Some of these concepts are as follows:

- theme
- characterization

- retelling and summarizing literary text
- determining the meanings of literary words and phrases
- discussing stories, dramas, and poems
- point of view in literary text
- analyzing illustrations
- comparing and contrasting literary text

Theme   Fourth- and fifth-graders should be able to determine the theme of a story, drama, or poem based on details in the text. After teaching the concept of theme (such as friendship, honesty, etc.), we can gather examples of picture books, poems, and fables and have students group them according to what the themes seem to be. We can then ask students to explain their decisions and justify their thinking when deciding the theme for a particular group of texts.

Another way to help students determine theme is to use higher-order questioning (Peterson & Taylor, 2012). For example, after reading an excerpt from *Because of Winn-Dixie* (DiCamillo, 2000), we can ask students questions such as "How do you know someone is your friend? What does he or she say? Can you be friends with people who are different from you? Why or why not?" (Peterson & Taylor, 2012, p. 297). We can teach students to look for the qualities of friendship within the story and ask questions such as "How did the author show that Opal was a friend?" By taking this a step further and asking students to find and cite evidence in the text that shows how the author demonstrates that Opal was a good friend, we are also helping students meet Reading Standard 1.

Understanding Characters   Characterization is an important component of the Key Ideas and Details category of Literature standards in grades 3–5. Understanding the characters in a story or drama is essential to understanding the author's message. Often, the author reveals his or her intent through the dialogue or actions of characters (Roser et al., 2007). The setting helps establish the tone and mood of a story. Students should be able to describe characters, settings, and events and include important details in their descriptions.

One way we can help students develop skills to analyze character traits, thoughts, motivations, feelings, and interactions is to involve them in an activity called Hot Seat. This activity is often used in drama groups to help actors develop their characters. To use Hot Seat to foster comprehension, have students read a selected text. Next, form small groups of three to five students, and ask each student to choose a character from the story. Each student studies his or her chosen character carefully and prepares for an interrogation from the rest of the class. All of the students also prepare questions to ask the other characters, based on information about those characters in the story. During the Hot Seat activity, the student takes on the persona of his or her prepared character and answers questions from that character's perspective. We may choose to arrange for individual students to be on the Hot Seat, or students may sit on a panel to answer questions as their characters. The class may also choose to use puppets, masks, or props in this activity.

Retelling and Summarizing   Third-graders are expected to be able to recount (retell) stories, with a particular focus on fables, folktales, and myths from diverse cultures. Fourth- and fifth-grade students should be able to summarize a literary text. When students write a summary of a literary text, they include the important parts of the story line: the beginning, setting, characters, problem, sequence of events, resolution, and ending.

Creating a story map can help students think through the major parts of a story when they prepare to retell or summarize (McLaughlin & Overturf, 2013a). An interactive story map is available at the website ReadWriteThink (www.readwritethink.org). Students can use this story map to help them think through the storyline in a more detailed way. At the ReadWriteThink site, students can use story maps that focus on character, setting, conflict, and resolution to help them analyze and summarize a story. (More information about summarizing can be found in Chapter 5.)

Determining the Meanings of Literary Words and Phrases   Students should possess strategies to be able to determine the meanings of unfamiliar words and phrases as they are used in a text. In third grade, students should be able to distinguish literal from nonliteral language, such as figures of speech and idioms. Fourth-grade students should be able to determine the meanings of words that allude to significant characters found in mythology. (See Chapter 8 for ways to teach this standard.) In fifth grade, students should be able to understand figurative language, such as metaphors and similes. Determining the meanings of unfamiliar words is so important that Language Standards 4–6 delineate specific expectations for vocabulary development. (More information about these concepts in vocabulary instruction can be found in Chapter 3.)

One activity for developing vocabulary that fosters comprehension of narrative text is called Story Impressions (McGinley & Denner, 1987). Before students read a story, arrange them in pairs or small groups. Then provide each group with a stack of cards containing 8 or 10 key words and phrases from the story. (You can write the words on the board instead, but with cards, the activity becomes hands-on and students can rearrange the words as they discuss.) Students work in pairs to arrange the words in an order that makes sense to them. As an alternative, arrange the words on the board in the order they appear and draw downward arrows between them (McLaughlin & Overturf, 2013b). Doing this gives students more of a scaffold for thinking about the storyline.

For example, for the children's book *Uncle Jed's Barbershop* (Mitchell, 1993), the word cards might include the following words from the story:

barbershop	clippers	lathered
sharecroppers	separate	barber
operation	segregation	Great Depression

While arranging and discussing the words, students can use reference materials to find the meanings of any words they don't know.

After completing the card activity, students can then write their own stories based on the words or write their general impression of what the story will be about. After students have created their story impressions, ask them to share their stories. Then have them read or hear the story read aloud and compare and contrast their versions with the original. Also have students discuss the words and how they are used in the story.

Discussing Stories, Dramas, and Poems   When students discuss stories, poems, and plays, they should be able to use the correct terminology. For instance, in discussing the structure of a literary work, they should use terms such as *chapter, stanza,* and *scene.*

Robert Frost's classic poem "Stopping by Woods on a Snowy Evening" is included as a text exemplar in the grades 2–3 text complexity band, but it is appropriate for much older students because of the deeper ways it can be interpreted. To introduce the poem, share the beautiful picture book *Stopping by Woods on a Snowy Evening,* illustrated by Susan Jeffers (Frost, 2001).

After reading aloud the picture book to allow students to hear the expressive language, encourage them to discuss the meaning of the poem. Then explicitly teach the concepts of rhythm and rhyme in the poem. For example, when listening to the poem, it is easy to imagine the rhythm of a horse trotting, with sleigh bells jingling. By experimenting with rhythm instruments, students can better understand the definition of *rhythm* in poetry and how it sometimes adds to the meaning.

Next, discuss the rhyme. Frost wrote the poem with an AABA rhyme pattern. This means that the A lines rhyme, whereas the B line is different for each stanza until the last one. There, changing to an AAAA rhyme pattern and repeating the last lines serve to slow down the rhythm (much like a horse slowing down or a person falling asleep). Provide students with individual copies so they can practice reading the poem as a choral or echo reading.

As we lead students to discuss the meaning of the poem, we should also teach them to use terms such as *stanza, rhyme,* and *rhythm.* Expecting students to discuss literature using the correct terms for the structures of books, stories, poems, and dramas will help them begin to meet the expectations of this cluster of standards.

Point of View in Literary Text   Another expectation in the Reading standards is that students understand varied points of view. A favorite text to teach first-person point of view is *Voices in the Park* (Browne, 1998). At first glance, this is a picture book with text that seems more appropriate for younger children. In fact, however, this text has been used successfully with middle school students to teach perspective and point of view.

In *Voices in the Park,* an incident is told from four different perspectives. Each character tells the same story from his or her point of view, using a unique voice. The illustrations and fonts that appear in the book match the different characters' personalities and outlooks on life, from the snooty mother to her almost invisible son. We can replicate excerpts of the text using an appropriate font for each character. Then students can read the different characters' point of view without the illustrations and engage in discussions about who is talking and what is happening in the story. When students see the illustrations and read the story again, they pay particular attention to the point of view of each character. A book like *Voices in the Park* can become a touchstone text when discussing point of view of the characters or the narrator in a more complex text.

In the Common Core Classroom

Writing "I" Poems to Develop Characterization and Point of View

Melissa is a third-grade teacher in a rural school who taught her students to analyze character traits in literary text. She prepared for this lesson by rereading the article "'I' Poems: Invitations for Students to Deepen Literary Understanding," by Linda Kucan (2007). An "I" poem is narrated in first person from the point of view of a person, place, or object.

According to Kucan, having students write "I" poems can help deepen their understanding of character, setting, plot, and point of view.

Melissa felt that guiding her third-graders to write "I" poems would help them explore character traits and begin to meet Reading Literature Standard 3.3: "Describe characters in a story (e.g., their traits, motivations, or feelings) and explain how their actions contribute to the sequence of events" (NGA & CCSSO, 2010, p. 12). She also realized that this lesson would help students develop skills for Reading Literature Standard 3.6: "Distinguish their own point of view from that of the narrator or those of the characters" (NGA & CCSSO, 2010, p. 12).

Melissa's class had discussed different ways to describe characters (e.g., their actions, their thoughts, what they say, what they look like, their feelings, etc.) for three days prior to this lesson. They had created an anchor chart about character traits and a flipchart to learn about the different ways they could analyze or describe a character. For today's lesson, Melissa wanted to use an easy text to scaffold her students' learning about characterization. She decided to use the book *Henry's Freedom Box: A True Story from the Underground Railroad* (Levine, 2007), which is the story of a slave who decides to mail himself to freedom. In using *Henry's Freedom Box,* Melissa planned to help students explore a character's thoughts, actions, and feelings as well as point of view. Next, she planned to invite her students to write "I" poems from Henry's point of view. Melissa felt that this activity would give each student a chance to show his or her individual creativity in describing the traits and point of view of the same character. To prepare for the lesson, Melissa created a new flipchart for students to use as a template for writing "I" poems (see Figure 2.4. She wrote several sentence stems on the chart to help students begin thinking like the character.

Melissa began the lesson by introducing the student learning target: "I can describe how a character in a story might think." The class reviewed the anchor chart about character traits and the flipchart about ways to analyze or describe a character. Then Melissa introduced the book *Henry's Freedom Box* (Levine, 2007). She read the story aloud and conducted a think-aloud (Davey, 1983) about Henry, the main character of the story. Periodically, she asked students to turn and talk with a partner about Henry. After reading the story, Melissa invited students to describe Henry in their reading journals. When students had finished, they shared what they had written with the other students at their table.

Next, Melissa introduced the "I" poem and the flipchart with the template (see Figure 2.4). She invited students to write their own "I" poems from the viewpoint of Henry. She knew

---

FIGURE 2.4 ● Flipchart Providing "I" Poem Template

I am_____

I wonder _____

I hear _____

Source: Kucan (2007).

FIGURE 2.5 ● Derek's "I" Poem

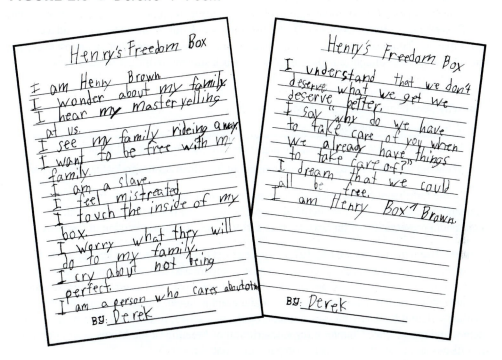

Henry's Freedom Box

I am Henry Brown
I wonder about my family
I hear my master yelling
at us.
I see my family rideing away.
I want to be free with my
family.
I am a slave.
I feel mistreated
I touch the inside of my
box.
I worry what they will
do to my family.
I cry about not being
perfect.
I am a person who cares aboutoth

BY: Derek

Henry's Freedom Box

I understand that we don't
deserve what we get we
deserve better.
I say "why do we have
to take care of you when
we already have things
to take care of?"
I dream that we could
all be free.
I am Henry Box Brown.

BY: Derek

a few students would have trouble writing many lines, so she decided to give the students a choice in deciding how many lines the poem could be, with the stipulation that it had to be at least six lines. Melissa's students responded with enthusiasm! They loved the story and were excited to write their own poems from Henry's point of view. As Melissa circulated through the room and began reading the students' poems, she was amazed. Every student was engaged and describing Henry by focusing on key events in the story.

Melissa assessed her students by observing them during discussion and while they were writing in their reading journals. She observed that each student was able to write an "I" poem with no problems. She assessed students' work against the expectations of the CCSS by analyzing each child's "I" poem. By carefully studying the students' work, Melissa could determine if they really understood the character of Henry and could put themselves in his position. She also noted the different ways that students chose to describe him. Some poems were insightful and in-depth. Several of her students really got into the mind of the character and made inferences about what it must have been like to be a slave. Figure 2.5 presents Derek's "I" poem about the character of Henry.

Analyzing Illustrations   Literary texts at the elementary level often include illustrations that help tell the story. In third grade, students are expected to explain how illustrations contribute to the mood, aspects of a character, or setting of a text. O'Neil (2011) used picture books to help elementary students develop visual literacy for comprehension, emphasizing that artists use color, line, shape, size, and style to help tell the story. She also described four modes of picture/text interaction.

The study of text illustrations can involve sophisticated comprehension skills. For example, in *A Sweet Smell of Roses* (Johnson, 2005), two girls sneak out of the house to attend a civil rights march. The illustrations, by Eric Velasquez, are pencil drawings, but on almost every page, one small object is colored red. Questions we may ask student to discuss include these:

- How does the artist portray the mood of the story?
- Why does he use pencil as a medium?
- What does the color red stand for?
- What does it mean that three of the pages are completely black and white?
- What are the motifs (i.e., recurring images) in the illustrations, and what do they mean?

In the fourth and fifth grades, students not only analyze illustrations, but they also compare and make connections in the elements between the text and a visual, oral, or multimedia presentation of the text, such as a video, play, or movie version of the story.

Comparing and Contrasting Literary Text   Once students have learned to determine the theme of a text, they are expected to learn to compare and contrast themes, characters, settings, and plots. One way to develop this skill is to compare and contrast different versions of the same story, such as a text-only version and a graphic novel. Other ways are to compare and contrast different books by the same author, books in a series, or different treatments of similar themes and topics. (See Chapter 6 for a description of Meeting of the Minds, a strategy that uses discussion to teach students to compare and contrast texts.)

Teaching Reading Standards for Informational Text

Students' comprehension of informational texts will be deeper if they understand the following concepts, which are emphasized in grades 3–5:

- main idea and supporting details
- summarizing
- relationships among concepts
- meanings of domain-specific words and phrases
- text features and structures
- point of view in literature and author's purpose in informational text
- interpreting information from print and digital sources
- supporting an opinion
- integrating information from multiple texts

Main Idea and Supporting Details   Determining the main idea is a fairly traditional reading skill, but it is often difficult for students at this level. In reading informational text, we can teach students that one way to determine the main idea is to identify the words and concepts that are mentioned most often in the text. These words and concepts often represent what the text is about.

This is the idea behind visual Internet tools such as Wordle (www.wordle.net), which allow users to generate "word clouds" from text they provide. For example, Figure 2.6 is a word cloud that represents the main idea of a nonfiction article about the last orbit of the Hubble Space Telescope.

FIGURE 2.6 ● "Word Cloud" about Hubble Space Telescope

Another strategy, called Sticking to the Main Idea, is discussed by Herrera, Perez, and Escamilla (2010) as being effective for English language learners. To teach this strategy, generate a list of vocabulary words representing four to six key concepts in the text. Give each student four to six sticky notes, and ask him or her to write each vocabulary word at the top of one of the notes (one word per note). Then have the student draw a picture representing the word on the front of the sticky note, below the written word.

Once the sticky notes have been prepared, have each student read the text individually, looking for the specific words in the text. As the student comes across a sentence with one of the words, he or she writes the sentence on the back of the sticky note and places the note in the margin of the text. After each student has read the passage and completed working with the sticky notes, have them work in pairs or small groups to retell what they learned using their sticky notes as a guide.

Summarizing   Fourth- and fifth-graders are also expected to be able to summarize informational texts. Summarizing is a college- and career-readiness skill that students will need to meet the higher expectations in all content areas. When students summarize, they identify the main idea and key supporting details in a text. (See Chapter 5 on ways to write summaries of informational text.)

Relationships Among Concepts   Students in grades 3–5 are expected to be able to describe the relationship among items in a series of historical events, a set of scientific ideas or concepts, or the steps in a technical procedure. For example, the book *Build It! Activities for Setting Up Super Structures* (Good, 1999) is considered a technical text. In it, students read directions to be able to build three-dimensional objects, such as bridges and domes. Text is included that gives background information about the science underlying each structure and how it is used, and an ideas section helps students think creatively about projects they could do with the object. We can ask students to follow the directions to build the structure. We can then ask them to explain how the background information, the steps in the directions, and other information in the text is connected and helps them understand more about the structure they have built.

Meanings of Domain-Specific Words and Phrases   Vocabulary is a key to understanding concepts in science, social studies, and mathematics. Understanding domain-specific words and phrases in an informational text means being able to understand what the text is about. (Chapter 3 is focused on vocabulary development, including domain-specific words and phrases.)

An activity that can be used to develop vocabulary for comprehension in reading literature or informational text is creating an alphabet book that includes the key ideas and vocabulary in the text. Students can work in small groups to choose words or phrases related to the text that begin with each letter, and they can collaborate to illustrate the pages to show the definition of each word or phrase. This activity engages students in thinking about the meanings of words and phrases in a text before, during, and after reading.

Students can create a simple, structured electronic alphabet book by going to the website ReadWriteThink and using the interactive alphabet organizer (www.readwritethink.org). They can also use programs such as PowerPoint and Photo Story (both Microsoft products) to create electronic alphabet books that include scanned artwork, digital photos, approved Internet images, and recorded narration (Evers, Lang, & Smith, 2011).

Text Features and Structures   Informational text is often "inconsiderate" in terms of being written in a way that is unfamiliar and confusing to students (Armbruster, 2004). This includes the use of unfamiliar text features and structures. Being able to understand text features and structures is an important part of comprehending informational texts.

Text features include those elements of a story or article that are not part of the main body of the text. They include the table of contents and index, pictures or photographs with captions, headings, bold words, diagrams, maps, charts, and so on. Text features are added to provide more information about the text, yet we know that students often ignore them (Kelley & Clausen-Grace, 2010).

We can teach intermediate students to take a "text feature walk" before reading an informational text. First, we can do a think-aloud (Davey, 1983) to model how to think about each text feature. Next, we can have students work in small groups to identify text features, read and interpret them, and make predictions and draw conclusions about the main body of the text, based on their preview (Kelley & Clausen-Grace, 2010).

Understanding expository text structures is another key to comprehension of informational text for intermediate students. When students recognize text structures such as description, sequence, compare–contrast, cause–effect, and problem–solution, they are better able to navigate more difficult content area texts (Akhondi, Malayeri, & Samad, 2011; Dole et al., 1991).

We can teach common text structures using graphic organizers. We can also help students recognize signal words and phrases. For example, words such as *first, second,* and *third* signal a sequence (called a *chronology* in the CCSS), and the phrase *as a result* signals that the author is discussing cause and effect. (See McLaughlin and Overturf [2013b] for a thorough discussion of text structure in teaching the ELA Standards.)

Point of View or Author's Purpose   Students are expected to understand the point of view the author assumes when writing an informational text. One way to teach point of view in social studies is to introduce students to the idea of primary and secondary sources. For example, *American Documents: The Mayflower Compact* (Yero, 2006) uses images of original documents and photographs of locations to help tell the story of the Pilgrims' voyage to America. Another example is *Christopher Columbus (In Their Own Words)* (Roop & Roop, 2000), which tells the story of Columbus's voyages. The authors write about Columbus as biographers but include excerpts from Columbus's diary as firsthand accounts. Students can compare and contrast the perspectives of the two authors, discussing possible reasons for their differences. Student can then role-play the same event from different perspectives.

Interpreting Information from Print and Digital Sources   Research suggests that many students need to engage in focused instruction in visual literacy. McTigue and Flowers (2011) found that most of the students they studied in grades 2–8 had very little understanding of the diagrams in science texts. The researchers also found that elementary teachers tended merely to point to diagrams or to skip over diagrams in their instruction.

Science texts depend on diagrams and other images to help relay scientific information. Similarly, social studies texts include timelines, photographs, and charts to help relay information and explain events. We need to provide the time for students to study visual images closely in print and digital sources (Flynt & Brozo, 2010). Modeling how to study an image to help us learn can better help our students learn the purpose of images that have been included in text. Students can then work with partners to point out what they notice about a selected image and discuss how it relates to the text. We can invite students to describe an image in writing for deeper understanding.

Supporting an Opinion   One of the instructional shifts in the CCSS is the expectation that students learn to read and write arguments as a college-readiness skill. The term *argument* is first introduced in grade 6. Based on the standards for grades 3–5, we teach students to analyze an author's opinion and the supporting reasons and evidence he or she provides for that opinion. First, we model how to think through a text that includes an opinion. Then, we engage students in lessons in which they talk about how they think an author supported his or her opinion.

After students have had plenty of modeling and engaged in whole- and small-group discussions, we can provide them with copies of a text that contains an opinion and supporting evidence. Working with partners, students cut the article into parts representing the opinion and the evidence supporting it. The partners then arrange the pieces of the article onto a sheet of construction paper and explain how the author supported the opinion.

One of the best ways to teach students how to analyze an opinion is to have them write and support their own opinions. (See Chapter 5 for more on teaching students to write opinions.) We can also teach students to listen to a speaker and determine how he or she supported his or her opinion.

Integrating Information from Multiple Texts   Another expectation of the CCSS—most explicitly, the Writing Standards—is that students will conduct short research projects to be able to write and speak knowledgeably about a subject. This expectation is aligned with Writing Standards 7 and 8.

For students to meet these standards, our classrooms should be flooded with a variety of texts and digital sources. Students must have access to the resources they need to conduct research. We ensure that students have opportunities to integrate information and build knowledge about a topic when we plan for thematic instruction. We invite students to engage in projects requiring research when we set them on the path to finding an answer to an authentic question or problem. Along the way, we teach them to evaluate texts and websites as appropriate sources for their research. (Chapter 5 includes more about research and writing.)

Comprehension Assessment in a CCSS Classroom

IN CLASSROOMS IN WHICH TEACHERS KNOW THEIR STUDENTS and their students' needs well, assessment is part of the instructional plan. Both teachers and students have specific learning goals for specific students, and both work to help students attain those goals.

When we think about assessing comprehension, we often think about giving reading tests in which students answer questions about a text. Constructing good tests of this sort of tests takes expertise. Also, these tests don't usually tell us much about how well students can apply what they are learning. In the CCSS classroom, there is an emphasis not only on testing students' progress through summative assessment (e.g., tests) but also on using formative assessment. Formative assessment is part of our everyday instruction, when we step back to observe and reflect on students' understanding of skills and strategies.

Leahy et al. (2005) have described this type of classroom:

In a classroom that uses assessment to support learning . . . instruction and assessment blurs. Everything students do—such as conversing in groups, completing seatwork, answering and asking questions, . . . even sitting silently and looking confused—is a potential source of information. (p. 19)

To use formative assessment in the CCSS classroom, we carefully observe how students approach tasks and listen to their comments during discussions about texts. We analyze students' completed graphic organizers and writing in response to reading. We also give our students specific feedback about their progress and provide suggestions about how they might improve. Formative assessment is based on goals for learning, and students should be part of setting and working to meet those goals.

Classrooms That Support Comprehension Development

THE CCSS FOR READING, WRITING, SPEAKING AND LISTENING, and Language are intended to be integrated throughout literacy instruction (NGA & CCSSO, 2010). For students to develop literacy competence, we need to plan rich instructional tasks that address the expectations of the Standards. We also need to create a classroom environment that supports comprehension development.

According to Duke and Pearson (2002), classrooms that support comprehension have a number of instructional qualities. In these classrooms, students spend a lot of time reading, especially real texts for authentic purposes. Students read the different types of texts that their teachers want them to learn to comprehend. Teachers plan for vocabulary development, engaging students in reading, experience, and discussion of words and their meanings. Students learn to decode text accurately and automatically. Students spend a lot of time writing for others, and both teachers and students engage in deep discussions about text.

All of these qualities are readily supported by the ELA Standards. Figure 2.7 shows how the ELA Standards correlate with each of these components for comprehension development.

McLaughlin (2012) would add that we must motivate and engage students, teach reading comprehension strategies, encourage students to use multiple modes of representative thinking, embed formative assessments, and engage students in critical literacy experiences. Including all of these components in our classroom literacy plan will ensure that our students are learning to read and meeting the ELA Standards at a high level.

Thinking about Comprehension in Grades 3–5

COMPREHENSION INSTRUCTION IN A GRADES 3–5 CCSS CLASSROOM is multifaceted. We teach students to recognize unfamiliar multisyllabic words, develop fluency, understand academic vocabulary, and apply metacognitive strategies to build their foundational skills for comprehension. We frequently engage students in discussions and encourage them to write about complex texts so they learn to think deeply about the author's ideas and connect those ideas to what they know. In addition, we provide time for students' independent reading of texts they enjoy, so they will love to read. Our goal is to pave the way for a lifetime of reading and learning from text.

FIGURE 2.7 ● How the ELA Standards Support Comprehension Development
in the Classroom

Components of Environment That Supports Comprehension*	How Components are Supported in ELA Standards
Students spend a good deal of time reading.	Students are expected to read a variety of literature and informational texts and to use print and digital resources.
Students experience reading real texts for real reasons.	Students are expected to conduct short research projects to find answers to questions and solutions to problems.
Students experience reading the range of text genres that teachers want them to comprehend.	Students are expected to read a range of text genres (including stories, dramas, poetry, and literary nonfiction) and texts in history, science, and technical subjects.
Teachers plan an environment rich in vocabulary and concept development through reading, experience, and discussion of words and their meanings.	Vocabulary development is embedded in the standards for literature, informational text, writing, and language. Students are expected to use speaking and listening in all of these areas.
Students develop strong skills in the accurate and automatic decoding of text.	The Foundational Skills standards address word recognition, determining the meanings of multisyllabic words, and reading fluency.
Students spend a lot of time writing texts for others to read and comprehend.	The Writing standards set the expectation for students to write opinions, informative/explanatory texts, and narratives. Students are expected to write to share the results of their research and to write for publication.
Teachers and students engage in high-quality discussions about text.	The Speaking and Listening standards refer often to discussions about text.

*Based on Duke & Pearson (2002).

REFERENCES

Akhondi, M., Malayeri, F. A., & Samad, A. A. (2011). How to teach expository text structures to facilitate reading comprehension. *The Reading Teacher, 64*(5), 368–372.

Allington, R. L. (2009). *What really matters in fluency: Research-based practices across the curriculum.* Boston, MA: Allyn & Bacon.

Allington, R. L., & Johnston, P. H. (2002). *Reading to learn: Lessons from exemplary fourth-grade classrooms.* New York, NY: Guilford Press.

Anderson, R. C., & Pearson, P. D. (1984). A schema-theoretic view of basic processes in reading comprehension. *Handbook of reading research, 1,* 255–291.

Armbruster, B. B. (2004). Considerate texts. In D. Lapp, J. Flood, & N. Farnan (Eds.), *Content area reading and learning: Instructional strategies* (2nd ed., pp. 47–58). Mahwah, NJ: Erlbaum.

Bear, D. R., Invernizzi, M., Templeton, S., & Johnston, F. (2011). *Words their way: Word study for phonics, vocabulary, and spelling instruction* (5th ed.). Boston, MA: Allyn & Bacon.

Beck, I. L., & McKeown, M. G. (2001). Inviting students into the pursuit of meaning. *Educational Psychology Review, 13*(3), 225–241.

Blachowicz, C., & Fisher, P. J. (2010). *Teaching vocabulary in all classrooms.* Boston, MA: Allyn & Bacon.

Bluestein, N. A. (2010). Unlocking text features for determining importance in expository text: A strategy for struggling readers. *The Reading Teacher, 63*(7), 597–600.

Brown, A. L., Day, J. D., & Jones, R. S. (1983). The development of plans for summarizing texts. *Child Development, 54*(4), 968–979.

Ciardiello, A. V. (2007). Puzzle them first: Motivating adolescent readers with question-finding. Newark, DE: International Reading Association.

Davey, B. (1983). Think aloud: Modeling the cognitive processes of reading comprehension. *Journal of Reading, 27*(1), 44–47.

Dewitz, P., Jones, J., & Leahy, S. (2009). Comprehension strategy instruction in core reading programs. *Reading Research Quarterly, 44*(2), 102–126.

Dole, J. A., Duffy, G. G., Roehler, L. R., & Pearson, P. D. (1991). Moving from the old to the new: Research on reading comprehension instruction. *Review of Educational Research, 61*(2), 239–264.

Duke, N. K., & Pearson, P. D. (2002). Effective practices for developing reading comprehension. In A. E. Farstrup & S. J. Samuels (Eds.), *What research has to say about reading instruction* (3rd ed., pp. 205–242). Newark, DE: International Reading Association.

Durkin, D. (1978). What classroom observations reveal about reading comprehension instruction. *Reading research quarterly,* 481–533.

Evers, A. J., Lang, L. F., & Smith, S. V. (2011). An ABC literacy journey: Anchoring in texts, bridging language, and creating stories. *The Reading Teacher, 62*(6), 461–470.

Fisher, D., & Frey, N. (2008). What does it take to create skilled readers? Facilitating the transfer and application of literacy strategies. *Voices from the Middle, 15*(4), 16–22.

Flynt, E. S., & Brozo, W. (2010). Visual literacy and the content classroom: A question of now, not when. *The Reading Teacher, 63*(6), 526–528.

Formative Assessment for Students and Teachers (FAST), State Collaborative on Assessment and Student Standards (SCASS). (2008, October). *Attributes of effective formative assessment.* Paper prepared for the Formative Assessment for Teachers and Students State Collaborative on Assessment and Student Standards of the Council of Chief State School Officers. Washington, DC: Council of Chief State School Officers.

Fountas, I. C., & Pinnell, G. S. (2001). *Guiding readers and writers, grades 3-6: Teaching comprehension, genre, and content literacy.* Westport, CT: Heinemann.

Goodwin, A., Lipsky, M., & Ahn, S. (2012). Word detectives: Using units of meaning to support literacy. *The Reading Teacher, 65*(7), 461–470.

Hasbrouk, J., & Tindal, G.A. (2006). Oral reading fluency norms: A valuable assessment tool for reading teachers. *The Reading Teacher, 59*(7), 636–644.

Hasbrouck, J., & Tindal, G. A. (2012). Fluency norms chart. *Reading Rockets.* Retrieved from http://www.readingrockets.org/article/31295/.

Harvey, S., & Goudvis, A. (2007*). Strategies that work: Teaching comprehension for understanding and engagement, second edition.* Portland, ME: Stenhouse.

Herrera, S. G., Perez, D. R., & Escamilla, K. (2010). *Teaching reading to English language learners: Differentiated strategies.* Boston, MA: Allyn & Bacon.

Kelley, M. J., & Clausen-Grace, N. (2010). Guiding students through expository text with text feature walks. *The Reading Teacher, 64*(3), 191–195.

Kieffer, M. J., & Lesaux, N. K. (2007) Breaking down words to build meaning: Morphology, vocabulary, and comprehension in the urban classroom. *The Reading Teacher, 61*(2), 134–144.

Kucan, L. (2007). "I" poems: Invitations for students to deepen literary understanding. *The Reading Teacher, 60*(6), 518–525.

LaBerge, D., & Samuels, J. (1974). Towards a theory of automatic information processing in reading. *Cognitive Psychology, 6,* 293–323.

Leahy, S., Lyon, C., Thompson, M., & William, D. (2005). Classroom assessment: Minute by minute, day by day. *Educational Leadership, 63*(3), 19–24.

Lewin, L., & Shoemaker, B. J. (1998). *Great performances: Creating classroom-based assessment tasks.* Alexandria, VA: Association for Supervision and Curriculum Development.

Marzano, R. J., Pickering, D. J., & Pollock, J. E. (2001). *Classroom instruction that works: Research-based strategies for increasing student achievement.* Alexandria, VA: ASCD.

McGinley, W. J., & Denner, P. R. (1987). Story impressions: A prereading/writing activity. *Journal of Reading, 31*(3), 248–253.

McKeown, M. G., Beck, I. L., & Blake, R. G. K. (2009). Rethinking reading comprehension instruction: A comparison of instruction for strategies and content approaches. *Reading Research Quarterly, 44*(3), 218–253.

McLaughlin, M. (2012). Reading comprehension: What every teacher needs to know. *The Reading Teacher, 65*(7), 432–440.

McLaughlin, M., & Allen, M. B. (2009). *Guided comprehension in grades 3-8* (comb. 2nd ed.). Newark, DE: International Reading Association.

McLaughlin, M., & DeVoogd, G. L. (2004). *Critical literacy: Enhancing students' comprehension of text.* New York, NY: Scholastic.

McLaughlin, M., & Overturf, B. J. (2013a). *The Common Core: Graphic organizers to teach K–12 students to meet the reading standards.* Newark, DE: International Reading Association.

McLaughlin, M., & Overturf, B. J. (2013b). *The Common Core: Teaching K–5 students to meet the reading standards.* Newark, DE: International Reading Association.

McTigue, E. M., & Flowers, A. C. (2011). Science visual literacy: Learners' perceptions and knowledge of diagrams. *The Reading Teacher, 64*(8), 578–589.

National Governors Association Center for Best Practices & Council of Chief State School Officers (NGA & CCSSO). (2010). *Common Core State Standards: English language arts and literacy in history/social studies, science, and technical subjects.* Washington, DC: Authors. Retrieved from http://www.corestandards .org/assets/CCSSI_ELA%20Standards.pdf.

National Institute of Child Health and Human Development (NICHD). (2000). *Report of the National Reading Panel. Teaching children to read: An evidence-based assessment of the scientific research literature on reading and its implications for reading instruction.* Retrieved from http://www.nichd.nih.gov/publications/ nrp/smallbook.htm.

O'Neil, K. E. (2011). Reading pictures: Developing visual literacy for greater comprehension. *The Reading Teacher, 65*(3), 214–223.

Ontario Ministry of Education. (n.d.). *Teacher resources—Comprehension in action: Evaluating (Module 2).* Literacy and Numeracy Secretariat Professional Learning Series. Retrieved from http://resources.curriculum .org/LNS/coaching/files/pdf/Comprehending_Resources_Module2.pdf.

Palincsar, A. S., & Brown, A. L. (1984). Reciprocal teaching of comprehension-fostering and comprehension-monitoring activities. *Cognition and Instruction, 2,* 117–175.

Pearson, P. D., & Gallagher, G. (1983). The gradual release of responsibility model of instruction. *Contemporary Educational Psychology, 8,* 112–123.

Peterson, D. D., & Taylor, B. M. (2012). Using higher order questioning to accelerate students' growth in reading. *The Reading Teacher, 65*(5), 295–304.

Pressley, M. (1976). Mental imagery helps eight-year-olds remember what they read. *Journal of Educational Psychology, 68,* 355–359.

Pressley, M. (2002). Metacognition and self-regulated comprehension. In A. E. Farstrup & S. J. Samuels (Eds.), *What research has to say about reading instruction* (3rd ed., pp. 291–309). Newark, DE: International Reading Association.

Pressley, M., Wharton-McDonald, R., Hampson, J. M., & Echevarria, M. (1998). The nature of literacy instruction in ten grade-4/5 classrooms in upstate New York. *Scientific Studies of Reading, 2,* 159–191.

Putnam, S. M., & Kingsley, T. (2009). The atoms family: Using podcasts to enhance the development of science vocabulary. *The Reading Teacher, 63*(2), 100–108.

Raphael, T. E., & Au, K. H. (2005). QAR: Enhancing comprehension and test-taking across grades and content areas. *The Reading Teacher, 59*(3), 206–221.

Rasinski, T. (2003). *The fluent reader: Oral reading strategies for building word recognition, fluency, and comprehension.* New York, NY: Scholastic.

Rasinski, T. (2012). Multidimensional fluency rubric. *Timothy Rasinski, Ph.D.* Retrieved from www.timrasinski .com

Rasinski, T., Padak, N., Newton, J., & Newton, E. (2011). The Latin-Greek connection: Building vocabulary through morphological study. *The Reading Teacher, 65*(2), 133–141.

ReadWorks. (2012). Books and passages: A final journey. *ReadWorks.org.* Retrieved from http://www .readworks.org/passages/final-journey.

Roser, N., Martinez, M., Fuhrken, C., & McDonnold, K. (2007). Characters as a guide to meaning. *The Reading Teacher, 60*(6), 548–559.

Rothstein, D., & Santana, L. (2011). Teaching students to ask their own questions: One small change can yield big results. *Harvard Education Letter, 27*(5). Retrieved from http://hepg.org/hel/article/507.

Shepard, L. A. (2005). Linking formative assessment to scaffolding. *Educational Leadership, 63*(3), 66–70.

Wilfong, L. G. (2008). Building fluency, word-recognition ability, and confidence in struggling readers: The Poetry Academy. *The Reading Teacher, 62*(1), 4–13.

Wilhelm, J. (1997). *You gotta BE the book: Teaching engaged and reflective reading with adolescents.* New York, NY: Teachers College Press.

Youngs, S., & Serafini, F. (2011). Comprehension strategies for reading historical fiction picture books. *The Reading Teacher, 66*(2), 115–124.

LITERATURE CITED

Bower, B., & Lobdell, J. (2001). Christopher Columbus. In *History alive! America's past.* Palo Alto, CA: Teachers Curriculum Institute.

Browne, A. (1998). *Voices in the park.* New York, NY: Dorling-Kindersley.

DiCamillo, K. (2000). *Because of Winn-Dixie.* Cambridge, MA: Candlewick Press.

Frost, R. (2001). *Stopping by woods on a snowy evening* (S. Jeffers, illus.). New York, NY: Dutton Children's Books.

Good, K. (1999). *Build it! Activities for setting up super structures.* Minneapolis, MN: Lerner.

Johnson, A. (2005). *A sweet smell of roses* (E. Velasquez, illus.). New York, NY: Simon & Schuster.

Levine, E. (2007). *Henry's freedom box.* New York, NY: Scholastic.

Mitchell, M. K. (1993). *Uncle Jed's barbershop.* New York, NY: Simon & Schuster.

Roop, P., & Roop, C. (2000). *Christopher Columbus (In their own words).* New York, NY: Scholastic.

Yero, J. L. (2006). *American documents: The Mayflower Compact.* Washington, DC: National Geographic Society.

chapter 3

Vocabulary Development

BUILDING STRONG VOCABULARY KNOWLEDGE IS A MUST! STUDENTS in grades 3–5 are past the early primary years of learning how to read. At this level, they must learn how to negotiate more difficult content area texts, more expressive and subtle narrative texts, and more sophisticated concepts. Having a growing vocabulary base helps students become better readers and learners.

Developing academic vocabulary is one of the instructional shifts associated with the Common Core State Standards (CCSS), and the English Language Arts (ELA) Standards have a particular focus on vocabulary development throughout all of the content areas. We need to provide intentional and consistent vocabulary instruction that will help our students be prepared for the challenges of middle school, as well as college and career.

Leslie Montgomery

Vocabulary and Academic Achievement

STUDY AFTER STUDY HAS INDICATED THAT VOCABULARY DEVELOPMENT correlates with reading comprehension and academic achievement (Anderson & Nagy, 1991; Dickinson & Tabors, 2001; Stahl & Fairbanks, 1986; White, Graves, & Slater, 1990). Stanovich (1986) found that children who come to school lacking in vocabulary development and oral language development usually do not progress in school as quickly as students who are better prepared. He used the term the "Matthew effect" to describe how early success leads to later success when it comes to vocabulary development and reading skill.

Teachers who have been in the classroom a number of years have probably seen this phenomenon. Students who come from more privileged backgrounds often are more equipped to meet the vocabulary demands of the content areas. These students often thrive in school. However, students from less privileged environments usually lack the same vocabulary base and are less likely to achieve at the same level. In fact, a study by Hart and Risley (1995) found a substantial gap in vocabulary knowledge between preschool students from lower versus higher socioeconomic backgrounds. Children who live in more affluent households and whose parents and caretakers have more education tend to have a higher level of vocabulary development, whereas children who live in poverty have usually not learned as many words. Explicit instruction in vocabulary development is especially necessary for English language learners (Echevarria, 1998) and for students living in poverty (Marulis & Neuman, 2011).

Most teachers know that vocabulary development is an important part of reading comprehension, but research shows that elementary teachers do not always include strong vocabulary instruction as part of their daily schedules (Beck, et al., 2002; Watts, 1995). Many teachers have good intentions but feel there is an overwhelming amount of information about vocabulary instruction and little guidance on how to actually teach vocabulary or structure elementary classrooms for vocabulary development. Teachers need to have a wide range of strategies at their fingertips to be able to teach vocabulary. They also need to know how to organize their classrooms so vocabulary development can happen.

Exploring Vocabulary in the ELA Standards

BECAUSE VOCABULARY DEVELOPMENT IS SUCH AN IMPORTANT PART of academic success, the CCSS include specific expectations for vocabulary knowledge and outline what students are expected to know and be able to do with words. However, at first glance, finding all of the vocabulary standards in the CCSS is a bit like playing Where's Waldo? Even though vocabulary development is a necessary part of reading development, the bulk of the vocabulary standards are not located in the Reading strands of the CCSS. Instead, the writers of the Standards placed the vocabulary standards in the Language strand in a cluster called Vocabulary Acquisition and Use. The idea is that vocabulary development runs through all parts of the literacy curriculum, from beginning kindergarten reading to high school science and social studies.

Although the word *vocabulary* appears infrequently in the CCSS, nine standards address the topic of *word meaning* in the intermediate grades: Reading Literature Standard 4, Reading Informational Text Standard 4, Reading Foundational Skills Standards 3 and 4, Writing Standards 2 and 3, and Language Standards 4, 5, and 6.

Tips for the Teacher

"VOCABULARY DEVELOPMENT IS EVEN MORE CRITICAL TO UNDERSTANDING reading because students are spending more time reading and analyzing complex text. I think in the past, teachers might have stopped at words here and there in the passage and questioned students about the meanings of those words. But now that we're engaging in close reading of harder texts, intentional vocabulary instruction is crucial."

—Margot, grade 5 teacher

In the rest of this chapter, we will explore the common topics found across the CCSS document in relation to determining word meaning. In grades 3–5, those topics are as follows:

- context
- morphology
- reference materials
- figurative language
- idioms, adages, and proverbs (grades 4 and 5)
- word relationships
- academic and domain-specific words

These are the vocabulary topics we want to teach to help our students in grades 3–5 meet the CCSS vocabulary expectations in reading, writing, foundational skills, speaking and listening, and language. We will discuss the standards that relate to each topic and strategies for teaching each component so that students can meet the standards.

Using Context to Determine Word Meaning

VARIOUS RESEARCHERS HAVE ESTIMATED THE NUMBER OF NEW words a student learns in school each year. The number of words is staggering, with some researchers putting the number at more than 3000 words per year (Graves, 2006). Obviously, teachers cannot teach all of these words to students directly, and students must learn words in other ways.

One of the ways students learn words is through the use of context. This fact explains the CCSS expectation that students learn to recognize what a word means through the use of the sentence- or passage-level context. Learning new words through the use of context is a highly important college- and career-readiness skill.

Standards That Refer to Use of Context

In the College and Career Readiness Anchor Standards for Language, Standard 4 states that students should be able to "Determine or clarify the meaning of unknown and multiple-meaning words and phrases by using context clues, analyzing meaningful word parts, and consulting general and specialized reference materials, as appropriate (NGA & CCSSO, 2010, p. 25). In this standard, it is clear that students should learn how to use context clues to determine the meanings of unknown words and phrases.

Figure 3.1 presents the standards that refer to using context to determine word meaning for grades 3, 4, and 5. The specific standards for each grade level that refer to the use of context are identified in the "Standard" column, and the precise skills that students should have at each grade level are identified in the "Indicators" column. The indicators in Language Standard 4 emphasize a problem-solving approach to determining word meanings through the general use of context clues at the sentence and passage levels. The indicators in Language Standard 5 deal with using context to determine the meanings of higher-level words and concepts.

FIGURE 3.1 ● Standards for Grades 3–5 That Refer to Using Context to Learn Words

Grade Level	Standard	Indicator
Grade 3	**Foundational Skills Standard 4:** Read with sufficient accuracy and fluency to support comprehension.	**c.** Use context to confirm or self-correct word recognition and understanding, rereading as necessary.
	Language Standard 4: Determine or clarify the meaning of unknown and multiple-meaning words and phrases based on grade 3 reading and content, choosing flexibly from a range of strategies.	**a.** Use sentence-level context as a clue to the meaning of a word or phrase.
	Language Standard 5: Demonstrate understanding of word relationships and nuances in word meanings.	**a.** Determine the literal and nonliteral meanings of words and phrases in context (e.g., *take steps*).
Grade 4	**Foundational Skills Standard 4:** Read with sufficient accuracy and fluency to support comprehension.	**c.** Use context to confirm or self-correct word recognition and understanding, rereading as necessary.
	Language Standard 4: Determine or clarify the meaning of unknown and multiple-meaning words and phrases based on grade 4 reading and content, choosing flexibly from a range of strategies.	**a.** Use context (e.g., definitions, examples, or restatements in text) as a clue to the meaning of a word or phrase.
	Language Standard 5: Demonstrate understanding of figurative language, word relationships, and nuances in word meanings.	**a.** Explain the meaning of simple similes and metaphors (e.g., *as pretty as a picture*) in context.
Grade 5	**Foundational Skills Standard 4:** Read with sufficient accuracy and fluency to support comprehension.	**c.** Use context to confirm or self-correct word recognition and understanding, rereading as necessary.

(continued)

FIGURE 3.1 • *(continued)*

Grade Level	Standard	Indicator
	Language Standard 4: Determine or clarify the meaning of unknown and multiple-meaning words and phrases based on grade 5 reading and content, choosing flexibly from a range of strategies.	**a.** Use context (e.g., cause/effect relationships and comparisons in text) as a clue to the meaning of a word or phrase.
	Language Standard 5: Demonstrate understanding of figurative language, word relationships, and nuances in word meanings.	**a.** Interpret figurative language, including similes and metaphors, in context.

Source: NGA & CCSSO (2010).

Strategies for Teaching Vocabulary in Context

For students to learn words through the use of context, they must be engaged in instruction that helps them learn this skill. Several strategies have been recommended to teach learning words in context, including teacher read-alouds, informal word learning, wide reading, and word problem solving.

Teacher Read-Alouds and Discussion   Reading aloud to third-, fourth-, and fifth-graders is one way to ensure that they have engaging experiences with interesting and evocative vocabulary. Reading aloud children's literature and fascinating content area texts—especially texts that are above student grade level—often allows students access to higher-level vocabulary.

An interactive read-aloud is one way to help students learn new words (Beck & McKeown, 2001; Brabham & Lynch-Brown, 2002). When we plan an interactive read-aloud, we identify stopping points to emphasize vocabulary as we read to students. Then we engage students in a discussion of the selected words and have students predict the words' meanings based on the context. Doing this can help students learn more about the meanings of academic vocabulary and how to determine the meanings of words in context.

Some texts are particularly well suited to vocabulary development. For example, try reading aloud excerpts from *Lemony Snicket's A Series of Unfortunate Events.* Lemony Snicket (2006), (whose real name is Daniel Handler), loves to play with language, vocabulary, and allusions to classic literature. The books in the series are appropriate for upper-elementary students, and vocabulary development is built right into them (Arter & Nilsen, 2009). Teachers can read aloud all kinds of more complex texts, both literary and informational text, to help students build vocabulary.

Informal Word Learning   Helping students develop word consciousness is another way to help them learn words through context. When teachers intentionally flood the environment with interesting and needed vocabulary through the use of texts, anchor charts, and attention-grabbing words in conversation (Blachowicz & Fisher, 2009; Brabham & Lynch-Brown, 2002), students become more aware of words.

One way to help students develop word consciousness is to deliberately insert fascinating words into the classroom conversation. For example, a teacher might say, "Please extract your writing implements and be disposed to commence your science endeavor" (i.e., "Please take out your pencils and be ready to begin your science project"). If this strategy is not overused, intermediate students will likely become intrigued by the use of words they don't know and begin emulating the teacher. Encouraging this pattern will help students build their word banks (Scott & Nagy, 2009).

Wide Reading   Wide reading is often recommended as a way for students to learn new words in context. There is evidence that students learn many new words by reading a large number of words in a variety of texts (Nagy, Herman, & Anderson, 1985). It seems obvious: For students to learn a lot of new words through context from books, magazines, websites, and instructions, they have to read a lot of texts! The theory is that wide reading makes readers better at determining unknown words in text. It follows that when students read a lot, they encounter more words, learn more words, and therefore get better at using context to figure out what the words mean.

To encourage wide reading, we can plan a time during the day when students have the opportunity to read texts of their choosing. While they read, we conference with them to find out what they are reading, gauge their comprehension, discuss vocabulary, determine any problems with which they might need help, and discuss the text. Research shows that independent reading outside the school day can also help increase students' vocabulary and comprehension (Anderson, Wilson, & Fielding, 1988).

Strategies for Word Problem Solving   We can teach individual words through context by introducing vocabulary using a cloze procedure (Blachowitz & Fisher, 2009; Carr, Dewitz, & Patberg, 1989; Overturf, Montgomery, & Smith, 2013). In a cloze activity, the teacher writes a sentence but leaves a blank where a vocabulary word should be inserted. For example, we may write "The horses went through the _____ between the mountains" on a chart or whiteboard and then present students with three possible choices of words: *passage, cave,* and *density.* When students are asked to predict the correct vocabulary word based on their prior knowledge and to justify their decisions through discussion, they are working on ways to understand words in context.

Students build skill inferring word meanings when they use problem-solving strategies to decide what word should be put in the blank. For example, the word *the* preceding the blank in the sample sentence indicates that the correct word is a noun or adjective. The word *through* is a clue that eliminates a word such as *cave* as a choice, because horses can go <u>*into*</u> a cave but not <u>*through*</u> a cave. Similarly, the word *through* eliminates a word such as *density,* because horses cannot go *through* density.

When students learn these types of word-problem solving strategies, as well as the concept of using context for comprehension, they are better able to determine the meanings of unfamiliar words. When the cloze procedure uses words and sentences from social studies or science, having a class discussion about what words should be placed in the blanks also helps students learn content knowledge.

Developing Morphological Awareness

MORPHOLOGY IS ANOTHER IMPORTANT AREA IN THE CCSS for developing vocabulary in grades 3–5. *Morphology* is the study of the meanings of parts of words, such as affixes (e.g., prefixes and suffixes), and common Greek and Latin root words. Intermediate students need to develop morphological awareness to be able to determine the meanings of multisyllabic words in context and to increase comprehension (Moats, 2011).

Learning about common prefixes, suffixes, and root words begins in the K–2 ELA Standards. In the upper-elementary grades, students are expected to use their knowledge of the meanings of prefixes, suffixes, and roots as clues to the meanings of words. White, Sowell, and Yanagihara (2009) have discussed the most appropriate prefixes and suffixes to teach in elementary school. When students learn the meanings of these word parts, it helps them unlock the meanings of hundreds of words.

Learning about Greek and Latin roots begins in fourth grade in the CCSS. Many of the words used in disciplinary texts are derived from Greek and Latin origins. Intermediate students should learn the meanings of common Greek and Latin roots to determine the meanings of unfamiliar multisyllabic words. Rasinski et al. (2011) have done an extensive study of the Latin–Greek connection to word study for elementary students and suggest that "the next quantum leap for vocabulary growth . . . will come when the systematic study of Latin–Greek derivations is embedded into vocabulary programs for the elementary . . . grades" (p. 135).

Knowledge of the meaning of one Greek or Latin root can often unlock the meanings of as many as 20 words. For example, the Latin root *vac* (meaning "empty") is the basis of a number of words: *vacuum, vacate, vacancy, vacation, evacuate,* and so on. As students learn the meanings of root words, their comprehension of text across the curriculum increases. Lists of Greek and Latin roots can be found in articles and books about morphology, as well as many websites. A list of the most common prefixes, suffixes, and roots found in academic texts can be found on the website of the Center for Development and Learning (www.cdl.org).

To help our students understand how to use word parts to determine meaning, we can engage them in activities where they play with prefixes, suffixes, and roots. They can segment and build words using morphemes, build compound words, and use morphemes to improve spelling. English language learners can identify cognates to help them understand the meanings of English words (Goodwin, Lipsky, & Ahn, 2012).

Standards That Refer to Morphology

For grades 3–5, two standards refer to the use of morphology: Foundational Skills Standard 3 and Language Standard 4. Each standard provides indicators with details about the morphological skills to be mastered at each grade level. Figure 3.2 shows the standards and indicators relating to morphology in the third, fourth, and fifth grades.

Strategies for Teaching Morphology

As educators' awareness of the importance of morphology continues to increase, more ideas are becoming available for teaching affixes and root words. In this section, we will discuss teaching ideas for building morphological awareness with students in grades 3–5.

Nifty Thrifty Fifty   To help students decode and determine the meanings of unfamiliar multisyllabic words, many teachers have students learn the Nifty Thrifty Fifty: a set of 50 words developed by Cunningham and Hall (1998) that are composed of common prefixes, root words, and suffixes. Once students learn these words (including definitions), they can use them to pronounce and determine the meanings of hundreds of other words. Examples of these words are *composer* (*compose, pose*) and *encouragement* (*encourage, courage*). Ways to intentionally teach the Nifty Thrifty Fifty can be found in Cunningham and Hall's book *Month-by-Month Phonics for the Upper Grades* (1998).

FIGURE 3.2 ● Standards for Grades 3–5 That Refer to Knowledge of Morphology

Grade Level	Standard	Indicator(s)
Grade 3	**Foundational Skills 3:** Know and apply grade-level phonics and word analysis skills in decoding words.	**a.** Identify and know the meaning of the most common prefixes and derivational suffixes. **b.** Decode words with common Latin suffixes.
	Language Standard 4: Determine or clarify the meaning of unknown and multiple-meaning words and phrases based on grade 3 reading and content, choosing flexibly from a range of strategies.	**b.** Determine the meaning of the new word formed when a known affix is added to a known word (e.g., *agreeable/disagreeable, comfortable, uncomfortable, care/careless, heat/preheat*). **c.** Use a known root word as a clue to the meaning of an unknown word with the same root (e.g., *company/companion*).
Grade 4	**Foundational Skills 3:** Know and apply grade-level phonics and word analysis skills in decoding words.	**a.** Use combined knowledge of all letter-sound correspondences, syllabication patterns, and morphology (e.g., roots and affixes) to read accurately unfamiliar multisyllabic words in context and out of context.
	Language Standard 4: Determine or clarify the meaning of unknown and multiple-meaning words and phrases based on grade 4 reading and content, choosing flexibly from a range of strategies.	**d.** Use common, grade-appropriate Greek and Latin affixes and roots as clues to the meaning of a word (e.g., *telegraph, photograph, autograph*).
Grade 5	**Foundational Skills 3:** Know and apply grade-level phonics and word analysis skills in decoding words.	**a.** Use combined knowledge of all letter-sound correspondences, syllabication patterns, and morphology (e.g., roots and affixes) to read accurately unfamiliar multisyllabic words in context and out of context.

(continued)

FIGURE 3.2 • *(continued)*

Grade Level	Standard	Indicator(s)
	Language Standard 4: Determine or clarify the meaning of unknown and multiple-meaning words and phrases based on grade 5 reading and content, choosing flexibly from a range of strategies.	**b.** Use common, grade-appropriate Greek and Latin affixes and roots as clues to the meaning of a word (e.g., *photograph, photosynthesis*).

Source: NGA & CCSSO (2010).

Thinking about Word Parts   To help students become interested in learning the meanings of common prefixes, suffixes, and Greek and Latin roots, we can engage them in activities to think about the meanings of word parts. Overturf et al. (2013) developed an activity called Crystal Ball Words. To begin, the teacher chooses a multisyllabic word containing a common prefix, Greek or Latin root, and suffix. The teacher introduces the meaning of each word part and then invites students to "gaze deep inside" a multisyllabic word to brainstorm all of the words they can think of that contain the same prefix, root, or suffix. For example, for the word *television,* students learn the meanings of the prefix *tele-* (which means "distance" or "from afar"), the Latin root *vis* ("to see"), and the suffix *-sion* ("the act or process of"). As a group, students brainstorm all of the words they can think of that have the prefix *tele-* (*telephone, teleport,* etc.). Next, they think of words with the root *vis* (*visual, revise, invisible,* etc.), and finally, they contemplate words with the suffix *-sion* (*decision, division, confusion,* etc.). As students brainstorm, they talk about the possible meaning of each word. For example, the word *confusion* means "the act or process of being confused." The activity Crystal Ball Words helps students realize that the parts of most multisyllabic words have meanings, and knowing the meanings of those parts can help determine the meanings of long, unfamiliar words in text.

An activity called Be the Bard helps students recognize the Latin–Greek connection in determining the meanings of multisyllabic words (Rasinski et al., 2011). The teacher explains that Shakespeare created many of the unusual words he used in his plays and shows students some examples. (A list of words is available at the website Shakespeare Online: www.shakespeare-online.com/biography/wordsinvented.html.) The teacher then invites students to use the meanings of prefixes, roots, and suffixes to create and define their own interesting new words. This type of meaningful word play can help students understand how multisyllabic words are structured.

Morphology Word Sorts   Word sorts have been used with much success to help students learn *derivational relations,* which is the type of word knowledge possessed by advanced readers and writers (Bear et al., 2011). A *word sort* is a word study routine in which students compare and contrast words and word parts within and across categories. For example, we write prefixes on one set of cards, Greek and Latin roots on another set of cards, and suffixes on a third set of cards. Students arrange and rearrange the cards to form a variety of multisyllabic words. After learning the meanings of the prefixes, roots, and suffixes, students determine the meanings of the multisyllabic words they construct.

Using Reference Materials

IN GRADES 3–5, STUDENTS SHOULD MAKE REGULAR USE of reference materials to find the appropriate meanings of words used in text. This does not mean that vocabulary instruction should be limited to students using dictionaries to look up definitions and write sentences for a set of words. On the contrary, research has found that asking students to look up dictionary definitions and use words in sentences is counterproductive (Beck, McKeown, & Kucan, 2002). Students often write odd sentences, and word meanings become confused instead of clarified.

Instead, students should use reference materials such as glossaries, dictionaries, and thesauruses (both print and digital) for authentic purposes, such as clarifying the meaning of text, conducting research, or writing about a topic. The CCSS that refer to using reference materials are shown in Figure 3.3.

Understanding Figurative Language

INTERMEDIATE STUDENTS WILL ENCOUNTER MANY INSTANCES OF FIGURATIVE language, such as similes, metaphors, and idioms, in the texts they read. However, many students in grades 3, 4, and 5 are still literal thinkers. Most students need instruction in how to think about the figurative language they find in text.

FIGURE 3.3 ● Standards for Grades 3–5 That Refer to the Use of Reference Materials

Grade Level	Standard	Indicator
Grade 3	**Language Standard 4:** Determine or clarify the meaning of unknown and multiple-meaning words and phrases based on grade 3 reading and content, choosing flexibly from a range of strategies.	**d.** Use glossaries or beginning dictionaries, both print and digital, to determine or clarify the precise meaning of key words and phrases.
Grade 4	**Language Standard 4:** Determine or clarify the meaning of unknown and multiple-meaning words and phrases based on grade 4 reading and content, choosing flexibly from a range of strategies.	**c.** Consult reference materials (e.g., dictionaries, glossaries, thesauruses), both print and digital, to find the pronunciation and determine or clarify the precise meaning of key words and phrases.
Grade 5	**Language Standard 4:** Determine or clarify the meaning of unknown and multiple-meaning words and phrases based on grade 5 reading and content, choosing flexibly from a range of strategies.	**c.** Consult reference materials (e.g., dictionaries, glossaries, thesauruses), both print and digital, to find the pronunciation and determine or clarify the precise meaning of key words and phrases.

Source: NGA & CCSSO (2010).

Being able to interpret the expressive ways in which authors describe characters, settings, and events is necessary to be able to comprehend more complex texts. In addition, good writers use vivid words and phrases, which often include figurative language. We want our students to be strong writers—able to describe characters, settings, events, and topics in ways that others will want to read. Understanding how figurative language is used in text can help students become better writers.

Examples of figurative language include simile, metaphor, onomatopoeia, hyperbole, personification, alliteration, and assonance. Idioms are a special consideration. Adages and proverbs are included because they are components of expressive writing in some texts.

Standards That Refer to Figurative Language

References to figurative language can be found in three CCSS strands: Reading Literature, Writing, and Language. Figure 3.4 presents the standards that refer to figurative language.

Strategies for Teaching Figurative Language

We can teach figurative language through reading and discussing children's literature, such as stories, poems, and plays. Numerous websites provide lists of children's books and poems to use in teaching figurative language.

Similes, Metaphors, and Other Types of Figurative Language   Writers often use figurative language in descriptions. Here are definitions and examples of common types of figurative language:

- A *simile* is a comparison using the word *like* or *as: as soft as a kitten*.
- A *metaphor* compares two objects by stating that one thing is the other: *the ice was a sheet of glass*.
- *Onomatopoeia* is the use of a word or phrase that sounds like the sound being described: *Pop! went the cork*.
- *Hyperbole* is exaggeration: *We must have waited a million years*.
- *Personification* gives human characteristics to an inanimate object or animal: *The train trudged along the track*.
- *Alliteration* is the use of several words together that have the same consonant sound: *bouncing balls in the backyard*.
- *Assonance* is the use of several words close together that have the same vowel sound: *the moon is blue on Tuesday*.

In most cases, an author use a combination of types of figurative language in expressive writing.

High-quality children's literature is written expressively, often including numerous types of figurative language. An excellent example for intermediate students is the picture book *Duke Ellington: The Piano Prince and His Orchestra* (Pinkney, 2006). The author, Andrea Pinkney, writes vividly about Ellington's jazz, describing the blues as "deeper than the deep blue sea" and musical notes as "curling like a kite tail in the wind." Song lyrics often include examples of expressive similes and metaphors, as well. A fun song to use with students is "You're a Mean

FIGURE 3.4 ● Standards for Grades 3–5 That Refer to Figurative Language

Grade Level	Standard	Indicator(s)
Grade 3	**Reading Literature Standard 4:** Determine the meaning of words and phrases as they are used in a text, distinguishing literal from nonliteral language.	
	Language Standard 5: Demonstrate understanding of word relationships and nuances in word meanings.	**a.** Distinguish the literal and nonliteral meanings of words and phrases in context (e.g., *take steps*).
Grade 4	**Reading Literature Standard 4:** Determine the meaning of words and phrases as they are used in a text, including those that allude to significant characters found in mythology (e.g., Herculean).	
	Writing Standard 3: Write narratives to develop real or imagined experiences or events using effective technique, descriptive details, and clear event sequences.	**d.** Use concrete words and phrases and sensory details to convey experiences and events precisely.
	Language Standard 5: Demonstrate understanding of figurative language, word relationships, and nuances in word meanings.	**a.** Explain the meaning of simple similes and metaphors (e.g., *as pretty as a picture*) in context. **b.** Recognize and explain the meaning of common idioms, adages, and proverbs.
Grade 5	**Reading Literature Standard 4:** Determine the meaning of words and phrases as they are used in a text, including figurative language such as metaphors and similes.	
	Writing Standard 3: Write narratives to develop real or imagined experiences or events using effective technique, descriptive details, and clear event sequences.	**d.** Use concrete words and phrases and sensory details to convey experiences and events precisely.

(continued)

FIGURE 3.4 • *(continued)*

Grade Level	Standard	Indicator(s)
	Language Standard 5: Demonstrate understanding of figurative language, word relationships, and nuances in word meanings.	**a.** Interpret figurative language, including similes and metaphors, in context. **b.** Recognize and explain the meaning of common idioms, adages, and proverbs.

Source: NGA & CCSSO (2010).

One, Mr. Grinch," from the movie *How the Grinch Stole Christmas*. Who can resist such rotten lyrics as examples of figurative language?

Poetry, by its very nature, usually includes examples of expressive and unusual comparisons. The book *Hailstones and Halibut Bones* (O'Neill, 1961/1990) is a favorite of many teachers. It is a book of poems about the color spectrum and includes a number of similes and metaphors within its pages. Students can read the poems and discuss O'Neill's use of figurative language. After reading, students can use paint samples from the hardware store to inspire their own color poems about topics of their own choice, such as objects in nature or perhaps cars or monsters. Writing and illustrating poems that contain descriptive similes and metaphors helps students contemplate the use of figurative language in the texts they read.

Idioms   Expectations for knowledge of idioms, adages, and proverbs are found only in Language Standard 5 for grades 4 and 5. An *idiom* is an expression in which the sum of the words means something different from what is suggested by the definitions of the individual words. In other words, it's a nonliteral use of language. Idiomatic expressions such as "It's raining cats and dogs" and "I can't get a word in edgewise" are part of our daily speech. Idioms are tricky for many students, especially English language learners. Often, students need more targeted instruction in common idioms used in the English language.

A number of children's books can serve as enjoyable resources for learning about idioms, including *More Parts* (Arnold, 2003), *Even More Parts* (Arnold, 2007), *There's a Frog in My Throat: 440 Animal Sayings a Little Bird Told Me* (Street, 2003), and *In a Pickle and Other Funny Idioms* (Terban, 2007). After reading and discussing the language in these texts, students will enjoy illustrating the literal and nonliteral meanings of interesting idioms (e.g., "I lost my head!"). Students can also dramatize their interpretations of idioms and the literal meanings of these expressions.

Proverbs and Adages   An *adage* is a saying that is considered true by many people and is often metaphorical. Examples of adages are "Don't count your chickens before they're hatched," and "A chain is only as strong as its weakest link." A *proverb* is a short, pithy statement that expresses a common truth. An old Chinese proverb that may be familiar is "Give a man a fish, and you feed him for a day. Teach a man to fish, and you feed him for a lifetime." Another well-known proverb that is attributed to Benjamin Franklin is "Early to bed and early to rise, makes a man healthy, wealthy, and wise."

The point is not for students to learn the definitions of the words *adage* and *proverb*. Rather, students should learn the meanings of common expressions and be able to decipher the meanings of other expressions when they see them in print or hear them in speech. A number of websites provide proverbs that most English speakers know. Students can explore these proverbs and discuss or dramatize the meanings.

Another way to teach the concept of adages and proverbs is to do a study of Benjamin Franklin, which is a natural part of the social studies curriculum in many intermediate classrooms. Use books such as *Ben Franklin: His Wit and Wisdom from A–Z* (Schroeder, 2011), which is an alphabet book that has more complex text and examples of Franklin's proverbs on almost every page. A classic intermediate-level chapter book that contains a number of Franklin's proverbs is *Ben and Me: An Astonishing Life of Benjamin Franklin by His Good Mouse Amos* (Lawson, 1988), a story told from the point of view of a mouse.

Recognizing Word Relationships

THE TERM *WORD RELATIONSHIPS* REFERS TO THE NETWORK of words surrounding a specific vocabulary word, such as synonyms, antonyms, and homographs. Researchers in vocabulary development often emphasize the importance of not only teaching the meaning of a word but also providing experiences with synonyms and antonyms connected to the word. Using this approach helps students make connections to words and their meanings and helps them distinguish between subtle differences in word meanings. For example, the words *scream* and *yell* are considered synonyms but have slightly different meanings. Students need experiences with synonyms to distinguish word nuances.

Antonyms, in particular, seem important in helping students understand the deeper meanings of words (Stahl, 1999; Stahl & Nagy, 2006). Asking students to think about a nonexample of a word (even when the word does not have an antonym) helps them understand more about the meaning of the word. Students in grades 3–5 should have many opportunities to explore word relationships.

Standards That Refer to Word Relationships

Language Standard 5 is the standard that refers to word relationships. The expectations for students in grades 3–5 set by Language Standard 5, along with indicators of skill development, are shown in Figure 3.5.

Strategies for Teaching Word Relationships

When we teach word relationships, we want to ensure that students see how words are connected. Some ways to teach vocabulary words with their related synonyms and antonyms include mapping, creative thinking, and active engagement.

Mapping a Word   Students can learn to map words to show a visual representation of word relationships. Organizers such as the Frayer model (Frayer, Frederick, & Klausmeier, 1969) require students to think about the definition of a word and its characteristics, as well as examples and nonexamples. The Concept of Definition map (Schwartz & Raphael, 1985) requires students to write a definition in their own words, list characteristics, and provide examples.

FIGURE 3.5 ● Standards for Grades 3–5 That Refer to Word Relationships

Grade Level	Standard	Indicator(s)
Grade 3	**Language Standard 5:** Demonstrate understanding of word relationships and nuances in word meanings.	**a.** Distinguish the literal and nonliteral meanings of words and phrases in context (e.g., *take steps*). **b.** Identify real-life connections between words and their use (e.g., describe people who are *friendly* or *helpful*). **c.** Distinguish shades of meaning among related words that describe states of mind or degrees of certainty (e.g., *knew, believed, suspected, heard, wondered*)
Grade 4	**Language Standard 5:** Demonstrate understanding of figurative language, word relationships, and nuances in word meanings.	**c.** Demonstrate understanding of words by relating them to their opposites (antonyms) and to words with similar but not identical meanings (synonyms).
Grade 5	**Language Standard 5:** Demonstrate understanding of figurative language, word relationships, and nuances in word meanings.	**c.** Use the relationship between particular words (e.g., synonyms, antonyms, homographs) to better understand each of the words.

Source: NGA & CCSSO (2010).

Creative Thinking   Asking students to think creatively about words and their synonyms and antonyms can encourage them to explore word relationships. An interesting way to think about synonyms and antonyms is by writing a diamante poem. (Visit the website ReadWriteThink for an interactive resource for writing diamante poems: www.readwritethink.org).

A *diamante* poem is a seven-line poem in the shape of the diamond in which each line uses specific types of words. Interestingly, this type of poem has two topics, and a transfer is made from one to the other through the language of the poem. The first line states the beginning topic. The second line provides two adjectives about the beginning topic, and the third line includes three -*ing* words about the beginning topic. The fourth line includes four nouns or a short phrase about both the beginning and ending topics. The next line includes three -*ing* words about the ending topic. The sixth line includes two adjectives about the ending topic, and finally, the last line states the ending topic.

A synonym diamante poem changes from one synonym to another, and an antonym poem shows the differences between two opposite topics. Use a diamante poem to describe synonyms and antonyms for a vocabulary word by beginning with a vocabulary word and building to a synonym or antonym. Figure 3.6 shows an antonym diamante poem that uses vocabulary words from social studies.

FIGURE 3.6 ● Diamante Poem Using Antonyms from Social Studies Vocabulary

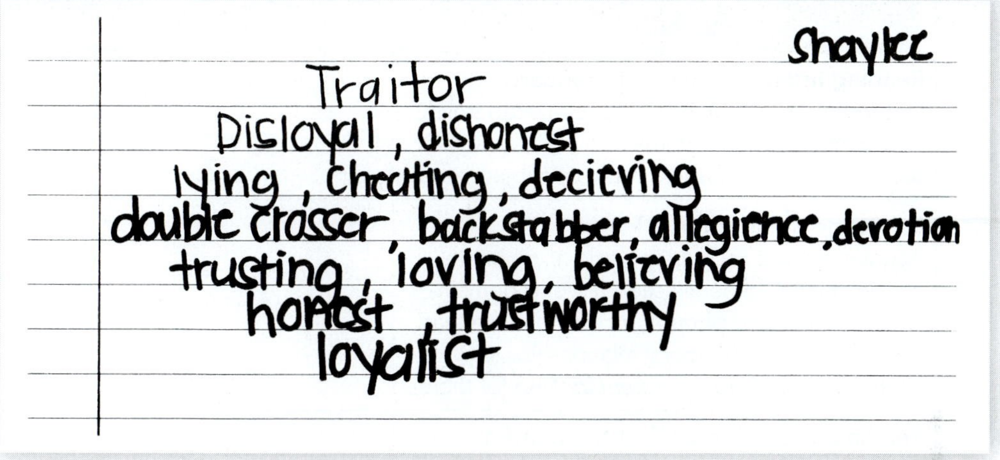

Shaylee

Traitor
Disloyal, dishonest
lying, cheating, decieving
double crosser, backstabber, allegience, devotion
trusting, loving, believing
honest, trustworthy
loyalist

Active Engagement Strategies   Vocabulary strategies that involve art, music, or movement are always popular in grades 3–5. Students can take on the persona of a vocabulary word and "introduce" themselves to their synonyms and antonyms, create human concept maps as they link vocabulary words and related words, or role-play vocabulary words and nuances (Overturf et al., 2013).

Learning General Academic and Domain-Specific Words

LEARNING VOCABULARY IN CONTENT AREAS SUCH AS SOCIAL studies, science, and mathematics is one of the keys to learning important concepts in these areas. Students are expected to determine the meanings of grade-appropriate, general academic and domain-specific words and phrases. Figure 3.7 shows the Reading Informational Text and Language Standards that refer to general academic and domain-specific words and phrases.

Strategies for Teaching General Academic and Domain-Specific Words

Many of the vocabulary strategies that have already been described in this chapter are appropriate for teaching general academic and domain-specific words. For example, the Frayer model (Frayer et al., 1969) can be used with content area words, and diamante poems can be written using general academic words. Words from the content areas can be introduced in context through the use of cloze sentences, and students can analyze the morphology of numerous content area words.

A specific example of a concept map that is especially appropriate for the content areas is the Concept of Definition map (McLaughlin & Allen, 2009; Schwartz & Raphael, 1985). A Concept of Definition map asks students to analyze a focus word by answering these questions

FIGURE 3.7 ● Standards for Grades 3–5 That Refer to Academic and Domain-Specific Vocabulary

Grade Level	Standard	Indicator
Grade 3	**Reading Informational Text Standard 4:** Determine the meaning of general academic and domain-specific words and phrases in a text relevant to a grade 3 topic or subject area.	
	Language Standard 6: Acquire and use accurately grade-appropriate conversational, general academic, and domain-specific words and phrases, including those that signal spatial and temporal relationships (e.g., *After dinner that night we went looking for them*).	
Grade 4	**Reading Informational Text Standard 4:** Determine the meaning of general academic and domain-specific words or phrases in a text relevant to a grade 4 topic or subject area.	
	Writing Standard 2: Write informative/explanatory texts to examine a topic and convey ideas and information clearly.	**d.** Use precise language and domain-specific vocabulary to inform about or explain the topic.
	Language Standard 6: Acquire and use accurately grade-appropriate general academic and domain-specific words and phrases, including those that signal precise actions, emotions, or states of being (e.g., *quizzed, whined, stammered*) and that are basic to a particular topic (e.g., *wildlife, conservation*, and *endangered* when discussing animal preservation).	
Grade 5	**Reading Informational Text Standard 4:** Determine the meaning of general academic and domain-specific words and phrases in a text relevant to a grade 5 topic or subject area.	
	Writing Standard 2: Write informative/explanatory texts to examine a topic and convey ideas and information clearly.	**d.** Use precise language and domain-specific vocabulary to inform about or explain the topic.

(continued)

FIGURE 3.7 • *(continued)*

Grade Level	Standard	Indicator
	Language Standard 6: Acquire and use accurately grade-appropriate general academic and domain-specific words and phrases, including those that signal contrast, addition, and other logical relationships (e.g., *however, although, nevertheless, similarly, moreover, in addition*).	

Source: NGA & CCSSO (2010).

about it: What is it? What is it like? What are some examples? What is a comparison? Students use information from the text to find the answers to these questions about the word. After completing the map and revisiting and revising it, each student uses the map as a guide to write a summary about the focus word.

In the Common Core Classroom
Mapping Domain-Specific Words

Leslie is a fifth-grade teacher whose students are reading an informational article about child labor in Ecuador as part of their social studies lesson. Before asking students to read the passage, Leslie introduced five new words that students would encounter in their reading. One of the five words she introduced was the word *union*. First, she invited students to make predictions about the meaning of the word in the context of a sentence. Leslie's students have had a great deal of experience with this process and had little problem making these types of predictions. Based on the sentence context, students predicted that union might mean "group," "family," or "community." A student wrote the class predictions on a chart.

Leslie then asked the students to read the article with a focus on the key vocabulary. She arranged students into mixed-ability partnerships. Each student read and discussed the text with a partner. Because students had had experience with the vocabulary words before reading the text, they recognized the word when it appeared in the passage. After students had read and discussed the article, Leslie facilitated a whole-class discussion about the vocabulary words. Based on the passage context, the students decided that the word *group* was the only one that fit with *union*, and Leslie asked a student to remove the other two possibilities from the chart.

After the class had closely and carefully discussed the article, Leslie invited each student to create a word definition map for one of the vocabulary words he or she had learned in the practice activities. Figure 3.8 shows a fifth-grader's word definition map of the word *union*. Leslie assessed the students' word definition maps and noted which students had a grasp of the vocabulary and which students still needed more instruction.

FIGURE 3.8 ● Fifth-Grade Student's Word Definition Map and Summary Paragraph

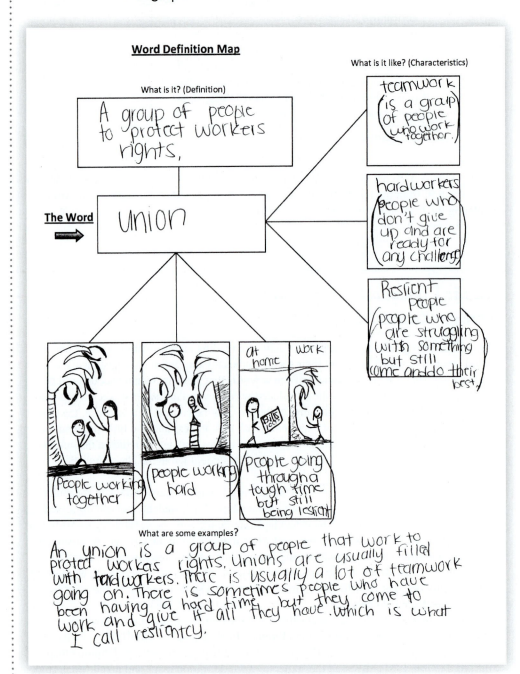

Vocabulary Websites   Literally hundreds of websites provide resources that can help increase vocabulary knowledge for students in grades 3, 4, and 5. An excellent website for practicing vocabulary is Free Rice (www.freerice.com). By choosing the correct vocabulary word to complete a blank, students actually contribute grains of rice to feed people who are hungry. The word list can be adjusted based on the needs of the student. Intermediate students often find this website motivating, as it appeals to their sense of compassion.

A number of vocabulary games can be found on the Internet. For example, see the variety of games at the website Vocabulary.co.il for students at different grade levels, including third grade (www.vocabulary.co.il/third-grade-vocabulary-games), fourth grade (www.vocabulary.co.il/fourth-grade-vocabulary-games), and fifth grade (www.vocabulary.co.il/fifth-grade-vocabulary-games).

Another way to build content vocabulary is to go on virtual field trips (Blachowicz & Obrochta, 2005). Taking field trips helps students build background knowledge and learn new words. There are many places we might like to take our students but could never visit. A virtual visit is the next best thing. Students can explore places such as Sea World, the Louvre, and Gettysburg by going online. As students explore websites about these and other places, they learn new vocabulary words about the topic and content area. Some sites are actually designed to host free virtual field trips for elementary students—for example, SimpleK12 (www.simplek12.com/virtualfieldtrips) and Teacher Tap (http://eduscapes.com/tap/topic35.htm) both host field trip resources.

Although not a virtual field trip, the National Center for Family Literacy (NCFL) hosts the website Wonderopolis (http://wonderopolis.org), which provides resources that can help build vocabulary. Each day, a different topic of interest is posted for upper-primary and intermediate students. The Wonder of the Day includes a video, text, key vocabulary, and activities students can do to explore the topic further.

Thinking about Vocabulary in Grades 3–5

THE IMPORTANCE OF VOCABULARY DEVELOPMENT FOR THIRD-, FOURTH-, and fifth-graders cannot be overstated. These students are learning about the world through language, literature, science, social studies, mathematics, and the arts. Vocabulary study helps them build deep understanding of concepts, which leads to increased comprehension and academic success. We need to plan for intentional and strategic vocabulary instruction and assessment so that students develop the ability to understand the meanings of words in complex text. This will help students meet the expectations of the ELA Standards.

REFERENCES

Allen, J. (1999). *Words, words, words: Teaching vocabulary in grades 4–12*. York, ME: Stenhouse.

Allington, R. L. (2011). *What really matters for struggling readers? Designing research-based programs* (3rd ed.). Boston, MA: Pearson.

Anderson, R. C., Wilson, P. T., & Fielding, L. G. (1988). Growth in reading and how children spend their time outside of school. *Reading Research Quarterly, 23*(3), 285–303.

Anderson, R. C., & Nagy, W. E. (1991). Word meanings. In R. Barr et al. (Eds.), *Handbook of reading research* (Vol. 2, pp. 690–724). New York, NY: Longman.

Arter, L. M., & Nilsen, A. P. (2009). Using Lemony Snicket to bring smiles to your vocabulary lessons. *The Reading Teacher, 63*(3), 235–238.

Bear, D. R., Invernizzi, M., Templeton, S., & Johnston, F. (2011). *Words their way: Word study for phonics, vocabulary, and spelling instruction* (5th ed.). Boston, MA: Allyn & Bacon.

Beck, I. L., & McKeown, M. G. (2001). Text Talk: Capturing the benefits of read-aloud experiences for young children. *The Reading Teacher, 55*(1), 10–20.

Beck, I. L., McKeown, M. G., & Kucan, L. (2002). *Bringing words to life: Robust vocabulary instruction.* New York, NY: Guilford Press.

Blachowicz, C., & Fisher, P. J. (2009). *Teaching vocabulary in all classrooms* (4th ed.). Boston, MA: Allyn & Bacon.

Blachowicz, C., Fisher, P. J., Ogle, D., & Watts-Taffe, S. (2006). Vocabulary: Questions from the classroom. *Reading Research Quarterly, 41*(4), 524–539.

Blachowicz, C., & Obrochta, C. (2005). Vocabulary visits: Virtual field trips for content vocabulary development. *The Reading Teacher, 59*(3), 262–268.

Brabham, E. G., & Lynch-Brown, C. (2002). Effects of teachers' reading-aloud styles on vocabulary acquisition and comprehension of students in the early elementary grades. *Journal of Educational Psychology, 94*(3), 465–473.

Bromley, K. (2012). *The next step in vocabulary instruction: Practical strategies and engaging activities that help all learners build vocabulary and deepen comprehension.* New York, NY: Scholastic.

Carlisle, J. F., McBride-Chang, C., Nagy, W., & Nunes, T. (2010). Effects of instruction in morphological awareness on literacy achievement: An integrative review. *Reading Research Quarterly, 45*(4), 464–483.

Carr, E., Dewitz, P., & Patberg, J. (1989). Using cloze for inference training with expository text. *The Reading Teacher, 42*(6), 380–385.

Carr, E., & Wixson, K. K. (1986). Guidelines for evaluating vocabulary instruction. *Journal of Reading, 29,* 588–595.

Cunningham, P., & Hall, D. (1998). *Month-by-month phonics for the upper grades: A second chance for struggling readers and students learning English.* Greensboro, NC: Carson-Dellosa.

Dickinson, D. K., & Tabors, P. O. (2002, March). Fostering language and literacy in classrooms and homes. *Young Children,* 10–18.

Echevarria, J. (Ed.). (1998, December). *Teaching language minority students in elementary school* (Research Brief no. 1). Washington, DC: Center for Research in Education, Diversity, and Excellence.

Frayer, D., Frederick, W.C., & Klausmeier. (1969). *A schema for testing the level of cognitive mastery.* Madison, WI: Wisconsin Center for Education Research.

Gambrell, L. B. (1996). Creating classroom cultures that foster motivation to read. *The Reading Teacher, 50*(1), 4–25.

Goodwin, A., Lipsky, M., & Ahn, S. (2012). Word detectives: Using units of meaning to support literacy. *The Reading Teacher, 65*(7), 461–470.

Graves, M. F. (2006). *The vocabulary book: Learning and instruction.* New York, NY: Teacher's College Press.

Hart, B., & Risley, T. R. (1995). *Meaningful differences in the everyday experiences of young American children.* Baltimore, MD: Paul H. Brookes.

Kieffer, M. J., & Lesaux, N. K. (2007). Breaking down words to build meaning: Morphology, vocabulary, and comprehension in the urban classroom. *The Reading Teacher, 61*(2), 134–144.

Lane, H. B., & Allen, S. A. (2010). The vocabulary-rich classroom: Modeling sophisticated word use to promote word consciousness and vocabulary growth. *The Reading Teacher, 63*(5), 362–370.

Marulis, L. M. & Neuman, S. (2011, Spring). *How do vocabulary interventions affect young at-risk children's word learning: A meta-analytic review.* Paper presented at a meeting of the Society for Research on Educational Effectiveness. Washington, DC.

McLaughlin, M., & Allen, M.B. (2009). *Guided comprehension in grades 3–8* (Combined 2nd ed.). Newark, DE: International Reading Association.

Moats, L. C. (2011). *Speech to print: Language essentials for teachers* (2nd ed.). Baltimore, MD: Paul H. Brookes.

Mountain, L. (2007). Synonym success—Thanks to the thesaurus. *Journal of Adolescent & Adult Literacy, 51*(4), 318–324.

Nagy, W. E., Herman, P. A., and Anderson, R. C. (1985). Learning words from context. *Reading Research Quarterly, 20*(2), 233–253.

Nagy, W. E., & Hiebert, E. H. (2010). Toward a theory of word selection. In M. L. Kamil et al. (Eds.), *Handbook of reading research* (Vol. 4; pp. 388–404). New York, NY: Longman.

Nagy, W., & Townsend, D. (2012). Words as tools: Learning academic vocabulary as language acquisition. *Reading Research Quarterly, 47*(1), 91–108.

National Governors Association Center for Best Practices & Council of Chief State School Officers (NGA & CCSSO). (2010). *Common Core State Standards: English language arts and literacy in history/social studies, science, and technical subjects.* Washington, DC: Authors. Retrieved from http://www.corestandards.org/assets/CCSSI_ELA%20Standards.pdf.

Overturf, B. J, Montgomery, L. H., & Smith, M. H. (2013). *Word nerds: Teaching all students to learn and love vocabulary.* Portland, ME: Stenhouse.

Rasinski, T., Padak, N., Newton, J., & Newton, E. (2011). The Latin–Greek connection: Building vocabulary through morphological study. *The Reading Teacher, 65*(2), 133–141.

Scott, J. A., & Nagy, W. E. (2009). Developing word consciousness. In M. Graves (Ed.), *Essential readings in vocabulary instruction* (pp. 102–113). Newark, DE: International Reading Association.

Stahl, S. A. (1999). *Vocabulary development.* Cambridge, MA: Brookline Books.

Stahl, S. A. & Fairbanks, M. M. (1986). The effects of vocabulary instruction: A model-based meta-analysis. *Review of Educational Research, 56*(1), 72–110.

Stanovich, K. (1986). Matthew effects in reading: Some consequences of individual differences in the acquisition of literacy. *Reading Research Quarterly, 21,* 360–401.

Schwartz, R., & Raphael, T. (1985). Concept of definition map: A key to improving students' vocabulary. *The Reading Teacher, 39,* 198–205.

Tharp, R. G., & Gallimore, R. (1991). *The instructional conversation: Teaching and learning in social activity* (Research Report no. 2). Santa Cruz, CA: National Center for Research on Cultural Diversity and Second Language Learning.

Watts, S.M. (1995). Vocabulary instruction during reading lessons in six classrooms. *The Journal of Reading Behavior, 27*(3), 399–424.

White, T. G., Graves, M. F., & Slater, W. H. (1990). Development of recognition and reading vocabularies in diverse sociolinguistic and educational settings. *Journal of Educational Psychology, 82,* 281–290.

White, T. G., Sowell, J., & Yanagihara, A. (2009). Teaching elementary students to use word-part clues. In M. Graves (Ed.), *Essential readings in vocabulary instruction* (pp. 83–89). Newark, DE: International Reading Association.

LITERATURE CITED

Arnold, T. (2003). *More parts.* London, UK: Puffin Books.

Arnold, T. (2007). *Even more parts.* London, UK: Puffin Books.

Lawson, R. (1988). *Ben and Me: An astonishing life of Benjamin Franklin by his good mouse Amos.* New York, NY: Little, Brown.

O'Neill, M. (1990). *Hailstones and halibut bones.* New York, NY: Doubleday Books for Young Readers. (Original work published 1961)

Pinkney, A. (2006). *Duke Ellington: The piano prince and his orchestra.* New York, NY: Hyperion Books.

Schroeder, A. (2011). *Ben Franklin: His wit and wisdom from A–Z.* New York, NY: Holiday House.

Snicket, L. (2006). *The complete wreck: A series of unfortunate events, books 1–13.* New York, NY: HarperCollins.

Street, P. (2003). *There's a frog in my throat: 440 animal sayings a little bird told me.* New York, NY: Holiday House.

Terban, M. (2007). *In a pickle and other funny idioms.* San Aselmo, CA: Sandpiper.

chapter 4

Text Complexity

THE ISSUE OF TEXT COMPLEXITY IS ONE THAT causes a lot of discussion and maybe a bit of consternation among educators as they work to understand the expectations of the English Language Arts (ELA) Common Core State Standards (CCSS). A common first reaction is "More complex text? Our kids can't read the texts we ask them to read now!" In fact, some researchers have pointed out that third-grade students are still learning to read in primary and some may have a difficult time reaching the current levels of text complexity (Hiebert, 2011/2012). However, the ELA Standards state that students are expected to acquire the "habits of reading independently and closely, which are essential to their future success" (NGA & CCSSO, 2010a, p. 10). The expectation for students to read more challenging texts is one of the instructional shifts in the CCSS.

Cassaundra L. Watkins

To help us decide what texts to use at each grade level, a list of example texts has been provided (NGA & CCSSO, 2010b). At first glance, the titles of the texts provided as guidance for understanding text complexity for each grade level band may seem surprising. The expectation for complex texts has teachers in grades 3–5 thinking about the kinds of texts to use for instruction and wondering about questions such as these: Why is text complexity emphasized in the Standards? How is text complexity determined? What kinds of materials should we use in the classroom? How and when should we teach our students to read complex texts? We will explore these questions in this chapter.

The CCSS Focus on Text Complexity

SOME TEACHERS MAY RECALL BEING CHILDHOOD READERS OF complex texts. We remember spending golden summer afternoons in a barn with a girl, a pig, and a spider as we read E. B. White's *Charlotte's Web* (1952/2006) or entering the wardrobe with Peter, Susan, Edmund, and Lucy while reading *The Lion, the Witch, and the Wardrobe* (Lewis, 1950/2010). We read student newspapers, such as *Weekly Reader,* and we used nonfiction books and reference materials to find answers to questions about the world (or at least to write reports for school). We regularly spent time in the local library. We were willing to do the hard work of reading complex texts as a matter of course.

Other teachers may recall that they didn't enjoy reading. Even as children, however, they knew that reading complex texts was important for school success, and so they worked a little harder and did their best. However, many students entering college today have been surprised that they need to enroll in remedial programs to be prepared for the demands of reading and writing in college coursework. There is much speculation about the reasons for this lack of college and career readiness. Research cited in Appendix A of the ELA Standards suggests that college texts have become more difficult while K–12 texts have actually become easier over the years (NGA & CCSSO, 2010b). Another finding is that teachers have gradually decreased their expectations for students to be accountable for reading complex texts, independently or otherwise. As a result, today's students are not able to read at the text levels of similarly aged readers in the past (NGA & CCSSO, 2010b, p. 3).

In order for students to be ready for college, the expectation is for students to have many experiences reading more challenging texts as they progress through school. The goal is for students to be equipped to read complex texts independently by the end of high school.

Understanding the Text Complexity Standard

IN THE CCSS, EACH GRADE LEVEL IS A step on a staircase leading to the ability to read complex texts independently and proficiently. College and Career Readiness Anchor Standard 10 is considered the text complexity standard for both literary and informational text. It states that students will, "Read and comprehend complex literary and informational texts independently and proficiently." This is the goal at each grade level.

Meeting the text complexity standard does not mean achieving a finite and discrete grade level at each year. In other words, students in third grade aren't expected to match neatly with third-grade texts. Instead, students are expected to read and improve their reading within a two-year text complexity band. At the beginning of each text complexity band, students should be provided with a lot of support and scaffolding. The expectation is that they will increase their reading ability over a two-year span until they are independently and proficiently reading the types of challenging texts included within their text complexity bands.

For grades 3–5, the expectations of Reading Standard 10 in the Literature strand are as follows:

- **Grade 3:** By the end of the year, read and comprehend literature, including stories, dramas, and poetry, *at the high end* of the grades 2–3 text complexity band independently and proficiently.
- **Grade 4:** By the end of the year, read and comprehend literature, including stories, dramas, and poetry, in the grades 4–5 text complexity band proficiently, *with scaffolding as needed at the high end* of the range.
- **Grade 5:** By the end of the year, read and comprehend literature, including stories, dramas, and poetry, *at the high end* of the grades 4–5 text complexity band independently and proficiently. [Italics added] (NGA & CCSSO, 2010)

For the same grades, the expectations of Reading Standard 10 in the Informational Text strand are as follows:

- **Grade 3:** By the end of the year, read and comprehend informational texts, including history/social studies, science, and technical texts, *at the high end* of the grades 2–3 text complexity band independently and proficiently.
- **Grade 4:** By the end of the year, read and comprehend informational texts, including history/social studies, science, and technical texts, in the grades 4–5 text complexity band proficiently, *with scaffolding as needed at the high end* of the range.
- **Grade 5:** By the end of the year, read and comprehend informational texts, including history/social studies, science, and technical texts, *at the high end* of the grades 4–5 text complexity band independently and proficiently. [Italics added]

Appendix B of the CCSS (NGA & CCSSO, 2010c) provides a list of texts that serve as examples for each text complexity band. These are *not* mandated texts. Rather, they are meant to be used as examples of the expected difficulty levels of texts and to guide us in making decisions about what challenging materials we select for our own classroom instruction and assessment.

In the grade K–1 text exemplars, teacher read-alouds or read-alongs of complex text comprise much of the text complexity focus for early primary students. In grades 2 and 3, as students become more independent readers, they are expected to read and comprehend more challenging text independently. However, the major leap in the difficulty level of the text exemplars seems to be at grade 4. In the grades 2 and 3 text complexity band, a book such as *Charlotte's Web* (White, 1952/2006) is still a read-aloud. In the grades 4 and 5 text complexity band, students are expected to read texts such as *Alice's Adventures in Wonderland and Through the Looking Glass* (Carroll, 1865/2012) independently and proficiently by the end of fifth grade.

Choosing Complex Texts for Grades 3–5 Classrooms

ACCORDING TO HIEBERT (2012A), SEVERAL FACTORS WORK TOGETHER to make a text complex, and texts can vary in complexity, even for proficient readers. Hiebert suggests seven actions that educators can take to address text complexity:

1. Focus on knowledge acquisition in the classroom.
2. Choose texts that help students connect to existing and new knowledge.

3. Choose texts that have the potential to activate students' passion.

4. Choose texts that help students develop vocabulary.

5. Increase the volume of reading in the classroom.

6. Help students build stamina by giving them extended time to read.

7. Work together as teachers to review text and determine benchmark texts appropriate at different points across grade levels to help track student progress.

The ELA Standards describe a three-part model for educators to use in deciding how easy or difficult a particular text will be for a particular student or group of students. In this model, a text is measured by three components: quantitative measures, qualitative measures, and considerations of the reader and the task (CCSSO & NGA, 2010b, p. 4). As we decide which complex texts to use for instruction and assessment in our classrooms, we should follow these steps:

1. Use quantitative measures to assign a text to a specific grade band.

2. Use qualitative measures to locate a text within a specific grade band.

3. Use professional judgment to decide how well suited a text is for a specific instructional purpose with a particular set of students (CCSSO & NGA, 2012).

According to the Standards, all three of these components are equally important when selecting texts to use for instruction (NGA & CCSSO, 2010b, p. 4). A brief summary of each component of text complexity follows.

Quantitative Measures of Text Complexity

The quantitative measure of text complexity applies to the readability of a text. For years, teachers and reading specialists have determined the readability of a text by using one or more readability formulas. A readability formula helps a teacher decide the grade level of a particular text so it can be matched appropriately with students' reading abilities.

Examples of readability formulas that have been available for some time include the Flesch-Kincaid, the Fry Readability Graph, the New Dale-Chall formula, and the Spache formula. These formulas are based on word and sentence lengths and the numbers of syllables in words. The Fry Readability Graph is one of the easiest for teachers to use. By counting the number of words in a 100-word passage, determining the average number of syllables and sentences, and then plotting the data on the Fry Readability Graph (available online), the teacher can calculate a rough estimate of the grade level of a text.

Newer tools for determining text complexity depend on numbers of words and sentence lengths but also consider sentence and passage coherence and text structure. These tools are complicated and much more suited to calculations by a computer than a human. One popular text complexity tool that has been used extensively is the Lexile Framework for Reading (www .Lexile.com) from MetaMetrics. At the beginning of the initiative, the CCSS focused on Lexiles as an appropriate quantitative measure of text complexity. As a result, Lexile levels have been recalibrated to better correlate with the expectations of the CCSS. For example, when we enter a text we are considering into Lexiles' online Quick Book Search, we may be surprised to find that texts we have used in the past are now rated as more appropriate for a lower grade level.

Supplemental information for Appendix A of the CCSS (NGA & CCSSO, 2012) reports research findings on a variety of tools that are now available to determine text complexity. Some

FIGURE 4.1 ● Text Complexity Bands for Grades 3–5

Common Core Band	ATOS	Degrees of Reading Power®	Flesch-Kincaid	The Lexile Framework®	Reading Maturity	SourceRater
2nd – 3rd	2.75 – 5.14	42 – 54	1.98 – 5.34	420 – 820	3.53 – 6.13	0.05 – 2.48
4th – 5th	4.97 – 7.03	52 – 60	4.51 – 7.73	740 – 1010	5.42 – 7.92	0.84 – 5.75

Source: NGA & CCSSO, 2012, p. 4

of these tools analyze samples of text that are entered or pasted in, and some have already rated entire books for text complexity. The following is a list of text complexity tools available online:

- ATOS, by Renaissance Learning (www.renlearn.com/atos/default.aspx)
- DRP Analyzer, by Questar Assessment (www.questarai.com/products/drpprogram/pages/drp_analyzer.aspx)
- Flesch-Kincaid (public domain) (http://office.microsoft.com/en-us/word-help/test-your-document-s-readability-HP010148506.aspx)
- Lexile Framework, by MetaMetrics (www.lexile.com/)
- Reading Maturity, by Pearson Education (www.readingmaturity.com/)

Each of these text complexity tools can give us an idea of the readability of text for use in the classroom. Figure 4.1 includes the CCSS text complexity bands for grades 2–5 within each of these text leveling systems.

We first use quantitative measures, such as those provided by text complexity tools, to assign a text to a grade band. Then, we turn to the qualitative measures of the text.

Qualitative Measures of Text Complexity

Qualitative measures are just as important as readability in determining text complexity. Qualitative measures are those factors that are best attended to by an attentive human reader, rather than a computer. After deciding the text complexity band using a text complexity analyzer, we look at these qualitative measures:

1. levels of meaning or purpose
2. structure
3. language conventionality and clarity
4. knowledge demands

Levels of Meaning or Purpose   In evaluating a literary text, one of the qualitative measures we consider is levels of meaning. A literary text that tells a straightforward story is easier to understand than a text in which the meaning is more subtle. For example, Jane Yolen's *Encounter* (1996) is a picture book with a Lexile level of 760L, making it appropriate for the higher end of the grades 2–3 text complexity band and the lower end of the grades 4–5 band. The book tells the story of Christopher Columbus's landing in San Salvador and his interaction with the Taino people. It can be understood at a literal level, but it takes a great deal of inference to truly understand the message of the author about the subjugation of the native people.

Thought-provoking text found in excellent children's literature often has several layers of meaning to consider—a factor we must consider when using such a text with students. A number of children's books appropriate for upper-elementary students require interpretation of layers of meaning for the reader to comprehend the text at a deeper level. A more complex literary work may also include more complex illustrations to be interpreted.

Informational texts can be difficult for many reasons. An informational text with an obvious purpose is easier to understand than an informational text with a more subtle purpose. When we evaluate an informational text for use in the classroom, we need to think about how straightforward the writing is. Is it easy to understand the author's purpose for the text, or will it take some work to figure out? Informational texts also often include visuals (e.g., maps, graphs, charts, diagrams, etc.) that may be easy to understand or difficult to interpret. Some visuals add to the meaning of a text, but some can be distracting, having little purpose beyond decoration.

Structure   In literature, a story with a simple structure follows a traditional pattern (often called a *story grammar*) that includes an introduction, problem, sequence of events, resolution, and ending. This type of story is usually considered easier to read than a text with an unconventional structure. In addition to the story structure, other literary devices—such as flashbacks, foreshadowing, and switching point of view—can make a text more difficult to comprehend. A rhyming poem written for children may have a more familiar structure than a non-rhyming poem that includes a number of literary devices, such as metaphors and assonance.

When authors write informational texts, they often use a variety of text structures that may be challenging for students. A text is considered "inconsiderate" when it is written in a way that is difficult for students to follow or when the sentences the author uses do not follow typical patterns (Armbruster, 2004). A well-written informational text will be written with a variety of sentence structures yet be coherent, clear, and logical to its readers. Such a text will also often include graphics that help relay information to and inform readers.

Language Conventionality and Clarity   Language and lack of clarity can also make a text hard to read. When evaluating a text for use in the classroom, teachers should ask: How clear and coherent is the language in the text? Does it include contemporary language that students can easily understand, or is the language old fashioned? Does the text include unfamiliar vocabulary?

Emily Dickinson's "A Bird Came Down the Walk" is one of the poems used as a text exemplar for grades 4–5. Consider the language and vocabulary used in the poem:

A Bird Came Down the Walk

A bird came down the walk—
He did not know I saw;
He bit an angleworm in halves
And ate the fellow, raw.

And then he drank a dew
From a convenient grass,
And then hopped sidewise to the wall
To let a beetle pass.

He glanced with rapid eyes
That hurried all abroad—
They looked like frightened beads, I thought—
He stirred his velvet head—

Like one in danger; cautious,
I offered him a crumb,
And he unrolled his feathers
And rowed him softer home

Than oars divide the ocean,
Too silver for a seam,
Or butterflies, off banks of noon,
Leap, plashless, as they swim.

Even though the poem uses fairly simple language for the most part, it still poses a number of vocabulary challenges (e.g., *convenient, cautious*). Also, the unconventional uses of language that characterize Dickinson's poem are probably unfamiliar to many 9- and 10-year-olds (e.g., "drank a dew"). Dickinson's poems are considered complex because they contain archaic language and structure, as well as multiple layers of meaning.

Informational texts often contain domain-specific vocabulary words representing concepts important to the related content area. Teachers should consider questions such as these: Does the author assume that readers know the vocabulary, or are important words highlighted with bold type and their definitions provided in a glossary or embedded in the text? How heavy is the vocabulary load? Informational texts also include a variety of text features that students must use to comprehend what they read, such as headings, captions, graphs and charts, tables of contents, indexes, and summaries.

Knowledge Demands   What kind of background knowledge does the reader need to comprehend a text? Text comes with knowledge demands. A literary text that describes the setting or historical context in student-friendly terms is easier to comprehend than a text that assumes the reader has adequate background knowledge.

For instance, the picture book *Grandfather's Journey* (Say, 1993) has very few words and is written using short, simple sentences. However, truly comprehending the story requires a great deal of background knowledge about Japanese customs and World War II in Japan. The Lexile level for *Grandfather's Journey* is AD650, which puts it in the grades 2–3 text complexity band, but the book is identified as needing "Adult Direction" for deep comprehension because of the knowledge demands.

Likewise, an informational text that leaves much to the reader's imagination instead of providing the necessary background information is more demanding in terms of knowledge level. The teacher should consider these questions: How much background information has the author provided? What assumptions does the author make about what the reader knows?

Qualitative Measures Rubrics   Rubrics are available for teachers' use that align with the CCSS in determining qualitative measures of both literary and informational texts. These rubrics were created by teachers and literacy leaders collaborating from a number of states and were facilitated by the Council of Chief State School Officers (CCSSO). Teachers can use these rubrics when evaluating texts for use in the classroom for qualitative measures. Figure 4.2 presents the Qualitative Measures Rubric for Literary Text (SCASS, 2013). Figure 4.3 shows the Qualitative Measures Rubric for Informational Text (SCASS, 2013).

FIGURE 4.2 • Qualitative Measures Rubric for Informational Text

Text Complexity: Qualitative Measures Rubric[1]

LITERATURE

Text Title _____   Text Author _____

	Exceedingly Complex	Very Complex	Moderately Complex	Slightly Complex
TEXT STRUCTURE	• **Organization:** Is intricate with regard to such elements as point of view, multiple time shifts, multiple characters, storylines and detail • **Use of Graphics:** If used, illustrations or graphics are essential for understanding the meaning of the text	• **Organization:** May include subplots, time shifts and more complex characters • **Use of Graphics:** If used, illustrations or graphics support or extend the meaning of the text	• **Organization:** May have two or more storylines and occasionally be difficult to predict • **Use of Graphics:** If used, a range of illustrations or graphics support selected parts of the text	• **Organization:** Is clear, chronological or easy to predict • **Use of Graphics:** If used, either illustrations directly support and assist in interpreting the text or are not necessary to understanding the meaning of the text
LANGUAGE FEATURES	• **Conventionality:** Dense and complex; contains abstract, ironic, and/or figurative language • **Vocabulary:** Complex, generally unfamiliar, archaic, subject-specific, or overly academic language; may be ambiguous or purposefully misleading	• **Conventionality:** Fairly complex; contains some abstract, ironic, and/or figurative language • **Vocabulary:** Fairly complex language that is sometimes unfamiliar, archaic, subject-specific, or overly academic	• **Conventionality:** Largely explicit and easy to understand with some occasions for more complex meaning • **Vocabulary:** Mostly contemporary, familiar, conversational; rarely unfamiliar or overly academic	• **Conventionality:** Explicit, literal, straightforward, easy to understand • **Vocabulary:** Contemporary, familiar, conversational language

(continued)

FIGURE 4.2 • (continued)

	Exceedingly Complex	Very Complex	Moderately Complex	Slightly Complex
MEANING	**Sentence Structure:** Mainly complex sentences with several subordinate clauses or phrases; sentences often contain multiple concepts	**Sentence Structure:** Many complex sentences with several subordinate phrases or clauses and transition words	**Sentence Structure:** Primarily simple and compound sentences, with some complex constructions	**Sentence Structure:** Mainly simple sentences
	Meaning: Multiple competing levels of meaning that are difficult to identify, separate, and interpret; theme is implicit or subtle, often ambiguous and revealed over the entirety of the text	**Meaning:** Multiple levels of meaning that may be difficult to identify or separate; theme is implicit or subtle and may be revealed over the entirety of the text	**Meaning:** Multiple levels of meaning clearly distinguished from each other; theme is clear but may be conveyed with some subtlety	**Meaning:** One level of meaning; theme is obvious and revealed early in the text.
KNOWLEDGE DEMANDS	**Life Experiences:** Explores complex, sophisticated or abstract themes; experiences portrayed are distinctly different from the common reader	**Life Experiences:** Explores themes of varying levels of complexity or abstraction; experiences portrayed are uncommon to most readers	**Life Experiences:** Explores several themes; experiences portrayed are common to many readers	**Life Experiences:** Explores a single theme; experiences portrayed are everyday and common to most readers
	Intertextuality and Cultural Knowledge: Many references or allusions to other texts or cultural elements	**Intertextuality and Cultural Knowledge:** Some references or allusions to other texts or cultural elements	**Intertextuality and Cultural Knowledge:** Few references or allusions to other texts or cultural elements	**Intertextuality and Cultural Knowledge:** No references or allusions to other texts or cultural elements

Source: State Collaborative on Assessment and Student Standards (SCASS). (2013). Text complexity: Qualitative measures rubric: Literature. Achievethecore. org. Retrieved from http://achievethecore.org/content/upload/SCASS_Text_Complexity_Qualitative_Measures_Lit_Rubric_2.8.pdf
[1]Adapted from Appendix A: Research Supporting Key Elements of the Standards, Common Core State Standards for English Language Arts and Literacy in History/ Social Studies and Science and Technical Subjects (2010).

FIGURE 4.3 ● Qualitative Measures Rubric for Literature

Text Complexity: Qualitative Measures Rubric

INFORMATIONAL TEXTS

Text Title _____   Text Author _____

	Exceedingly Complex	Very Complex	Moderately Complex	Slightly Complex
TEXT STRUCTURE	● **Organization:** Connections between an extensive range of ideas, processes or events are deep, intricate and often ambiguous; organization is intricate or discipline-specific ● **Text Features:** If used, are essential in understanding content ● **Use of Graphics:** If used, intricate, extensive graphics, tables, charts, etc. are integral to making meaning of the text; may provide information not otherwise conveyed in the text	● **Organization:** Connections between an expanded range of ideas, processes or events are often implicit or subtle; organization may contain multiple pathways or exhibit some discipline-specific traits ● **Text Features:** If used, directly enhance the reader's understanding of content ● **Use of Graphics:** If used, graphics, tables, charts, etc. support or are integral to understanding the text	● **Organization:** Connections between some ideas or events are implicit or subtle; organization is evident and generally sequential or chronological ● **Text Features:** If used, enhance the reader's understanding of content ● **Use of Graphics:** If used, graphic, pictures, tables, and charts, etc. are mostly supplementary to understanding the text	● **Organization:** Connections between ideas, processes or events are explicit and clear; organization of text is chronological, sequential or easy to predict ● **Text Features:** If used, help the reader navigate and understand content but are not essential to understanding content. ● **Use of Graphics:** If used, graphic, pictures, tables, and charts, etc. are simple and unnecessary to understanding the text but they may support and assist readers in understanding the written text

(continued)

FIGURE 4.3 ● *(continued)*

	Exceedingly Complex	Very Complex	Moderately Complex	Slightly Complex
LANGUAGE FEATURES	● **Conventionality:** Dense and complex; contains considerable abstract, ironic, and/or figurative language ● **Vocabulary:** Complex, generally unfamiliar, archaic, subject-specific, or overly academic language; may be ambiguous or purposefully misleading ● **Sentence Structure:** Mainly complex sentences with several subordinate clauses or phrases and transition words; sentences often contains multiple concepts	● **Conventionality:** Fairly complex; contains some abstract, ironic, and/or figurative language ● **Vocabulary:** Fairly complex language that is sometimes unfamiliar, archaic, subject-specific, or overly academic ● **Sentence Structure:** Many complex sentences with several subordinate phrases or clauses and transition words	● **Conventionality:** Largely explicit and easy to understand with some occasions for more complex meaning ● **Vocabulary:** Mostly contemporary, familiar, conversational; rarely overly academic ● **Sentence Structure:** Primarily simple and compound sentences, with some complex constructions	● **Conventionality:** Explicit, literal, straightforward, easy to understand ● **Vocabulary:** Contemporary, familiar, conversational language ● **Sentence Structure:** Mainly simple sentences
PURPOSE	● **Purpose:** Subtle and intricate, difficult to determine; includes many theoretical or abstract elements	● **Purpose:** Implicit or subtle but fairly easy to infer; more theoretical or abstract than concrete	● **Purpose:** Implied but easy to identify based upon context or source	● **Purpose:** Explicitly stated, clear, concrete, narrowly focused

FIGURE 4.3 ● *(continued)*

KNOWLEDGE DEMANDS	Exceedingly Complex	Very Complex	Moderately Complex	Slightly Complex
	Subject Matter Knowledge: Relies on extensive levels of discipline-specific or theoretical knowledge; includes a range of challenging abstract concepts **Intertextuality:** Many references or allusions to other texts or outside ideas, theories, etc.	**Subject Matter Knowledge:** Relies on moderate levels of discipline-specific or theoretical knowledge; includes a mix of recognizable ideas and challenging abstract concepts **Intertextuality:** Some references or allusions to other texts or outside ideas, theories, etc.	**Subject Matter Knowledge:** Relies on common practical knowledge and some discipline-specific content knowledge; includes a mix of simple and more complicated, abstract ideas **Intertextuality:** Few references or allusions to other texts or outside ideas, theories, etc.	**Subject Matter Knowledge:** Relies on everyday, practical knowledge; includes simple, concrete ideas **Intertextuality:** No references or allusions to other texts, or outside ideas, theories, etc.

Source: State Collaborative on Assessment and Student Standards (SCASS). (2013). Text complexity: Qualitative measures rubric: Informational Texts. *Achievethecore.org.* Retrieved from http://achievethecore.org/content/upload/SCASS_Info_Text_Complexity_Qualitative_Measures_Info_Rubric_2.8.pdf

Before we decide to use a text with a particular group of students, we have to consider their knowledge and needs. After we have used quantitative and qualitative measures to determine text complexity, we must examine a text through a third lens: reader and task measures.

Reader and Task Measures

Quantitative and qualitative measures are not enough when determining the appropriate text complexity for a group of students. The CCSS clearly state that when determining appropriate texts for a classroom, teachers must also use professional judgment about the class and the students (NGA & CCSSO, 2010b). Our students come to us with different cognitive abilities, interests, and motivations, as well as reasons for reading and expected outcomes of reading. We must carefully consider how the texts we plan to use are suited to our particular students. The expectation is that *all* students will be engaged in lessons on how to read complex texts. We need to consider students who are struggling readers, who are learning English, who need accommodations for disabilities, and who are reading at higher levels to determine the types of supports they will need when engaging in CCSS reading lessons with complex texts.

The CCSSO has published a set of suggested questions we should ask when evaluating the reader and task components of text complexity. With our unique group of students in mind, we need to review these considerations before making a decision to use a particular text. The "Guiding Questions for Reader and Task Considerations" can be found at ccsso.org (CCSSO, 2012c).

There are now a number of tools available to help educators with the task of determining text complexity. The Council of Chief State School Officers has developed a website called *Navigating Text Complexity* (http://www.ccsso.org/Navigating_Text_Complexity.html). Another excellent collection of resources on determining text complexity can be found on the Kansas State Department of Education website (www.ksde.org/Default.aspx?tabid=4778). Fisher, Frey, and Lapp (2012) also provide a thorough discussion of the issue of text complexity.

Text Complexity Across the School Year

THE WRITERS OF THE CCSS DID NOT EXPECT that complex texts would be used for all lessons, although this point often gets lost in the discussion. We do need to use complex texts frequently so that students engage in experiences in reading and comprehending text at a high level, but complex texts should not be the only texts used in the grades 3–5 classroom. In Appendix A of the CCSS, the "Readers and Tasks" section states the following:

> Students' ability to read complex text does not always develop in a linear fashion. Although the progression of Reading Standard 10 . . . defines required grade-by-grade growth in students' ability to read complex text, the development of this ability in individual students is unlikely to occur at an unbroken pace. Students need opportunities to stretch their reading abilities but also to experience the satisfaction and pleasure of easy, fluent reading within them, both of which the Standards allow for. . . . Such factors as students' motivation, knowledge, and experiences must also come into play in text selection. Students deeply interested in a given topic, for example, may engage with texts on that subject across a range of complexity. Particular tasks may also require students to read harder texts than they would

normally be required to. Conversely, teachers who have had success using particular texts that are easier than those required for a given grade band should feel free to continue to use them so long as the general movement during a given school year is toward texts of higher levels of complexity. (NGA & CCSSO, 2010b, p. 9).

The document goes on to say that the CCSS must be complemented by a well-developed, content-rich curriculum consistent with the expectations of the Standards.

It is clear that a variety of texts should be included in a curriculum that meet the needs of all learners and helps students build knowledge. So, when should complex text be used? In a comprehensive literacy classroom, there are times when we read aloud, times when students read to themselves, times when the class reads together, times when small groups read together, and times when students read to find information. Writing Standard 8 states the expectation that students will be involved in brief research projects across the school year, and students will need to engage in reading complex text to find information both in print and digital sources. Sometimes, we read aloud a challenging literary text and involve students in discussions focusing on identifying key details, character traits and motivations, and problem/resolution, and sometimes we read aloud a challenging informational text and teach students how to work through comprehending such a text. We also plan lessons that engage students in comprehending complex texts in which they read and discuss the text and the content. Figure 4.4 identifies the types of reading experiences that should be included in a literacy plan for grades 3–5.

FIGURE 4.4 ● Types of Reading Experiences in Grades 3–5 CCSS Classroom

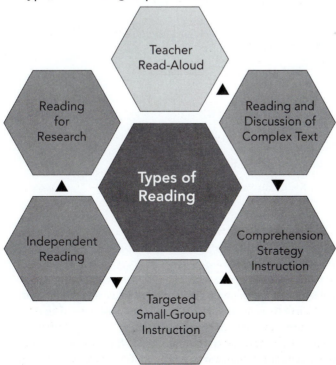

Text Complexity and Literary Text

By the time students reach third grade, most of them are familiar with simple stories, poems, and dramas. They can probably follow the storyline of a narrative text: beginning, setting, characters, problem, sequence of events, resolution, and ending. Even though students may not know the words to describe the parts of a storyline, they have likely spent many hours subconsciously absorbing this information.

The key expectation of the Reading Standards for Literature is for students to tackle challenging literary texts, which have more complex characters and details and more nuanced stories. In poetry, students are expected to read poems with more complex ideas and meanings beyond the actual words on the page.

Literature Text Types for Grades 3–5

The types of literature specifically mentioned in the CCSS for grades K–5 are stories, drama, and poetry. In grades 3–5, the genres mentioned in the Standards are as follows:

Stories

Children's adventure stories

Folktales

Legends

Fables

Fantasy

Realistic fiction

Myths

Books in a series

Graphic novels

Mysteries

Drama

Simple plays

Staged dialogue with brief familiar scenes

Poetry

Narrative poems

Limerick poems

Free-verse poems

Literary text exemplars are examples of stories, dramas, and poems that we can compare with literary texts we may be considering for use in our classrooms. The text exemplars that have been provided are not texts mandated by the CCSS; rather, they are only meant to serve as examples of the levels of difficulty appropriate for CCSS lessons. When we examine the text exemplars found in the ELA Standards (NGA & CCSSO, 2010a, p. 32) and in Appendix B

FIGURE 4.5 ● Exemplar Texts for Literature, Grades K–5

	Literature: Stories, Drama, Poetry
K	● *Over in the Meadow* by John Langstaff (traditional) (c1800) ● *A Bay, a Dog, and a Frog* by Mercer Mayer (1967) ● *Pancakes for Breakfast* by Tomie DePaola (1978) ● *A Story, A Story* by Gail E. Haley (1970) ● *Kitten's First Full Moon* by Kevin Henkes (2004)
1	● "Mix a Pancake" by Christina G. Rossetti (1893) ● *Mr. Popper's Penguins* by Richard Atwater (1938) ● *Little Bear* by Else Holmelund Minarik, illustrated by Maurice Sendak (1957) ● *Frog and Toad Together* by Arnold Lobel (1971) ● *Hi! Fly Guy* by Tedd Arnold (2006)
2–3	● "Who Has Seen the Wind?" by Christina G. Rossetti (1893) ● *Charlotte's Web* by E. B. White (1952) ● *Sarah, Plain and Tall* by Patricia MacLachlan (1985) ● *Tops and Bottoms* by Janet Stevens (1995) ● *Poppleton in Winter* by Cynthia Rylant, illustrated by Mark Teague (2001)
4–5	● *Alice's Adventures in Wonderland* by Lewis Carroll (1865) ● "Casey at the Bat" by Ernest Lawrence Thayer (1888) ● *The Black Stallion* by Walter Farley (1941) ● "Zlateh the Goat" by Isaac Bashevis Singer (1984) ● *Where the Mountain Meets the Moon* by Grace Lin (2009)

Source: NGA & CCSSO, 2010a, p. 32

(NGA & CCSSO, 2010c), we see a combination of traditional and classic literary works and more contemporary selections. The primary trait that underlies all of these texts is that students must analyze and think deeply about them to determine the author's message.

Text exemplars for literature for K–5 (NGA & CCSSO, 2010a) are shown in Figure 4.5. An expanded list of text exemplars can be found in Appendix B of the CCSS (NGA & CCSSO, 2010c).

In the Common Core Classroom
Creating Trading Cards about Complex Text

Taylor teaches fourth grade at an urban elementary school. One-third of her class is composed of English language learners, and there are also several struggling readers in her class. Taylor has planned to teach a lesson using complex text and selected the short story

"Tuesday of the Other June," by Norma Fox Mazer. This story centers on two girls named June, one of whom bullies the other. The story is considered a complex text for fourth-graders, but Taylor felt this story would resonate with her students.

Taylor made the decision to scaffold this lesson by beginning with a read-aloud. Taylor reads aloud to her students every day, and regardless of students' reading level, they thoroughly enjoy being read to and are usually fully engaged throughout the reading.

Prior to the lesson, Taylor designated places in the text where she planned to stop and have students "turn and talk" to describe the characters, make inferences, and determine the meanings of unfamiliar words and phrases. To accommodate her English language learners and struggling readers, Taylor identified several words and phrases, including examples of figurative language, that she thought students might need help defining or understanding.

Taylor was careful not to tell her students too much about the story before the reading. She told them that it was the story of a girl about their age named June and that June had a problem on Tuesdays. Then Taylor read the story aloud, using her voice and actions to make the narrative as animated as possible. The students were highly engaged throughout the story and listened attentively.

As Taylor read, she stopped at the places she had designated so students could discuss with their partners. She was prepared to prompt students as needed, but she found that students were able to infer quite a bit on their own, talking with one another about what they thought was happening and predicting what was going to happen in the story. Taylor gave students an opportunity to ask questions and answer them for each other. As she listened in on their partner discussions, she was surprised at students' willingness to share their thoughts about the text and help each other through parts that some of them found confusing.

After Taylor finished the story and students had discussed it, she introduced the second part of the lesson, which was for students to create trading cards that depicted their favorite characters from the story. She found the idea for the Trading Card Creator on the ReadWriteThink website (www.readwritethink.org). The idea is for students to create trading cards about fictional or real people, places, events, or vocabulary. The original lesson suggested that students complete their cards electronically, but this was not an option for Taylor's students because she has only a few classroom computers. Instead, Taylor printed out copies of the trading card planning sheet and gave one to each student.

Taylor introduced the trading card activity. She did not give students very many instructions for completing the planning card sheet or trading card illustration, as she wanted to see what they would do on their own. She did, however, give them a few simple instructions, such as "Read the directions and questions carefully," "Answer each question the best you can," and "Take your time so that you can think clearly, write neatly, and draw a detailed illustration."

Taylor planned for students who needed to work with partners to do so, while students who were more independent readers worked on their own. As students worked on their trading cards, Taylor circulated the room, monitoring their comprehension and offering support when necessary. She noticed that some students were struggling to answer several of the questions and assumed this might be due to the format of the planning sheet and the wording of the questions. She provided a bit of clarification or paraphrasing, which allowed students to continue working independently or with partners.

Taylor assessed her students' work informally through observation during large- and small-group discussions, as well as one on one with students during partner and independent work time. As she stopped to talk with each student about his or her trading card, she asked one or two questions from the planning sheet and determined the student's level of comprehension based on the details included in his or her responses. A sample trading card planning sheet, completed by one of Taylor's fourth-graders, is shown in Figure 4.6.

FIGURE 4.6 • Student's Completed Character Trading Card Planning Sheet

Student's name: Tera

Date: 10-26-12

CHARACTER TRADING CARDS
PLANNING SHEET

Directions: Use this planning sheet to prepare for the online Character Trading Cards activity by filling in information for each side of the trading card. Since space on the trading card is limited, you will need to summarize your information.

Character's name: June T.

Story title: Tuesday of the other June

1. Description

Setting: Where does the story take place?
In school and swimming class

Appearance: What does the character look like?
Black, long hair, skinny, tall
Brown eyes, light brown skin

Personality: How would you describe the character's personality (funny, shy, daring)?

2. Insights

Thoughts: What are the character's most important thoughts?
to get away from June M.

Feelings: What are the character's most important feelings?
she is happy when she stands up to June M.

read·write·think Copyright 2006 IRA/NCTE. All rights reserved. International Reading Association NCTE marcopolo ReadWriteThink materials may be reproduced for educational purposes.

3. Development

Problem: What is the character's problem at the beginning of the story?
June M. is bullying June T.

Goal: What does the character want to happen by the end of the story?
for June M. to leave her alone.

Outcome: How does the end of the story affect the character?
She stands up to June M. and feels so happy to do it

4. Statements and Actions

Statements: What is the most important or memorable thing the character says?
"good bye good riddane to bad trash"

Actions: What is the character's most important action?
When she stands up to June M.

Interactions: How does the character get along with other characters?
She really doesn't get along with everyone

5. My Impressions

Like: What do you like most about this character?
how she stands up to June M.

Dislike: What do you dislike most about this character?
that she didn't stand up for herself earlyer

Personal connection: Whom does this character remind you of and why?
of when I was geting bullied over the summer and how I standed up for myself and

Source: Reprinted with permission by International Reading Association, Delaware.

After analyzing the planning sheets and trading card illustrations, Taylor realized that her students needed more practice with recording evidence from the text to support their answers to text-based questions. After seeing the finished products, Taylor was pleased to see that her students had made a good start in thinking about complex text. She also noted that she would need to schedule a bit more time for her next lesson, in which students would read the text themselves.

Text Complexity and Informational Text

It is common knowledge that the type of text read most often in elementary classrooms has traditionally been narrative text. Children who watch television programs and movies and who read literary texts find the concept of a storyline familiar. In contrast, elementary students have often spent much less time watching documentaries and reading informational texts. One of the instructional shifts in the CCSS is to provide a balance between the reading of literary and informational texts.

Teachers sometimes think that students don't enjoy informational texts. However, children are naturally curious. If students' interest is piqued, most of them enjoy learning about the world. Well-written and interesting informational texts are usually appealing to boys, who are often hard to motivate when it comes to literacy activities. In fact, Jon Scieszka, the well-known children's author, has founded an initiative called Guys Read (www.guysread.com). He claims that many boys would be more likely to engage in reading if the texts were more appealing to them and advocates for providing boys with access to nonfiction, among other types of texts. Research supports the theory that boys often prefer nonfiction (Brozo, 2010).

When students read informational texts to find information for a WebQuest, research paper, or community project, they often get excited about finding and reading texts on topics or projects that have a purpose for them. Every classroom should be filled with intriguing picture books about content area topics, plus nonfiction books, magazines, articles, newspapers, and technology that provides access to quality websites. Informational texts should be available during self-selected reading time, connected to content area instruction, and selected for teacher read-alouds. We should share thought-provoking informational texts just as often as we share literary stories to motivate students to read.

Informational Text Types for Grades 3–5

Types of informational texts specifically mentioned in the CCSS for grades K–5 are literary nonfiction and historical, scientific, and technical texts. Most of these text types are listed in the CCSS section on Reading Standard 10 (NGA & CCSSO, 2010a, p. 32):

- biographies and autobiographies
- books about history, social studies, science, and the arts
- technical texts, including directions, forms, and information displayed in graphs, charts, and maps
- digital sources on a range of topics

Again, text exemplars for informational texts for grades 3–5 are intended for use in comparison to texts we may be considering for our own students. Text exemplars for informational texts for K–5 (NGA & CCSSO, 2010a) are shown in Figure 4.7. Appendix B of the CCSS (NGA & CCSSO, 2010c) also includes an expanded list of exemplars for informational texts.

Reading Complex Text Closely

STUDENTS IN GRADES 3–5 ARE EXPECTED TO ENGAGE in numerous experiences with complex texts to meet the CCSS. To meet Reading Standard 1, elementary students are expected to ask and answer questions about key details in a text, to refer to the text when asking and answering

FIGURE 4.7 ● Exemplar Texts for Informational Texts, Grades K–5

	Informational Texts: Literary Nonfiction and Historical, Scientific, and Technical Texts
K	• *My Five Senses* by Aliki (1962) • *Truck* by Donald Cnews (1980) • *I Read Signs* by Tana Hoban (1987) • *What Do You Do With a Tail Like This?* by Steve Jenkins and Robin Page (2003) • *Amazing Whales!* by Sarah L. Thomson (2005)
1	• *A Tree Is a Plant* by Clyde Robert Bulla, illustrated by Stacey Schuett (1960) • *Starfish* by Edith Thacher Hurd (1962) • *Follow the Water from Brook to Ocean* by Arthur Dorros (1991) • *From Seed to Pumpkin* by Wendy Pfeffer, illustrated by James Graham Hale (2004) • *How People Learned to Fly* by Fran Hodgkins and True Kelley (2007)
2–3	• *A Medieval Feast* by Aliki (1983) • *From Seed to Plant* by Gail Gibbons (1991) • *The Story of Ruby Bridges* by Robert Coles (1995) • *A Drop of Water: A Book of Science and Wonder* by Walter Wick (1997) • *Moonshot: The Flight of Apollo It* by Brian Floca (2009)
4–5	• *Discovering Mars: The Amazing Story of the Red Planet* by Melvin Berger (1992) • *Hurricanes: Earth's Mightiest Storms* by Patricia Lauber (1996) • *A History of US* by Joy Hakim (2005) • *Horses* by Seymour Simon (2006) • *Quest for the Tree Kangaroo: An Expedition to the Cloud Forest of New Guinea* by Sy Montgomery (2006)

Source: NGA & CCSSO, 2010a, p. 32

questions, to make logical inferences, and to quote accurately when citing textual evidence by the end of fifth grade.

This standard comes from College and Career Readiness Anchor Standard 1, which states, "Read closely to determine what the text says explicitly and to make logical inference from it; cite specific textual evidence when writing or speaking to support conclusions drawn from the text" (NGA & CCSSO, 2010a, p. 10). The texts students read should match the expectation of Reading Standard 10 for text complexity. Reading Standards 2 through 9 support Reading

Tips for the Teacher

"WITH THE COMMON CORE STANDARDS, students need to be able to look beyond the surface level. They need to be able to read critically and have an understanding about the author and the author's thinking. It is almost as if the expectations of the Reading Standards are a communication between the student and the author."

—Leslie, grade 5 teacher

Standards 1 and 10. Standards for Writing, Speaking and Listening, and Language will usually also be addressed in close reading tasks.

According to the writers of the CCSS, "Students who meet the Standards readily undertake the close, attentive reading that is at the heart of understanding and enjoying complex works of literature. They habitually perform the critical reading necessary to pick carefully through the staggering amount of information available today in print and digitally" (NGA & CCSSO, 2010a, p. 3). The expectation is that students will read a complex text closely, engaging in a productive struggle with it to decipher the author's intended meaning (Coleman & Pimentel, 2012) and discussing with classmates and writing about the text. According to Brown and Kappes (2012),

> Close reading involves an investigation of a short piece of text, with multiple readings done over multiple instructional lessons. Through text-based questions and discussion, students are guided to deeply analyze and appreciate various aspects of the text, such as key vocabulary and how its meaning is shaped by context; attention to form, tone, imagery and/or rhetorical devices; the significance of word choice and syntax; and the discovery of different levels of meaning as passages are read multiple time. (p. 2).

In close reading tasks, the Reading, Writing, Speaking and Listening, and Language Standards are integrated. Students work in groups to learn how to think about text and engage in discussion and writing to contemplate ideas and new and challenging vocabulary presented by the text. Supportive information about implementation of the CCSS shows that these kinds of more independent close reading experiences should be a regular part of a third grade classroom (Student Achievement Partners, 2012a).

Teaching students how to read and think critically can enhance comprehension (McLaughlin & DeVoogd, 2004). When students are engaged in critical literacy, they look at the text from different perspectives, examining the author's bias and challenging the ideas presented. As McLaughlin and DeVoogd (2004) state, "Even though the author has the power to create and present the message, readers have the power and the right to be text critics, by reading, questioning, and analyzing the author's message" (p. 21). In close reading, students read carefully and critically and use evidence in the text to support their understanding, which can lead to deeper comprehension.

Reading the Text Multiple Times

The Reading Standards are divided into four clusters:

1. Key Ideas and Details
2. Craft and Structure
3. Integration of Knowledge and Ideas
4. Range of Reading and Level of Text Complexity (NGA & CCSSO, 2010)

Shanahan (2012b) suggests that students should read a complex text three times in a close reading. Each reading should accomplish a separate purpose. In the first reading, students explore the big question: "What did the text say?" as they read for key ideas and details. In the second reading, students explore how the text works by thinking about the question "How did the text say it?" as they read for craft and structure. The third reading helps students evaluate the quality of the text and understand how it connects to other texts. In this reading, students explore these questions: "What does the text mean? What is its value? How does the text connect other texts?" as they read to integrate knowledge and ideas. Shanahan further suggests that while students are the ones doing the reading and interpretation, the teacher's major role is to ask text-dependent questions that help guide students through the text. The text may be brief, but the close reading may take several days to accomplish.

Gallagher (2004) describes teaching his students to do first-draft, second-draft, and third-draft reading. In first-draft reading, the reader reads to understand what the text says. In second-draft reading, the reader explores the author's craft, such as structure and language. In third-draft (or more) reading, students contemplate the ideas in the text more fully. Gallagher has found that students in grades 4–12 comprehend a text in a much deeper way when they explore it multiple times. Robb (2003) discusses the concept of close reading in different content areas, in which "students become cameras and silently zoom in on words, phrases, sentences, paragraphs, graphs, illustrations, to figure out what the author means" (p. 146).

Text-Dependent Questions

When we ask text-dependent questions, we ask questions that can be answered only by reading the text. When students write or discuss answers to text-dependent questions, they don't discuss their personal experiences with a similar topic. Instead, they read, ask and answer questions, make logical inferences, and refer to information and clues in the text as the bases of their answers.

For example, suppose a fifth-grade class is reading a passage from *Tuck Everlasting* (Babbitt, 2007) in which the main character, Winnie Foster, is walking alone in the woods. Questions such as "Have you ever been alone in the woods?" and "How did it feel to be there?" are not considered text-dependent questions (and even though these questions might help students activate prior knowledge, make connections, and visualize being in the woods, they are better suited for lessons outside a close-reading lesson). Text-dependent questions include questions like these: "How did Winnie feel to be in the woods?" "How do you know?" and "What words does the author use to help you know how Winnie felt?" Questions such as these require students to consult the text and make logical inferences to answer. Fifth-graders are also expected to quote accurately while citing textual evidence, according to Reading Standard 1.

Figure 4.8 provides guidelines for creating text-dependent questions for close analytic reading of texts (Student Achievement Partners, 2012b).

Prereading in Close Reading Lessons

One of the criticisms of current instructional practices in reading is that when teachers teach how to make connections to background knowledge, they sometimes spend too much time preparing students to read a text and too little time having students actually read the text (Coleman, 2011). For example, Shanahan (2012a) observed elementary teachers who spent 20 minutes preparing students for reading but allowed only 5 minutes for students to read the

FIGURE 4.8 ● Guidelines for Creating Text-Dependent Questions for Close
Reading of Texts

An effective set of text dependent questions delves systematically into a text to
guide students in extracting the key meanings or ideas found there. They typically
begin by exploring specific words, details, and arguments and then moves on to
examine the impact of those specifics on the text as a whole. Along the way they
target academic vocabulary and specific sentence structures as critical focus points
for gaining comprehension.

While there is no set process for generating a complete and coherent body of text
dependent questions for a text, the following process is a good guide that can serve
to generate a core series of questions for close reading of any given text.

Step One: Identify the Core Understandings and Key Ideas of the Text

As in any good reverse engineering or "backwards design" process, teachers
should start by identifying the key insights they want students to understand from
the text—keeping one eye on the major points being made is crucial for fashioning
an overarching set of successful questions and critical for creating an appropriate
culminating assignment.

Step Two: Start Small to Build Confidence

The opening questions should be ones that help orientate students to the text and
be sufficiently specific enough for them to answer so that they gain confidence to
tackle more difficult questions later on.

Step Three: Target Vocabulary and Text Structure

Locate key text structures and the most powerful academic words in the text that are
connected to the key ideas and understandings, and craft questions that illuminate
these connections.

Step Four: Tackle Tough Sections Head-on

Find the sections of the text that will present the greatest difficulty and craft
questions that support students in mastering these sections (these could be sections
with difficult syntax, particularly dense information, and tricky transitions or places
that offer a variety of possible inferences).

Step Five: Create Coherent Sequences of Text Dependent Questions

The sequence of questions should not be random but should build toward more
coherent understanding and analysis to ensure that students learn to stay focused on
the text to bring them to a gradual understanding of its meaning.

(continued)

FIGURE 4.8 • *(continued)*

Step Six: Identify the Standards That Are Being Addressed

Take stock of what standards are being addressed in the series of questions and decide if any other standards are suited to being a focus for this text (forming additional questions that exercise those standards).

Step Seven: Create the Culminating Assessment

Develop a culminating activity around the key ideas or understandings identified earlier that reflects (a) mastery of one or more of the standards, (b) involves writing, and (c) is structured to be completed by students independently.

Source: Student Achievement Partners, 2012c.

text. In addition, Shanahan noted that some teachers gave students so much information about the text that students had no reason to read it. A controversy about prereading (to preread or not to preread?) has been buzzing in the literacy field (Gewertz, 2012).

The goal of prereading instruction is to teach students to make connections to what they already know about a topic before they read independently. We still need to teach students *how* to activate their own background knowledge before reading, set a purpose for reading, monitor their own comprehension when reading independently, and work on vocabulary knowledge, such as strategies for developing morphology. But these tasks should be taught in separate lessons outside close reading experiences. In close reading for grades 3–5, we want to keep prereading brief, emphasizing just enough to help students set a purpose for reading and to motivate them to read without telling them too much or revealing information that will destroy any real reasons for reading the text.

See Chapter 7 for ideas about how to structure an upper-elementary classroom curriculum to support both comprehension development and deeper, more critical literacy.

Close Reading Model Lessons

Close reading model lessons have been posted on several websites for teachers to use as guides (Student Achievement Partners, 2012a). In the close reading model lessons for elementary grades, each lesson is conducted in a whole-class setting using a brief text, such as a folktale or an excerpt from a novel. Each lesson takes several days of instruction. The directions to the teacher are to limit before-reading discussion or instruction.

In these lessons, students read the text at least three times. In the first reading, students read the text or a section of the text independently without assistance. In the second reading, the teacher or a competent peer reads aloud the entire passage so that all students can hear the text. (In the grade 3 model lessons, it is suggested that the text be read aloud in the first reading.) During the second reading, the teacher may stop for discussions about domain-specific vocabulary, context, or sentence structure. After the second reading, the teacher poses text-dependent questions, in which students must use the text to find and discuss the answers. In the third reading, students read the text and work alone or with partners to find evidence to answer the text-dependent questions.

In some of the elementary model lessons, students engage in an activity using art, music, drama, or graphic organizers to visualize parts of text or engage in more extended vocabulary instruction. Most of the lessons end with an assessment in which students develop a concise, single sentence to answer each teacher-dependent question or write an analysis of the text supported by evidence from it.

In the Common Core Classroom
Reading Informational Texts Closely

Leslie teaches fifth grade at an urban school with a diverse population. To help her students meet the expectations of the CCSS, she has increased the amount of informational text that she includes in her classroom instruction. She also has focused more on text complexity, text-dependent questions, independent thinking, and peer discussion. Leslie has observed that her students still struggle with quoting from text accurately. She has planned to model text-dependent questioning for the students and how to find accurate quotes to support their answers. Leslie plans to teach a lesson in which she asks students to engage in a "productive struggle" with complex informational text. She plans to scaffold her text-dependent questions to build support for the struggling readers in her class.

Leslie based her text questions on the idea of green-light, yellow-light, and red-light questions, an adaptation of question–answer relationships (Raphael & Au, 2005). Green-light questions are those that have "right there" answers. Yellow-light questions require students to pause and infer based on what they already know or understand from information in the text. Red-light questions require students to stop and consider what they already know against what is stated in the text to think critically about the text.

For this lesson, Leslie chose an informational article entitled "Hard at Work: Many Kids in Ecuador Go to Work Instead of School" (Upadhyay, 2005). To begin the lesson, Leslie showed students a world map and asked if they could find Ecuador. It took the students a while to locate this country. The class then predicted what they might know about Ecuador based on where it was located in the world and what they already know about the environment there. The students were able to tell that the country is in South America, which is below the equator. Based on this, they inferred that the climate must be hot and possibly even humid. Leslie asked students to predict what types of food might grow in this type of climate. The students predicted oranges, because they knew oranges grow in Florida.

After a discussion about key vocabulary in the article (see Chapter 3), Leslie invited students to get out their highlighters and notebooks. She asked the students to read the first section of the article silently. She then began by asking green-light, text-dependent questions based on information in the first paragraph. As a group, the class read to find the answer to this green-light question: "How old was Wilbur when he began working on the banana plantation?" The class found the evidence together, and each student highlighted it in his or her copy of the article.

The article stated, "One in every four children is working." Leslie encouraged her students to use their math skills to determine what that statement meant in terms of the students in their classroom. The students determined that if there were 20 students in the room, then 5 of them would be working. Leslie was delighted to see that one of the students noted that could be expressed as the fraction 5/20, and another realized that was one-fourth of the class.

Students read the second section of the article and Leslie then moved to a yellow-light question. She asked, "Why did Mr. Sinchi's children have to go to work on the plantation instead of going to school?" She modeled for students how to find the answer and highlighted the evidence in the text. Next, she asked students another yellow-light question: "Why are people paid higher wages in Costa Rica?" This time, Leslie invited each student to draw a T-chart in his or her notebook. Then, working with partners, the students found evidence for the answer to the question in the passage and highlighted it. Each student wrote the answer in his or her own words on the left side of his or her T-chart. On the right side, each student provided his or her evidence from the passage. When students had finished, Leslie asked them to exchange partners and share their answers with new partners. Then they had an opportunity to revise their answers, in their own words, at the bottom of the page. Many students were able to get to the answer that the existence of unions helps workers to earn reasonable wages.

On day 2 of this lesson, Leslie and the class revisited the map of Ecuador and discussed their new knowledge about the country, child labor, and unions. The students also discussed their thoughts about child labor so far. Many stated that child labor was wrong and that it was sad that the children couldn't go to school. However, some students said that the children should feel proud that they get to play a role in putting food on the table. Students then reread the passage independently.

Leslie posed the red-light question: "What point is the author trying to make in this article?" Using their highlighters and working independently, students wrote their answers in their own words on the left sides of their T-charts and provided evidence from the passage to support their answers on the right sides of the charts. Figure 4.9 presents a student's T-chart, showing an answer to a higher-level question and evidence to support the answer.

Once students had finished with their T-charts, they teamed with different partners to discuss their findings. Leslie then gave students an opportunity to revise their thinking in their own words. Answers ranged from higher-level thinking, such as "The article is to bring awareness of the issue," to more literal thinking, such as "The author wanted to share about Ecuador."

Leslie has observed that many students struggle with thinking critically about what they read and feels that students having conversations with multiple partners is a critical piece of this lesson. At no time did Leslie tell students the point the author was trying to make. Students arrived at their own conclusions through reading the text, finding evidence, and having critical discussions about the topic.

The goal was not for all students to arrive at the same conclusion. Rather, the goal was for all students to arrive at some conclusion and be able to back it with evidence from the text. A secondary goal was for students to begin to have critical discussions with peers that fostered their thinking beyond the text. When students had critical discussions with partners, their thinking became clearer and they contemplated multiple points of view about the same subject.

Leslie assessed this lesson through whole-group discussion, peer conversation/partner work, notebooks, highlighted evidence, and over-the-shoulder conferencing. She was thrilled to see some of her most-struggling students engaged in academic conversation and providing evidence that supported their thinking!

FIGURE 4.9 ● Student's Completed T-Chart for Citing Textual Evidence

Shaylee
August 23, 12

Question- What is the point the author is
trying to make?

My answer	Evidence
The point the author is trying to make is child labor is really out in this world. Also, it's not just in foreign places it's also in the United States of America. It's also telling me that child labor is forcing parents to make a decision for their kids to go to school or work.	I found my first piece of evidence on page 2 in the section where it says "Child Labor in the U.S.A" it says "The mistreatment of child workers isn't just a foreign problem." It also states that if we raise awareness we could help invest in education.

Revised answer— My revised answer is
that the author is trying to make
the point that child labor exists all
over the world but if we help raise
awareness of child labor we can most
likely find a way to stop parents from having to
decide to send their child to school or work.

Basal Alignment Project, Grades 3–5

One of several projects that have come about as the result of the CCSS is the Basal Alignment Project (Students Achievement Partners, 2012d). Teachers of third-, fourth-, and fifth-grade students from several states have collaborated to review the lessons included in a number of basal reading series. These teachers have then worked together to revise the lessons to better align with the expectations of the CCSS. After participating in extensive professional learning about close reading and text-dependent questions, these teachers have created guides for close reading for many of the stories and articles found in materials that are already being used in their schools. The lessons are free and available for all teachers. Because the texts included in basal reading series are usually excerpts from books and novels and articles published elsewhere, the lessons are valuable for understanding the concept of close reading with a variety of materials.

Close Reading and Text Complexity

To plan for close reading experiences with our students, we first need to select a text of appropriate complexity, contemplating both quantitative and qualitative measures and considering readers and tasks. We need to read and think critically about the texts we use and create text-dependent questions for the text that are appropriate for our particular group of students. Then we need to plan a lesson sequence that requires students to dig deeply into one text over the course of several days. And finally, we need to guide our students through the text in a way that ensures they are engaged and learning at high levels.

Thinking about Text Complexity in Grades 3–5

THE WRITERS OF THE CCSS ACKNOWLEDGE THAT SKILLFUL teaching is required for students to accomplish the goal of reading more complex texts. They writers state, "Many students will need careful instruction—including effective scaffolding—to enable them to read at the level required by the Common Core State Standards" (Coleman & Pimentel, 2012, p. 8). Students in grades 3–5 are just beginning to read more complex texts. For them to read at expected levels and think critically about the text, we must be willing to do the hard work of thinking and planning to teach them in new ways.

REFERENCES

Armbruster, B. B. (2004). Considerate texts. In D. Lapp, J. Flood, & N. Farnan (Eds.), *Content area reading and learning: Instructional strategies* (2nd ed., pp. 47–58). Mahwah, NJ: Erlbaum.

Brown, S., & Kappes, L. (2012). *Implementing the Common Core State Standards: A primer on the "close reading of text"* Washington, DC: Aspen Institute.

Brozo, W. G. (2010). *To be a boy, to be a reader: Engaging teen and preteen boys in active literacy.* Newark, DE: International Reading Association.

Coleman, D. (2011, July 31). *Close reading of text: Letter from a Birmingham jail, Martin Luther King, Jr.* New York, NY: EngageNY. Retrieved from http://vimeo.com/27056255

Coleman, D., & Pimentel, S. (2012). *Revised publishers' criteria for the Common Core State Standards in English language arts and literacy, grades 3–12.* Washington, DC: National Governors Association, Council of Chief State School Officers, Achieve, Council of Great City Schools, & National Association of State Boards of Education. Retrieved from http://www.corestandards.org/assets/Publishers_Criteria_for_3-12.pdf.

Council of Chief State School Officers (CCSSO). (2013). Suggested considerations for reader and task. *Library of additional resources on text complexity.* Retrieved from http://www.ccsso.org/Navigating_Text_Complexity/Accelerate_with_Additional_Resources.html

Fisher, D., Frey, N., & Lapp, D. (2012). *Text complexity: Raising rigor in reading.* Newark, DE: International Reading Association.

Gallagher, K. (2004). *Deeper reading: Comprehending challenging texts, 4–12.* Portland, ME: Stenhouse.

Gewertz, C. (2012, April 25). Common standards ignite debate over student "prereading" exercises. *Education Week, 31*(29), 1, 22–23.

Hiebert, E. H. (Dec. 2011/Jan. 2012). The Common Core's staircase of text complexity: Getting the size of the first step right. *Reading Today, 29*(3), 26–27.

Hiebert, E. H. (2012a). Seven actions that teacher can take right now: Text complexity. *Text Matters.* TextProject. Retrieved from http://textproject.org/teachers/text-matters/7-actions-that-teachers-can-take-right-now-text-complexity/.

Hiebert, E. H. (2012b). Readability and the Common Core's staircase of text complexity. *Text Matters.* TextProject. Retrieved from http://textproject.org/teachers/text-matters/readability-and-the-common-core-staircase-of-text-complexity/.

Kansas State Department of Education. (2012). ELA and literacy resources for the Kansas Common Core Standards. *Kansas College and Career Ready Standards.* Retrieved from http://www.ksde.org/Default.aspx?tabid=4778.

McLaughlin, M., & DeVoogd, G. L. (2004). *Critical literacy: Enhancing students' comprehension of text.* New York, NY: Scholastic.

National Governors Association Center for Best Practices & Council of Chief State School Officers (NGA & CCSSO). (2010a). *Common Core State Standards: English language arts and literacy in history/social studies, science, and technical subjects.* Washington, DC: Authors. Retrieved from http://www.corestandards.org/assets/CCSSI_ELA%20Standards.pdf.

National Governors Association Center for Best Practices & Council of Chief State School Officers (NGA & CCSSO). (2010b). Appendix A: Research supporting key elements of the standards and glossary of key terms. *Common Core State Standards.* Washington, DC: Authors. Retrieved from http://www.corestandards.org/assets/Appendix_A.pdf.

National Governors Association Center for Best Practices & Council of Chief State School Officers (NGA & CCSSO). (2010c). Appendix B: Text exemplars and sample performance tasks. *Common Core State Standards.* Washington, DC: Authors. Retrieved from http://www.corestandards.org/assets/Appendix_B.pdf.

National Governors Association Center for Best Practices & Council of Chief State School Officers (NGA & CCSSO). (2012). *Supplemental information for Appendix A of the Common Core State Standards for English language arts and literacy: New research on text complexity.* Washington, DC: Authors. Retrieved from http://corestandards.org/assets/E0813_Appendix_A_New_Research_on_Text_Complexity.pdf.

Nelson, J., Perfetti, C., Liben, D., & Liben, M. (2012). *Measures of text difficulty: Testing their predictive value for grade levels and student performance.* Retrieved from http://www.ccsso.org/Documents/2012/Measures%20ofText%20Difficulty_final.2012.pdf.

Raphael, T. E., & Au, K. H. (2005). QAR: Enhancing comprehension and test taking across grades and content areas. *The Reading Teacher, 59*(3), 206-221.

Robb, L. (2003). *Teaching reading in social studies, science, and math: Practical ways to weave comprehension strategies into your content area teaching.* New York, NY: Scholastic.

Shanahan, T. (2012a). Part 2: Practical guidance on pre-reading lessons. *Shanahan on Literacy.* Retrieved from http://www.shanahanonliteracy.com/2012/03/part-2-practical-guidance-on-pre.html.

Shanahan, T. (2012b). Planning for close reading. *Shanahan on Literacy.* Retrieved from http://www.shanahanonliteracy.com/search/label/Close%20reading.

State Collaborative on Assessment and Student Standards (SCASS). (2013). Text complexity: Qualitative measures rubric: Literature. Achievethecore.org. Retrieved from http://achievethecore.org/content/upload/SCASS_Text_Complexity_Qualitative_Measures_Lit_Rubric_2.8.pdf

Student Achievement Partners. (2012a). Close reading model lessons. Retrieved from http://www.achievethecore.org/page/752/featured-lessons

Student Achievement Partners. (2012b). Guide to creating text-dependent questions. Retrieved from http://www
    .achievethecore.org/page/46/complete-guide-to-creating-text-dependent-questions
Student Achievement Partners. (2012c). Basal alignment project. BAP Project Page. Retrieved from http://www
    .achievethecore.org/page/751/bap-project-page

LITERATURE CITED

Babbitt, N. (2007). *Tuck everlasting*. New York, NY: Square Fish.
Carroll, L. (2012). *Alice's adventures in Wonderland and through the looking glass*. New York: Signet Classics.
    (Original work published 1865)
Lewis, C. S. (1950). *The chronicles of Narnia: The lion, the witch, and the wardrobe*. New York, NY:
    MacMillan.
Mazer, N. F. (1986). "Tuesday of the other June." In *Junior Great Books, Series 4, Book 1* (pp. 29–45). .
    Chicago, IL: Great Books Foundation.
Say, A. (1993). *Grandfather's journey*. Boston, MA: Houghton-Mifflin.
White, E. B. (2006). *Charlotte's web*. New York, NY: HarperCollins. (Original work published 1952)
Upadhyay, R. (2005). "Hard at work: Many kids in Ecuador go to work instead of school." In S. Harvey &
    A. Goudvis (Ed.). *The source book of short text* (pp. 84–85). Portsmouth, NH: Heinemann.
Yolen, J. (1996). *Encounter*. San Anselmo, CA: Sandpiper Press.

Writing

IN A COMMON CORE CLASSROOM, KIDS WRITE! They write to learn about science and social studies, to demonstrate their learning, to support their opinions, to inform or explain their thinking, and to express their feelings, tell a story, or describe an event. In a writing classroom, we teach students how to write clearly and logically as well as creatively. Students share and discuss their writing, and together, we set goals for improvement.

Writing is at the center of learning across the curriculum. The ability to express one's thoughts clearly in writing is unquestionably a foundation for college and career readiness and is therefore a major focus in the Common Core State Standards (CCSS).

Kelly Sraj Toms

Writing to Learn

THE ACT OF COMPOSING HELPS US ORGANIZE OUR thoughts and think about new ideas. It also helps us internalize learning. According to the National Commission on Writing (2003), "If students are to make knowledge their own, they must struggle with the details, wrestle with the facts, and rework raw information and dimly understood concepts into language they can communicate to someone else. In short, if students are to learn, they must write" (p. 9). Writing is not only used to show what students know; it is also a tool for thinking and learning deeply.

A classroom intent on developing grades 3–5 students as writers includes writing *for* students, *with* students, and *by* students. There must be writing *for* students as we model how to write different types of text, including those required by the CCSS. Interactive writing—in which we write *with* students to help them improve their skills and strategies—is another type of writing instruction that should be part of every classroom. It seems obvious, but for our students to be writers, they must have many opportunities to actually write. Writing *by* students includes writing to learn, to demonstrate learning, and to produce works for publication.

Students should also write for different purposes. The CCSS recommend that at the elementary level, 30% of writing should be to persuade, 35% to explain, and 35% to convey experience (NGA & CCSSO, 2010a, p. 5).

Writing to Read

WE HAVE KNOWN FOR SOME TIME THAT REQUIRING students to write increases both their writing ability and their content knowledge. Recent research suggests that the act of writing actually helps students become better readers. In a report from the Carnegie Foundation, entitled *Writing to Read: Evidence for How Writing Can Improve Reading,* Graham and Hebert (2010) discuss the effects of different writing practices on students' reading achievement. They found convincing evidence that when students write, it enhances their reading comprehension. According to Graham and Hebert, "The evidence is clear: writing can be a vehicle for improving reading. In particular, having students write about a text they are reading enhances how well they comprehend it. The same result occurs when students write about a text from different content areas, such as science and social studies" (p. 6). Graham and Hebert also make several recommendations for writing practices that enhance students' reading comprehension, as identified in Figure 5.1.

The *Writing to Read* report and the CCSS are very much aligned. In fact, the CCSS for writing include the recommendations of the *Writing to Read* report. In grades 3–5, students are expected to write about the texts they read. Students are expected to respond to texts they read in writing (including writing personal reactions and analyzing and interpreting the text), write summaries of texts, take notes about information in texts, answer questions about texts in writing, and create their own questions about texts. The CCSS Writing Standards also focus on the process of writing and outline the criteria for writing different types of texts. Students are expected to spell and write sentences correctly. The Standards also expect students to write a lot across the curriculum. Writing experiences are designed to help students increase reading comprehension and improve their ability to write.

FIGURE 5.1 ● Writing Practices That Enhance Reading Comprehension

Writing Practices That Enhance Students' Reading

This report identifies a cluster of closely related instructional practices shown to be effective in improving students' reading. We have grouped these practices within three core recommendations, here listed in order of the strength of their supporting evidence.

I.   **HAVE STUDENTS WRITE ABOUT THE TEXTS THEY READ.** Students' comprehension of science, social studies, and language arts texts is improved when they write about what they read, specifically when they

   ● Respond to a Text in Writing (Writing Personal Reactions, Analyzing and Interpreting the Text)
   ● Write Summaries of a Text
   ● Write Notes About a Text
   ● Answer Questions About a Text in Writing, or Create and Answer Written Questions About a Text

II. **TEACH STUDENTS THE WRITING SKILLS AND PROCESSES THAT GO INTO CREATING TEXT.** Students' reading skills and comprehension are improved by learning the skills and processes that go into creating text, specifically when teachers

   ● Teach the Process of Writing, Text Structures for Writing, Paragraph or Sentence Construction Skills (Improves Reading Comprehension)
   ● Teach Spelling and Sentence Construction Skills (Improves Reading Fluency)
   ● Teach Spelling Skills (Improves Word Reading Skills)

III. **INCREASE HOW MUCH STUDENTS WRITE.** Students' reading comprehension is improved by having them increase how often they produce their own texts

Source: Graham & Hebert, 2010. Reprinted with permission by Carnegie Corporation of New York.

A number of resources are dedicated to helping students develop into better expressive writers. Figure 5.2 lists a few recommended resources. However, this chapter focuses on the particular CCSS expectation to connect writing to the understanding of text and how to meet that expectation in the classroom.

The Writing Standards for Grades 3–5

BECAUSE WRITING IS SUCH AN IMPORTANT PART OF academic success, the CCSS outline specifically what students are expected to know and be able to do at each grade level. The expectations build to ensure the achievement of writing competence by the end of high school.

In grades K–2, there are just seven Writing Standards. In grade 3, two new Writing standards are introduced: Writing Standard 4, which is about writing pieces appropriate to

FIGURE 5.2 ● Resources for Teaching Expressive Writing

Resources to Help Students Become Better Writers

Dorfman, L. R., & Cappelli, R. (2009). *Nonfiction mentor texts: Teaching informational writing through children's literature, K–8*. Porland, ME: Stenhouse.

Duke, N., Caughlan, S., Juzwik, M., Martin, N. (2011). *Reading and writing genre with purpose in K–8 classrooms*. Portsmouth, NH: Heinemann.

Fletcher, R., & Portalupi, J. (2001). *Writing workshop: The essential guide*. Portsmouth, NH: Heinemann.

Hale, E. (2008). *Crafting writers K–6*. Portland, ME: Stenhouse.

Lattimer, H. (2003). *Thinking through genre: Units of study in reading and writing workshops 4–12*. Portland, ME: Stenhouse.

Tompkins, G. (2011). *Teaching writing: Balancing process and product, K–8* (6th ed.). Boston, MA: Allyn & Bacon.

the assignment task and purpose, and Writing Standard 10, which is about having students write routinely over both extended and shorter timeframes for a range of discipline-specific tasks, purposes, and audiences. In grade 4, Writing Standard 9 is introduced, which states the expectation that students will draw evidence from literary or informational texts to support analysis, reflection, and research. This makes a total of 10 writing standards by the end of fourth grade. Table 5.1 presents Writing Standards 1, 2, and 3 for grades 3–5, and Table 5.2 presents Writing Standards 4 through 10 for grades 3–5.

There are four clusters or categories of Writing standards:

1. Text Types and Purposes
2. Production and Distribution of Writing
3. Research to Build and Present Knowledge
4. Range of Writing

Each individual Writing standard is tightly interwoven with the other Writing standards, as well as the standards in Reading, Speaking and Listening, and Language. Appendix C of the English Language Arts (ELA) Standards (NGA & CCSSO, 2010b) provides examples of student writing that meet the Standards. The

Tips for the Teacher

"I THINK THE COMMON CORE STANDARDS ARE MORE difficult than our old standards. But I think the rigor is necessary for students to be able to perform writing tasks to prepare them for the next year, and to become individuals who can express their thoughts clearly in writing."

—Cassaundra, grade 4 teacher

TABLE 5.1 ● *Writing Standards 1–3 for Grades 3–5*

Grade 3 students:	Grade 4 students:	Grade 5 students:
Text Types and Purposes		

1. Write opinion pieces on topics or texts, supporting a point of view with reasons.

   a. Introduce the topic or text they are writing about, state an opinion, and create an organizational structure that lists reasons.

   b. Provide reasons that support the opinion.

   c. Use linking words and phrases (e.g., *because, therefore, since, for example*) to connect opinion and reasons.

   d. Provide a concluding statement or section.

1. Write opinion pieces on topics or texts, supporting a point of view with reasons and information.

   a. Introduce a topic or text clearly, state an opinion, and create an organizational structure in which related ideas are grouped to support the writer's purpose.

   b. Provide reasons that are supported by facts and details.

   c. Link opinion and reasons using words and phrases (e.g., *for instance, in order to, in addition*).

   d. Provide a concluding statement or section related to the opinion presented.

1. Write opinion pieces on topics or texts, supporting a point of view with reasons and information.

   a. Introduce a topic or text clearly, state an opinion, and create an organizational structure in which ideas are logically grouped to support the writer's purpose.

   b. Provide logically ordered reasons that are supported by facts and details.

   c. Link opinion and reasons using words, phrases, and clauses (e.g., *consequently, specifically*).

   d. Provide a concluding statement or section related to the opinion presented.

- -

2. Write informative/explanatory texts to examine a topic and convey ideas and information clearly.

   a. Introduce a topic and group related information together; include illustrations when useful to aiding comprehension.

   b. Develop the topic with facts, definitions, and details.

   c. Use linking words and phrases (e.g., *also, another, and, more, but*) to connect ideas within categories of information.

2. Write informative/explanatory texts to examine a topic and convey ideas and information clearly.

   a. Introduce a topic clearly and group related information in paragraphs and sections; include formatting (e.g., headings), illustrations, and multimedia when useful to aiding comprehension.

   b. Develop the topic with facts, definitions, concrete details, quotations, or other information and examples related to the topic.

2. Write informative/explanatory texts to examine a topic and convey ideas and information clearly.

   a. Introduce a topic clearly, provide a general observation and focus, and group related information logically; include formatting (e.g., headings), illustrations, and multimedia when useful to aiding comprehension.

   b. Develop the topic with facts, definitions, concrete details, quotations, or other information and examples related to the topic.

(continued)

TABLE 5.1 • *(continued)*

Grade 3 students:	Grade 4 students:	Grade 5 students:
Text Types and Purposes		

d. Provide a concluding statement or section.	c. Link ideas within categories of information using words and phrases (e.g., *another, for example, also, because*).	c. Link ideas within and across categories of information using words, phrases, and clauses (e.g., *in contrast, especially*).
	d. Use precise language and domain-specific vocabulary to inform about or explain the topic.	d. Use precise language and domain-specific vocabulary to inform about or explain the topic.
	e. Provide a concluding statement or section related to the information or explanation presented.	e. Provide a concluding statement or section related to the information or explanation presented.
3. Write narratives to develop real or imagined experiences or events using effective technique, descriptive details, and clear event sequences.	3. Write narratives to develop real or imagined experiences or events using effective technique, descriptive details, and clear event sequences.	3. Write narratives to develop real or imagined experiences or events using effective technique, descriptive details, and clear event sequences.
a. Establish a situation and introduce a narrator and/or characters; organize an event sequence that unfolds naturally.	a. Orient the reader by establishing a situation and introducing a narrator and/or characters; organize an event sequence that unfolds naturally.	a. Orient the reader by establishing a situation and introducing a narrator and/or characters; organize an event sequence that unfolds naturally.
b. Use dialogue and descriptions of actions, thoughts, and feelings to develop experiences and events or show the response of characters to situations.	b. Use dialogue and description to develop experiences and events or show the responses of characters to situations.	b. Use narrative techniques, such as dialogue, description, and pacing, to develop experiences and events or show the responses of characters to situations.
c. Use temporal words and phrases to signal event order.	c. Use a variety of transitional words and phrases to manage the sequence of events.	c. Use a variety of transitional words, phrases, and clauses to manage the sequence of events.
d. Provide a sense of closure.	d. Use concrete words and phrases and sensory details to convey experiences and events precisely.	d. Use concrete words and phrases and sensory details to convey experiences and events precisely.
	e. Provide a conclusion that follows from the narrated experiences or events.	e. Provide a conclusion that follows from the narrated experiences or events.

Source: NGA & CCSSO, 2010.

TABLE 5.2 ● *Writing Standards 4–10 for Grades 3–5*

Grade 3 students:	Grade 4 students:	Grade 5 students:
Production and Distribution of Writing		
4. With guidance and support from adults, produce writing in which the development and organization are appropriate to task and purpose. (Grade-specific expectations for writing types are defined in standards 1–3 above.)	4. Produce clear and coherent writing in which the development and organization are appropriate to task, purpose, and audience. (Grade-specific expectations for writing types are defined in standards 1–3 above.)	4. Produce clear and coherent writing in which the development and organization are appropriate to task, purpose, and audience. (Grade-specific expectations for writing types are defined in standards 1–3 above.)
5. With guidance and support from peers and adults, develop and strengthen writing as needed by planning, revising, and editing. (Editing for conventions should demonstrate command of Language standards 1–3 up to and including grade 3 on pages 28 and 29.)	5. With guidance and support from peers and adults, develop and strengthen writing as needed by planning, revising, and editing. (Editing for conventions should demonstrate command of Language standards 1–3 up to and including grade 4 on pages 28 and 29.)	5. With guidance and support from peers and adults, develop and strengthen writing as needed by planning, revising, editing, rewriting, or trying a new approach. (Editing for conventions should demonstrate command of Language standards 1–3 up to and including grade 5 on pages 28 and 29.)
6. With guidance and support from adults, use technology to produce and publish writing (using keyboarding skills) as well as to interact and collaborate with others.	6. With some guidance and support from adults, use technology, including the Internet, to produce and publish writing as well as to interact and collaborate with others; demonstrate sufficient command of keyboarding skills to type a minimum of one page in a single sitting.	6. With some guidance and support from adults, use technology, including the Internet, to produce and publish writing as well as to interact and collaborate with others; demonstrate sufficient command of keyboarding skills to type a minimum of two pages in a single sitting.
Research to Build and Present Knowledge		
7. Conduct short research projects that build knowledge about a topic.	7. Conduct short research projects that build knowledge through investigation of different aspects of a topic.	7. Conduct short research projects that use several sources to build knowledge through investigation of different aspects of a topic.

(continued)

TABLE 5.2 ● *(continued)*

Grade 3 students:	Grade 4 students:	Grade 5 students:
Production and Distribution of Writing		
8. Recall information from experiences or gather information from print and digital sources; take brief notes on sources and sort evidence into provided categories.	8. Recall relevant information from experiences or gather relevant information from print and digital sources; take notes and categorize information, and provide a list of sources.	8. Recall relevant information from experiences or gather relevant information from print and digital sources; summarize or paraphrase information in notes and finished work, and provide a list of sources.
9. (Begins in grade 4)	9. Draw evidence from literary or informational texts to support analysis, reflection, and research. a. Apply *grade 4 Reading standards* to literature (e.g., "Describe in depth a character, setting, or event in a story or drama, drawing on specific details in the text [e.g., a character's thoughts, words, or actions]."). b. Apply *grade 4 Reading standards* to informational texts (e.g., "Explain how an author uses reasons and evidence to support particular points in a text").	9. Draw evidence from literary or informational texts to support analysis, reflection, and research. a. Apply *grade 5 Reading standards* to literature (e.g., "Compare and contrast two or more characters, settings, or events in a story or a drama, drawing on specific details in the text [e.g., how characters interact]"). b. Apply *grade 5 Reading standards* to informational texts (e.g., "Explain how an author uses reasons and evidence to support particular points in a text, identifying which reasons and evidence support which point[s]").
Range of Writing		
10. Write routinely over extended time frames (time for research, reflection, and revision) and shorter time frames (a single sitting or a day or two) for a range of discipline-specific tasks, purposes, and audiences.	10. Write routinely over extended time frames (time for research, reflection, and revision) and shorter time frames (a single sitting or a day or two) for a range of discipline-specific tasks, purposes, and audiences.	10. Write routinely over extended time frames (time for research, reflection, and revision) and shorter time frames (a single sitting or a day or two) for a range of discipline-specific tasks, purposes, and audiences.

Source: NGA & CCSSO, 2010.

Vermont Writing Collaborative (2013), in collaboration with Student Achievement Partners and the Council of Chief State School Officers, has published examples of annotated student writing that aligns with the Writing Standards for each grade level. Elementary teachers may want to work together to plan an aligned writing curriculum, in which students experience appropriate writing and text types in all content areas (Engel & Streich, 2006).

Text Types and Purposes

The first three Writing Standards describe in detail the three types of student writing that are expected from students in grades 3–5:

- opinion pieces
- informative/explanatory texts
- narrative texts

Each text type has a purpose and place in the curriculum. Students will write opinion pieces across the curriculum about the texts they read, addressing the topic of the text and the author's style. They will write informative or explanatory texts to demonstrate their learning and to present their research findings. Narrative writing can help students understand the structure of a narrative text and help them learn to express their thoughts and emotions through the use of descriptive language.

Writing to Persuade: Opinion Writing   A special area in grades 3–5 is opinion writing, which is the precursor to argumentative reading and writing in grades 6–12. The concept of argument in writing does not mean bantering back and forth. *Argument* is also not the same as *persuasion*. In persuasion, the writer or speaker attempts to sway the beliefs of the reader or listener through emotions, instead of facts. Advertising often uses emotional techniques of persuasion, such as "Just do it!" (bandwagon technique) and "Choosy mothers choose Jif" (snob appeal).

A formal argument has a logical structure, in which a writer states an opinion and then uses reasons and evidence based on facts to support that opinion. A strong argument can usually be made for or against an issue by using facts. Just like a lawyer, a person who can make a good argument can argue either side of an issue, because he or she can produce convincing reasons and evidence for either side. In some respects, it doesn't even matter what the individual personally believes. Writing a strong argument supported by facts is still often called *persuasive writing*.

Beginning in grade 6, students learn to read and write arguments. In grades K–5, Writing Standard 1 lays the foundation for argumentative writing with the expectation that students write opinions about different topics, texts, and issues across the curriculum and support those opinions with reasons and evidence. When students read a complex text closely, we will sometimes ask them to write an opinion about the author, the author's style, the topic of the text, or the text itself. In other cases, students will write opinions about issues and ideas they have researched.

References to opinions, reasons, and evidence occur across the ELA Standards. For example, Reading Standard 8 for Informational Text for grades 4–5 emphasizes analysis of the text to explain how authors use reasons and evidence to support particular points. At grades 4–5, Speaking and Listening Standard 3 expects students to identify or summarize the reasons and evidence a speaker provides to support his or her point or claim. At grades 4–5, Writing Standard 9 expects students to explain in writing how an author uses reasons and evidence to support a particular point. The ability to write a supported opinion (argument) is a major emphasis in the CCSS.

Teachers should, note, however, that for grade 3, Reading Standard 8 for Informational Text does not emphasize author opinion, focusing instead on understanding text structure. For kindergarten, first grade, and second grade, Reading Standard 8 is about author opinion, as are fourth and fifth grades. Third-graders are expected to continue to read and write opinions but should also learn text structures that are important for comprehension, such as cause–effect and compare–contrast.

Strategies for Teaching Opinion Writing   Students in grades 3–5 need a variety of opportunities to read and write opinions. They also need explicit instruction. In order to write a credible opinion, students need to know the following:

- the difference between fact and opinion
- how to support an opinion with reasons and evidence
- how to write an opinion paragraph or essay

Fact versus Opinion   To teach students to write opinions supported by facts, we must first teach them the difference between a fact and an opinion. A *fact* is something that has actually happened or a statement that can be proven. A fact can be supported by evidence. An *opinion* is a belief and is subjective. An opinion is usually based on emotion, perspective, or someone's understanding of a topic. However, opinions can be supported by facts to make them more credible.

One way we can help students practice distinguishing between fact and opinion is to engage them in a whole-group activity. We can place two charts on opposite sides of the classroom: one with the heading "Facts" written at the top and one with the heading "Opinions" written at the top. After explaining the difference between a fact and an opinion, we hand out index cards, strips of paper, or sticky notes with statements of facts written on some and opinions written on others. Each student discusses his or her statement with another student, and together, they decide if the statement is a fact or an opinion. Both students should be able to justify the decisions for both statements. Students then switch statements, find new partners, and repeat the process. At a signal from us, the students holding fact statements line up on the "Facts" chart side of the room, and the students holding opinion statements line up on the other side. Each student explains why his or her statement is a fact or an opinion, justifies his or her answer, and attaches his or her statement to the appropriate chart. These charts can then serve as anchor charts, which students can refer back to as they continue to work on understanding facts and opinions.

Reasons and Evidence   When students write opinions, they must be able to state those ideas and support them with supportive reasons and evidence (facts). However, students often have difficulty understanding the difference among opinions, reasons, and evidence.

A good way to teach students this concept is through interpreting pictures (Hillocks, 2011). We can show students a photograph or piece of artwork that tells a story. We then ask students to tell what they think is happening in the picture, which is an opinion. Next, we ask them why they have that opinion, which provides the reasons for the opinion. And then we ask them to describe the details in the picture that made them think the way they do, which is the evidence.

An excellent strategy guide for K–5 persuasive writing is available at the website ReadWriteThink.org (www.readwritethink.org). The Persuasive Writing Strategy Guide (IRA, 2012b) is a collection of teaching ideas, websites, and interactive tools for teaching persuasive writing. For instance, a PowerPoint presentation about persuasive arguments can be used to introduce the concept of reasons versus evidence to students. The Persuasive Strategies PowerPoint includes information about stating a claim and then using the persuasive strategies of Big Names (opinions of important people or experts), Logos (data and statistics), Pathos (emotion), Ethos (trust), Kairos (importance of issue), and Research (results of studies). An interactive tool called the "Persuasion Map" helps students see the structure of an argument in a visual way. Students can use the map to plan and write their own opinions supported by reasons and facts to support the reasons.

Paragraph Frames and Organizers   Authors use certain types of organization when they write opinions. We can help our students understand these structures for opinion writing by introducing paragraph frames (Fowler, 1982; Nichols, 1980). Paragraph frames are scaffolds for writing that can be used with students who need this kind of support. By using paragraph frames that are structured for writing opinion paragraphs, we can help students learn how to write an opinion with a particular point of view and support it with reasons and other information. However, we should use paragraph frames only for a brief amount of time when students are first learning the structure (or longer with students who have special learning needs). When students have had adequate experience writing opinions through the use of paragraph frames, we should release the responsibility to them to write opinions on their own without such support. Figure 5.3 shows one example of a paragraph frame for writing an opinion after reading a text.

Another way we can scaffold student opinion writing is with an Oreo! OREO stands for Opinion, Reasons, Evidence, and Opinion. The Tennessee Curriculum Center (n.d.) has posted directions online for a primary OREO writing lesson that can be easily adapted for students in grade 3, 4, or 5. Both a video and a graphic organizer for an OREO lesson are available online (see the URL in the References.) In this lesson, the teacher creates a chart and corresponding graphic organizer that looks like the side view of an Oreo cookie. On the top cookie, the student writes his or her opinion. In the filling of the cookie, the student lists reasons and evidence for his or her opinion. On the bottom part of the cookie, the student restates the opinion.

Older students can use the OREO organizer as a guide for planning opinion paragraphs and essays. To write a paragraph, the student writes a lead sentence that introduces the opinion, reasons that support the opinion, at least one sentence for each reason that includes facts to

---

FIGURE 5.3 ● Example of a Paragraph Frame for Writing an Opinion Piece

After reading _____, my opinion is _____. First, I agree/disagree that_____ because _____ and _____. For example, _____. In addition, I think _____ because _____. Another reason I believe _____ is because _____. Therefore, _____.

FIGURE 5.4 ● Linking Words and Phrases for Use in Writing Opinion Pieces

Linking Words, Phrases, and Clauses Used in Writing Standard 1			
Grade 2	**Grade 3**	**Grade 4**	**Grade 5**
Because And Also	Because Therefore Since For example	For instance In order to In addition	Consequently Specifically

support the reason, and a closing sentence that restates the opinion. To write an essay, the student writes a paragraph that introduces the opinion, a separate paragraph for each reason and more detailed supporting evidence, and a closing paragraph that restates the opinion.

Linking Words, Phrases, and Clauses   In Writing Standard 1 for grades 3–5, students are expected to use linking words and phrases when they write opinions, such as *because, therefore, since,* and *for example.* When students learn to use linking words and phrases in their own writing, they may better comprehend texts that use similar language. Figure 5.4 identifies the linking words and phrases used as examples in Writing Standard 1 in the elementary grades.

In the Common Core Classroom

Reading and Writing Opinions—OREO Style!

Cassie is a resource teacher in a large city school. She has been working with fourth-graders on writing opinions, but some of them are having problems. Cassie discovered the OREO (Opinion, Reasons, Evidence, Opinion) organizer and decided to use it to teach a small group of students. She adapted the OREO organizer for fourth grade by increasing the number of reasons and pieces of evidence required. She also searched for a text that would motivate her students.

For this lesson, Cassie selected the article "All Split Up? Are All-Girls and All-Boys Classes a Good Idea?" (Weekly Reader Corporation, 2007), which she found on the ReadWorks website (www.readworks.org). This text fit the criteria for text complexity for Cassie's students, and she felt it was a good model of supporting an opinion. She decided to teach the lesson over three 30-minute sessions to scaffold her students' learning about writing opinions.

In the first session, Cassie modeled using a chart-sized OREO organizer. Her students loved the OREO organizer, because it made them think of cookies. Cassie asked the students to suggest an idea for "Ways to save the earth," and together they brainstormed examples they could use to support this idea. The students engaged in an enthusiastic and lively discussion about their opinions. Then Cassie passed out the article she had selected for this lesson. After she provided a very brief introduction, students read the article silently. When they were ready, Cassie facilitated a discussion about real-world examples of all-girls and all-boys schools in their local school district. Students shared their background knowledge and used examples from the text to begin forming their opinions about the topic. Cassie distributed copies of the OREO organizer, and demonstrated how to use it. Students began to complete the organizer, explaining their opinions about the topic.

In the second session, Cassie taught students how to include linking words and phrases when they write opinion pieces. She created sentence strips with examples of linking words and phrases appropriate for fourth-grade students. While she explained, she placed the sentence strips next to the chart-sized OREO organizer to demonstrate where linking words could be inserted into the writing. Cassie explained to the students that constantly using the word *because* to support an opinion makes reading the text boring and less enjoyable for the reader. Students practiced saying other linking words and phrases they could use instead.

For the third session, Cassie created an anchor chart of an opinion paragraph frame to provide a model for students to use as they transferred the information from their OREO organizers into written opinion paragraphs. She highlighted the linking words to ensure that students were aware of the importance of using different linking words and phrases.

A completed OREO graphic organizer, with linking words and phrases added as sticky notes

When Cassie felt students possessed the knowledge and skills they needed, she invited them to write opinion paragraphs about all-girl and all-boy settings. She invited students to use their OREO organizers, their knowledge of linking words and phrases, and the paragraph frame to support their opinions with reasons and evidence.

As students wrote, Cassie observed and conferenced with them, assessing the ways in which they developed and supported their opinions and demonstrated their development of the skills identified in Writing Standard 1. Cassie observed that once the students began writing, all of the students in the group formulated their own opinions, reasons, and evidence and worked independently. She felt that the lesson was successful based on students' ability to write independently and support their opinions without any additional explanation. When analyzing students' work, Cassie noted that each student took a personal stance on the issue of all-girls or all-boys schools and supported his or her opinion. Some students used background knowledge and details from the text to support their opinions, and some used only examples from the text. Figure 5.5 shows one student's opinion paragraph.

Cassie created a rubric to score her students' work and assess their progress toward meeting Writing Standard 1 for fourth grade (W.4.1). Although she expected students to use correct

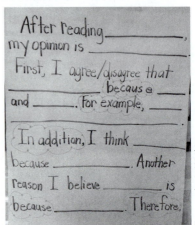

A paragraph frame provided as an anchor chart for students' use

FIGURE 5.5 ● Jeffrey's Opinion Paragraph

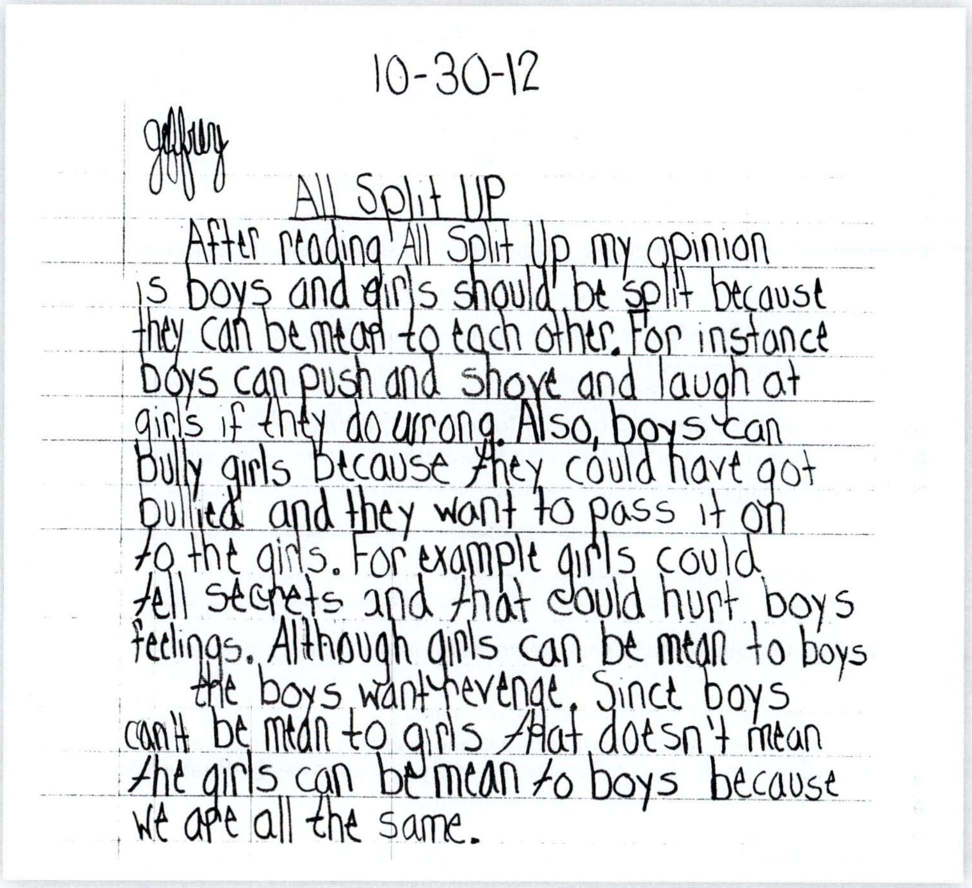

10-30-12

Jeffrey

All Split UP
After reading All Split Up my opinion
is boys and girls should be split because
they can be mean to each other. For instance
boys can push and shove and laugh at
girls if they do wrong. Also, boys can
bully girls because they could have got
bullied and they want to pass it on
to the girls. For example girls could
tell secrets and that could hurt boys
feelings. Although girls can be mean to boys
the boys want revenge. Since boys
can't be mean to girls that doesn't mean
the girls can be mean to boys because
we are all the same.

spelling and conventions in their writing, her assessment was centered on students' ability to write an opinion paragraph. Here is Cassie's rubric:

4	Student was able to state an opinion in response to the question stated in the text, provide two reasons and evidence to support the opinion, use at least two linking words or phrases in the opinion paragraph, and restate the opinion in the concluding statement.
3	Student was able to state an opinion in response to the question stated in the text, provide at least one reason to support the opinion, use at least one linking word or phrase in the opinion paragraph, and restate the opinion in the concluding statement.
2	Student was able to state an opinion, but it was either not in response to the text or unclear. Student's reasons were unclear or student did not provide reasons to support the opinion. No linking words were used or they were used incorrectly and/or there was no concluding restatement of the opinion.

(continued)

● Cassie's rubric (*continued*)

1	Student was able to state an opinion, but no reasons were given, no linking words were provided, and no concluding statement was provided.

Cassie believes that although students can find opinion writing difficult, they can succeed if they are provided with sufficient modeling, organizers, and an interesting grade-level text. She feels that the OREO organizer was a pivotal piece in her instruction, because it was visual and provided a perfect model for the opinion-writing process. She plans to use this lesson with other intermediate students to teach them to write opinions. She also plans to release the responsibility to students as they learn to write their own opinions and then support them independently.

Figure 5.6 identifies additional online resources for helping students learn to read and write opinions and arguments.

Writing to Explain: Informative/Explanatory Writing   When Josiah reads about the role Paul Revere played in the American Revolution, he writes about what he has learned. When Ana and Christina conduct an experiment that demonstrates the water cycle, they write

---

FIGURE 5.6 ● Online Resources for Reading and Writing Opinion Pieces

Lesson Plan, Can You Convince Me? Developing Persuasive Writing (grades 3–5)— ReadWriteThink
www.readwritethink.org/classroom-resources/lesson-plans/

Lesson Plan, Dear Librarian: Writing a Persuasive Letter (grades 3–5)—ReadWriteThink
www.readwritethink.org/classroom-resources/lesson-plans/

Lesson Plan, Voting! What's It All About? (grades 3–5)—ReadWriteThink
www.readwritethink.org/classroom-resources/lesson-plans/

Strategy Guide, Persuasive Writing (grades 3–5)—ReadWriteThink
www.readwritethink.org/professional-development/strategy-guides

Writing Workshop, Persuasive Writing (grades 3–5)—Scholastic
www.scholastic.com

Educator Resources and Lesson Plans/Student Activities, Argumentative Writing—Utah Education Network
www.uen.org/core/languagearts/writing/argumentative.shtml

Educator Resources and Lesson Plans/Student Activities, Persuasive/Opinion Writing— Utah Education Network
www.uen.org/core/languagearts/writing/persuasive.shtml

Lesson Plans and Teaching Resources, Argument—Web English Teacher
http://www.webenglishteacher.com/argument.html

to explain their experiment and the results. The ability to write to inform or to explain is another important CCSS expectation for students in grades 3–5. Students write informative and explanatory texts both to learn and to demonstrate their learning.

Writing Standard 2, which focuses on informative and explanatory writing, is connected to Reading Standard 2 for Informational Text, which focuses on main idea, key supporting details, and summarizing. Students will need to read and discuss a lot of informational text as we demonstrate how authors write about information. Writing Standard 2 states expectations for students to write to inform or to explain.

Strategies for Teaching Informative/Explanatory Writing   To meet Writing Standard 2, students need to learn how to write these types of texts:

- informative/explanatory paragraphs
- summaries
- multiparagraph essays and reports

Writing Informative/Explanatory Paragraphs   Paragraph structure is often tricky for elementary students. Research has shown that elementary students often think that a paragraph is a graphic that begins with an indentation (Garner et al., 1986). Many students need explicit instruction even to understand what a paragraph is. We can invite students to reconstruct paragraphs that have been cut into separate sentences as a way for them to experiment with paragraph structure. After students have arranged their cut-up sentences into a topic sentence, sentences that support the topic, and a restated topic sentence, they write the completed paragraph. Doing this helps students better understand the function of a paragraph.

When students write to inform or explain, they need to be able to discuss an idea and add details that will help the reader visualize the information or the steps of a process. In some writing, students synthesize information and come up with an idea that they explain. Our students need regular opportunities to write about information and explain processes. One way we can do this is by asking students to explain or dramatize a familiar process (e.g., brushing teeth or hitting a ball with a bat) and identifying the steps they use.

Another way is to employ a bit of acting ourselves! Invite students to describe in writing how to make a peanut butter and jelly sandwich (or another type of sandwich, if anyone has a peanut allergy). As each student reads his or her directions aloud, we can follow the directions literally. For example, if a student says "Put peanut butter on the bread," use a finger to put a dab of peanut butter on the top side of the bread. Students are usually eager to provide details to make it right. After the sandwich-making session, invite each student to write a paragraph about how to make a sandwich of his or her choice. This activity is a lot of fun and can help students remember to add pertinent details.

The Hamburger Paragraph is an instructional method that many teachers like to use to teach informative/explanatory paragraph writing. Much like the OREO organizer, this method provides students with a visual model of how a paragraph fits together. In this model, we relate the paragraph to the layers of a hamburger. The top bun introduces the topic. The layers of the hamburger (e.g., lettuce, tomato, cheese) are the key details. The meat is the most important idea. The bottom bun is the closing sentence. The bun holds the hamburger together, just as the introduction and the closing hold the paragraph together. By conducting a quick Internet search, you will find a variety of graphic organizers, charts, and video demonstrations of the Hamburger Paragraph method that you can use with students.

In the Common Core Classroom

Getting to the Root of Writing Informative Paragraphs

Kelly teaches third grade in a suburban elementary school. Since implementation of the CCSS in her state, Kelly has placed more emphasis on teaching her students to read and write informational texts. For this lesson, she decided to teach students to use informational texts to find information. She also decided to teach her students to write informative paragraphs that meet the expectations outlined in Writing Standard 3. Kelly feels it is important to integrate literacy skills into content area instruction, and so she designed this lesson to connect with a science unit on plants. She selected an online text entitled *The World of Plants* (Macceca, 2008) to use as the base of the lesson.

Kelly planned for this lesson to be a whole-group mini-lesson to be taught over two days. Her plans included using the gradual release of responsibility model, in which she would first model informational reading and writing for the students while they watch. Next, she would invite students to help her, and then, she would ask students work with partners. After students worked through their thinking with partners, she would invite them to work independently. By planning to gradually release responsibility to students, she would ensure they had opportunities to practice success.

Kelly began the lesson by discussing how readers determine what is important in a nonfiction text. The class had previously studied text features and how they help readers to recognize what is important in the text. For this lesson, Kelly reviewed subheadings and explained how they help readers to determine key ideas in the text. Then Kelly asked her students to follow along on their iPads while she read aloud a passage from the book about plants entitled "Stems and Stalks" (Macceca, 2008). She stopped periodically to think aloud about the text. As she read, she modeled taking notes about key ideas on a flipchart.

Before the next lesson, Kelly met with students who needed extra support. In small-group instruction, she made sure that each student had grasped the concept of using subheadings to determine key ideas and taking notes about these ideas.

On the second day, Kelly explained the concept of a main idea in an informational text and modeled how readers determine the main idea by doing a think-aloud. Students then located supporting details in the text, working with partners. Kelly explained that they were going to use their notes to write their own paragraphs about plants. The class discussed how writers compose paragraphs. Kelly explained that an author includes a main idea, supporting details, and a conclusion. She demonstrated this structure using paragraphs in the text.

Next, Kelly introduced the Hamburger Paragraph graphic organizer on a flipchart to

A Hamburger Paragraph graphic organizer prepared as a flipchart

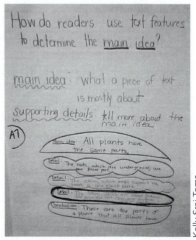

Kelly Sraj Toms

transition into paragraph writing. She modeled how she took the main idea from her notes on the flipchart and turned it into a main idea sentence. She wrote her main idea sentence in the "top bun" on the graphic organizer. The students looked for supporting details in Kelly's notes on the flipchart, and Kelly recorded these ideas in the graphic organizer in the "lettuce," "tomatoes," and "meat" sections. After discussing how the conclusion sentence is similar to the main idea sentence, Kelly and her students studied the graphic organizer to see how it could be used to organize a paragraph. Together, the students (with some help from Kelly) decided that the "bun," or main idea, needs to hold all of the information together. The details (e.g., lettuce, tomato, and meat) all tell more about the main idea.

Finally, students practiced writing paragraphs on their own. Kelly invited them to read a passage from *The World of Plants* about roots (Macceca, 2008). Students took their own notes while reading and determined the main idea of the passage based on the subheading.

FIGURE 5.7 ● A Student's Paragraph about a Text Passage on "Roots"

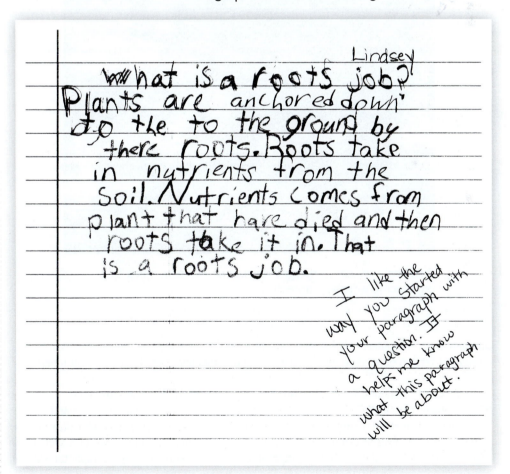

Then they completed their graphic organizers. Finally, they used their graphic organizers to write paragraphs to inform others about the topic. Figure 5.7 shows a third-grade writer's attempt at writing an informational paragraph.

As Kelly informally assessed her students through observation and conferencing, she noticed that most students demonstrated understanding of the important ideas in a text. Because the purpose for reading was set for students, they were able to find supporting details in the text they read. The transfer needed to use the information in the graphic organizer to write a clearly written paragraph—including a main idea and supporting details—was more of a struggle. Students demonstrated some frustration and had many questions about this process.

From teaching this lesson, Kelly learned that she had to model numerous times for her third-graders. To expand her students' learning about paragraph writing, Kelly planned to revisit this lesson throughout the year.

A student uses her completed Hamburger Paragraph graphic organizer to write a paragraph.

Kelly Sraj Toms

Summarizing   A *summary* is a particular type of informative text: one that provides a condensed version of another text. The CCSS expect students to be able to write summaries of texts.

The GIST method is an effective approach for students to use in summarizing (Cunningham, 1982). GIST stands for Generating Interactions between Schemata and Text. To begin, the student reads the first paragraph of a text and writes a sentence of 15 words or less to summarize the paragraph. After reading the second paragraph, the student writes a sentence of 15 words or less to summarize both paragraphs. After reading the third paragraph, the student again writes a sentence of 15 words or less to summarize all three paragraphs.

An engaging way to use the GIST method with intermediate students is to give them $1.50 in play money to spend on writing the summary and then make them pay 10 cents for every word they use. Depending on the length of the passage and the capabilities of the students, the amounts may need to change.

We can also use many other summarizing strategies with elementary students:

- **Interview summary:** Students ask the 5 Ws + H questions (*who, what, when, where, why, how*) about the text and then use the answers to the questions as a guide for writing a summary.

- **Somebody Wanted But So:** The SWBS method (Macon, Bewell, & Vogt, 1991) can be used to summarize a literary or social studies text. In every story and in most historical events, somebody wants something but something unexpected happens, so there is a consequence. In this method, students use a SWBS graphic organizer to think about the characters in the story or the individuals who were part of an event, and then use the organizer as a guide to writing a summary. Figure 5.8 shows a completed SWBS organizer for a social studies text about Christopher Columbus.

- **Very Important Points:** In the VIP approach (Hoyt, 2002), each student has one sticky note that he or she has cut into three to six equal-sized strips. When the student finds a main idea, he or she flags it with a sticky note strip. As students find more important pieces of information, they can change their minds and move the strips. Having a limited number of strips gives the students limited choices, so they can't choose the entire text. After students have selected their VIPs, they use these points to write a summary of the text.

- **Sticky note summarizing:** Each student has a few sticky notes and an informational text that contains headings and subheadings. The student turns each heading and subheading into a question. For each question, the student writes one sentence that answers the question on a sticky note and places it on the text under the subheading. When the student has finished with the article, he or she removes the sticky notes, closes the text, and arranges the sticky notes to summarize the text. The student then uses the sticky notes as a guide to write an organized summary.

- **Digital magazine covers:** A creative way to have students practice summarizing is to have them use technology to create magazine covers. Each magazine cover should contain the most important information found in the text (Assaf & Garza, 2007). After learning how to summarize, students use key words and phrases to develop their magazine covers. Making decisions about illustration, color, and layout helps students process their reading and summarization skills through visual imagery.

Writing a Multiparagraph Essay or Report   Sometimes, we will expect upper-elementary students to write ideas or information in a multiparagraph essay. We can help students understand

---

FIGURE 5.8 ● Somebody Wanted But So (SWBS) Graphic Organizer

Somebody	Wanted	But	So
Columbus	To find a route to India	He landed on San Salvador	He discovered America

the structure of an essay by using the Painted Essay method from the Vermont Writing Collaborative (n.d.). The Painted Essay uses color to teach elementary students how to relate main ideas and details to the overall essay structure and to plan an essay with a logical structure. Instructions and a downloadable template can be found online (see URL in References).

Other times, we may ask students to present results from their research by writing a report. Reports written by upper-elementary students usually include these elements:

1. a title page
2. a table of contents, with page numbers (depending on length)
3. a section or paragraph that introduces of the topic or problem
4. a body, made up of several sections or paragraphs with headings (Other text features may be embedded, such as illustrations, maps, charts, and graphs.)
5. a section that provides a conclusion
6. a references list or bibliography
7. appendices

When students create reports electronically, they can easily add appropriate visuals. Creative reports can be shared in a final form using PowerPoint, digital storytelling, or other technology.

Linking Words and Phrases in Informative/Explanatory Writing   In Writing Standard 2 for grades 3–5, indicator c provides examples of linking words and phrases students are expected to use in their informative/explanatory writing (NGA & CCSSO, 2010a, p. 20). Figure 5.9 includes these words and phrases.

Writing to Convey Experience: Narrative Writing   A third type of text students are expected to write is the narrative. In Writing Standard 3, students are expected to write real and imagined narratives. When student write real narratives, they write about experiences and events. Examples of real narratives are journal entries, personal narratives or memoirs, and expressive feature articles. When students write imagined narratives, they write stories, poems, plays, and paragraphs that are based on imagination.

Writing narratives can help students learn more about how authors write, which can in turn help them comprehend personal narratives and stories, poems, and plays. Narrative writing uses dialogue and description to help readers visualize an experience.

FIGURE 5.9 ● Linking Words and Phrases for Use in Informative/ Explanatory Writing

Grade 3	Grade 4	Grade 5
also	another	in contrast
another	for example	especially
and	also	
more	because	
but		

In teaching this type of writing, we ask students to convey experiences or write imaginatively using words and phrases that create sensory images: how something looked, sounded, smelled, and felt. When students write narratives, we want them to include figurative language, such as similes and metaphors, and to use nuances of language to describe a setting or event.

Creative written responses to reading, which are important for reading development, are often written in the narrative style outlined in Writing Standard 3. Opinion pieces on topics or texts follow the format outlined in Writing Standard 1.

Classrooms That Support Writing Achievement

STUDENTS WILL NEED TO WRITE IN RESPONSE TO reading, to write longer more polished pieces, and to be able to conduct research and write about what they find. For students to develop this type of writing ability, we need to plan frequent writing opportunities throughout the school day. To meet Writing Standards 4 through 9, we need to teach our students how to do the following:

- use a writing process
- conduct brief research projects
- write in response to reading

Standards-Based Writing

The introduction to the CCSS includes this statement: "The Standards do not mandate such things as a particular writing process" (NGA & CCSSO, 2010a, p. 4). Although the CCSS do not describe a specific writing process to help students develop their writing ability, they have the clear expectation that students will use some type of writing process to produce writing for publication. Writing Standards 4 through 6 all state the expectation that students will engage in a writing process to produce writing for an audience.

Language Standards 1 through 3 are intricately interwoven with the process of producing clear writing. Each Language standard includes a list of indicators particular to the grade level—for example, "Use abstract nouns" in third grade; "Use a comma before a coordinating conjunction in a compound sentence" in fourth grade; and "Use underlining, quotation marks, or italics to indicate titles of works" in fifth grade (NGA & CCSSO, 2010a, p. 28). By the end of the year, students are expected to know and use the skills identified by these indicators for their grade levels. (A few indicators are marked with asterisks, indicating that continued study is needed in higher grades, as texts become more sophisticated). Students will need explicit instruction in many of the indicators under each Language standard to be able to apply these skills as they write.

Writing Standard 6 focuses on students being able to use technology to produce and publish writing. In grade 3, the expectation is that students will still need guidance and support from adults. By grades 4 and 5, students are expected to work more independently to produce and publish writing using technology. Standard 6 also mentions using technology to interact and collaborate with others. A particular expectation for grades 4 and 5 in Writing Standard 6 is for students to have sufficient keyboarding skills to type a minimum of one page (fourth grade) or two pages (fifth grade) in a single sitting.

Using a Standards-Based Writing Process   When writers write, they engage in a process. The steps of this process are recursive; that is, they do not happen in a straight line. Instead, writers move back and forth among steps as they draft and polish a writing piece for publication. They write and revise many times until the writing seems clear and appropriate for a particular purpose and audience. Students need time and opportunity to engage in writing for authentic audiences and purposes and to learn to follow a writing process.

As noted earlier, the CCSS do not specify a particular writing process. However, the Writing Standards for grades 3–5 use terms such as *planning, revising, editing,* and *publishing* in describing the steps students should follow.

Planning   Writers plan their writing. They think about the different parts of their written pieces and make decisions before they begin to write. For instance, they consider the purpose for their writing and think about what their audience needs to know. They decide on the genre and structure of the piece. They make decisions about their reasons for writing before and as they begin to write.

Drafting   Writers create drafts, which are never their final pieces. Some writers write a draft and then go back and revise it. Some writers revise along the way but still make critical decisions about how to make their writing clearer to their readers. Sometimes, writers start over and try a new approach.

Most writers use technology to create their pieces, which makes it easy to experiment with writing. We should make every effort for students to draft pieces using technology, not just type their pieces on a word processor after they have finished writing. There is a clear expectation in the CCSS for students to be efficient in the use of technology and to develop keyboarding skills in writing. Technology will become increasingly important in CCSS assessments, as students demonstrate what they know.

Revising   Writers revise their pieces so that readers can read them more easily and understand what they are trying to say. This is the stage in which writers craft their writing.

We can teach students to "use their ARMS" to revise:

- Add details to make the writing more complete.
- Remove information that doesn't fit.
- Move words, sentences, and passages to other locations in the piece.
- Substitute dull, boring words for interesting, snappy words.

Choosing words, phrases, and punctuation for effect in writing is part of revision.

We should provide numerous opportunities for students to collaborate with others as they write and revise their work. Getting feedback from others helps writers understand what revisions might be needed to make their writing clearer and more interesting to the audience.

Editing Writers edit their writing so that readers are not distracted by typing mistakes, poor grammar, spelling, and awkward sentence structure. We can teach students to "call the COPS" to edit: Capitalization, Organization, Punctuation, and Spelling.

The first three Language Standards focus on the conventions of standard English—grammar, usage, capitalization, punctuation, and spelling—and clearly delineate the expected

FIGURE 5.10 ● Grades 3–5 Language Standards That Support Writing[*]

Language Standard 1: Demonstrate command of the conventions of standard English grammar and usage when writing or speaking.

Language Standard 2: Demonstrate command of the conventions of standard English capitalization, punctuation, and spelling when writing.

Language Standard 3: Use knowledge of language and its conventions when writing, speaking, reading, or listening.

[*]Also see particular grade-level indicators for each standard (NGA & CCSSO, 2010a, pp. 28–29).

level of proficiency for each grade level. Figure 5.10 presents the grades 3–5 Language Standards that support the writing process.

Publishing   When a student publishes a piece of writing, he or she has polished the writing so that it is ready for outside readers. A final piece is written so that it has a purpose and audience, and it possesses the characteristics of the form (i.e., a poem looks like a poem, etc.). The ideas are well developed, and the writing portrays voice. The piece is organized, contains transitional words and phrases, and has a clear ending. The sentences are varied in length and structure, are constructed effectively, and are complete and correct. The language contains correct grammar and usage, and the writer has used strong verbs and nouns, concrete or other sensory details, and language appropriate to the content, purpose, and audience (Education Northwest, 2013).

Sometimes, we publish students' writing on a bulletin board in a hallway or in a class book. Often, we post polished student writing on a secure website or some other electronic format for others to enjoy. In fact, students' writing can be published in many ways. Consider using one of these technology tools to help your students extend and publish their writing. Directions for posting writing are found on each website:

- **Animation-ish:** This software, which is the brainchild of children's author Peter Reynolds, allows students to animate drawings and thereby help illustrate a story or informational writing (free demo; www.fablevisionlearning.com)
- **Animoto:** Students can create custom presentations using images, music clips, music, and text (free). (http://animoto.com/pro/education)
- **GoAnimate for Schools:** This tool allows students to make animated videos of stories or presentations (free trial). (http://goanimate4schools.com/public_index)
- **Photo Story:** Students can use this Microsoft program to make a digital story of a piece of writing, including a voice recording and background music (free). (www.microsoft.com/en-us/download/details.aspx?id=11132)
- **Storybird:** Students can collaborate in a social network to create stories ("storybirds") with selected artwork (free). (http://storybird.com/)

Conducting Research

In the CCSS for grades 3–5, students are expected to conduct brief research projects. These projects are not the 20-page research papers typical of college courses. Instead, students are expected to gather information from credible sources to find answers to authentic questions or to build knowledge about a topic. Students will take notes from text sources (both print and digital) and write opinions, information, or explanations based on their research. They may write a brief research report, but the use of technology will broaden their modes of thinking and help them make their writing more interesting and engaging.

Standards for Conducting Research in Grades 3–5   Writing Standards 7 and 8 focus on conducting research and are especially connected to the Reading Standards for Informational Text. Students in grades 3–5 are expected to be able to recall information from experiences and gather information from print and digital sources, take notes, categorize information, and provide a list of sources. Fifth-graders are expected to summarize or paraphrase information in their notes and finished work.

Strategies for Conducting Research   Students at this age love to learn about the world! We need to offer them frequent opportunities to explore topics of interest and build knowledge in the content areas, and they are usually very motivated to do so. Whether we assign the topic for a brief research project in a content area or allow students to choose their own topics, we can have them generate questions about the topic and conduct research to find answers. In doing so, we are helping students meet the CCSS Reading and Writing Standards. Planning instruction around a theme is a natural way to embed opportunities for research.

Text Sets   Students need opportunities to connect information and build networks of knowl-edge. To encourage students to explore topics, we need to make a variety of texts available to them, including digital sources. For example, when we are working on an integrated thematic unit of study focused on a particular topic in a content area, we should gather text sets that represent a variety of writing styles and different kinds of information about the same topic. Students can conduct research to find answers or solve problems, write to remember what they found, and then write about their topics based on what they learned from various sources. Figure 5.11 features a text set that is focused on ecology and the environment.

QuIP   One way that we can help student organize research is through the QuIP (Questions Into Paragraphs) strategy (McLaughlin & Allen, 2009). In QuIP, students use a graphic organiz-er to write questions they would like to explore, list sources of information to find the answers to these questions, and write notes on the answers.

The QuIP Research Grid provides a framework for initiating research and structuring writing about the topic. Students generate three broad questions about their chosen topics. Then they locate and read at least two sources to find answers to their questions. Students write down the titles of the sources and take notes about the answers they find in them. Once students have completed their research, they synthesize the information by writing a paragraph.

Using QuIP with fifth-graders is an excellent way to integrate Reading Standard 7 for Informational Text ("Draw on information from multiple print or digital sources") and Reading Standard 9 for Informational Text ("Integrate information from several texts on the same topic") (NGA & CCSSO, 2010A, p. 14) with Writing Standards 7 and 8. A QuIP lesson plan and chart can be found on the website ReadWriteThink (IRA, 2010a).

FIGURE 5.11 ● Example Text Set on Ecology and the Environment

Literature

Durell, A., George, J. C., & Paterson, K. (1993). *The big book for our planet.* New York, NY: Dutton Children's Books.

History/Social Studies (Narrative Nonfiction)

Cherry, L. (1992). *A river ran wild.* San Diego, CA: A Gulliver Green Book.

Jeffers, S., & Chief Seattle. (1991). *Brother eagle, sister sky.* New York, NY: Dial Books.

Science Texts

Davis, B. (2007). *Biomes and ecosystems.* Milwaukee, WI: Gareth Stevens.

Gray, S.H. (2012). *Ecology: The study of ecosystems.* New York, NY: Scholastic.

Kelsey, E. (2010). Not *your typical book about the environment.* Toronto, ON: Owlkids Books.

Pollock, S. (2005). *Eyewitness: ecology.* New York, NY: Dorling Kindersley.

Technical Texts

Farndon, J. (2001). *Science experiments: Weather.* New York, NY: Marshall Cavendish.

McKay, K., & Bonnin, J. (2008). *True green kids: 100 things you can do to save the planet.* Washington, DC: National Geographic Society.

Walker, P., & Wood, E. (2005). *Ecosystem science fair projects using worms, leaves, crickets, and other stuff.* Berkeley Heights, NJ: Enslow.

Persuasive Texts

Knight, M. J. (2009). *Why should I care about nature?* Mankato, MN: Black Rabbit Books.

Knight, M. J. (2009). *Why should I recycle garbage?* Mankato, MN: Black Rabbit Books.

Knight, M. J. (2009). *Why should I switch off the light?* Mankato, MN: Black Rabbit Books.

Websites

Ecology Kids (www.ecology.com/ecology-kids/)

Kids Do Ecology (http://kids.nceas.ucsb.edu/)

TIME for Kids: Environment (www.timeforkids.com/minisite/environment)

In the Common Core Classroom

Researching Body Systems

Laura's fourth-graders have been learning about the body and its functions in a science unit. She wants to integrate literacy in science and address the fourth-grade Writing Standards on research. In Laura's classroom, students have access to iPads.

Students have already read information about body systems from two online sources that Laura decided were appropriate for them. Next, she has planned for them to have experiences that will develop the skills identified in Writing Standard 7, "Conduct short research projects that build knowledge through investigation of different aspects of a topic" (NGA & CCSSO, 2010a, p. 21). She has also planned to address the skills from Writing Standard 8, "Recall relevant information from experiences or gather relevant information from print and digital sources; take notes and categorize information, and provide a list of sources" (NGA & CCSSO, 2010a, p. 21). Laura has planned for her students to conduct research on three body systems. Each student will then compare and contrast resources, notes, and other texts to become an expert on one body system. The result will be an informative report to convince the reader that the writer is an expert on the topic.

To begin, Laura asked each student to select a body system on which to become an expert. Laura then guided students to create questions about their selected body systems. Students were excited by this challenge and thoroughly enjoyed creating their own questions. After students finished preparing questions, Laura asked them to reread their online sources and find answers to the questions. She provided a Get the GIST graphic organizer to guide students' thinking as they reread their online sources. The organizer directed students to follow these steps:

1. Read the article or section of text.
2. Fill in the questions below:
   - Who or what was this article about?
   - What were the main ideas in the article?
3. Write a GIST summary. In your own words tell what this article is all about.

Figure 5.12 shows Dylan's completed graphic organizer on the respiratory system.

Laura informally assessed her students' understanding of the research process and their ability to gather information from a text by observing them as they read their online sources and completed their GIST organizers. She saw that most students engaged in applying research strategies, including determining importance, organizing information collected, and citing sources. Laura observed that many students showed understanding when answering who or what the article was about but struggled to identify the main ideas.

Laura recognized this situation as an opportunity to remind the students to support their thinking with evidence from the text. Doing so prompted students to include more in their responses, but students still seemed confused as to what was sufficient. Laura also recognized that she needed to teach and model how to read different nonfiction text structures. Students were easily confused when they didn't understand how the writer organized the text. Laura noted to plan future lessons on text structure.

FIGURE 5.12 ● A Student's Completed GIST Graphic Organizer

#9

Get the GIST

Name Dylan

Title Respiratory system

Source Kids Health.org

1. Read the article or section of text.

2. Fill in the questions below

   Who or what was the article about:

   This artical was about your lungs, inhaling, exhaling, and the parts. also the respiratory system.

   What were the main ideas in the article:
   • where you lungs are   • The vocal cords
   • what parts
   • inhaling
   • exhaling

3. Write a GIST summary. In your own words tell what this article is all about.

   This article was about your lungs and how they work. For example it was about where the lungs are, what the parts are, inhaling, exhaling, and the vocal cords. At the end there was a short section to talk about what you learned. It was also about the respiratory system

To help students understand the concept of the main idea, Laura decided to teach a mini-lesson. She modeled finding the main idea, including how examining details helped clarify her thinking. She also modeled how making connections led to details that added to her understanding. Laura noted that the students demonstrated a deeper understanding after this short lesson. However, many students still needed prompting and guidance to successfully communicate their research findings in writing. Laura continued to model how rereading what you write can help you write a clearer explanation for an audience. This was something she had to model repeatedly, and the students seemed to grasp the concept only after she had demonstrated several times.

Laura then asked students to write reflection pieces about their new learning and how they might teach others about the discoveries they made in their research. Students used their organizers and draft writing to write about their research. To determine whether individual students had met the designated standards, Laura created a rubric to assess writing based on research.

Writing in Response to Reading

Writing Standard 9, which begins in fourth grade, refers to the ability to draw evidence from a text to support analysis, reflection, and research. One of the expectations of the CCSS is that students will be able to write text-based answers to text-dependent questions (see Chapter 4). In this way, the Writing Standards are closely aligned with the standards for Reading Literature and Reading Informational Text.

Drawing Evidence from Texts   In the Common Core classroom, students read complex texts closely and discuss text-dependent questions. Writing Standard 9 states that students are expected to write about texts, using evidence and clues in the text to support their analysis, reflection, and research. By the end of third grade, students should be able to refer to the text when asking and answering questions about it. In the fourth and fifth grades, students should be able to write about details and examples in the text to support their thinking about it. (For more information about teaching students about text-based evidence, see Chapters 2 and 4 of this book.)

Range of Writing

WRITING STANDARD 10, WHICH BEGINS IN GRADE 3, is the sole standard in the category Range of Writing. Beginning in grade 3, students are expected to "Write routinely over extended time frames (time for research, reflection, and revision) and shorter time frames (a single sitting or a day or two) for a range of discipline-specific tasks, purposes, and audiences" (NGA & CCSSO, 2010A, p. 21). Writing Standard 10 states the same expectations, using the same language, for students in grades 4–12.

Clearly, grade 3 is when students begin to develop routines for using writing as a learning tool throughout the school day. By the end of grade 3, students are expected to produce longer, more polished pieces of writing. They are also expected to write short, to-the-point pieces, such as responses to reading or summaries of content learning.

Writing Workshop

The Writing Workshop approach can provide the time, structure, and opportunity students need to engage in a writing process that helps them become better writers (Fletcher & Portalupi, 2001). It can also provide the time and opportunity for students to conduct research that supports their writing and learning.

A Writing Workshop usually lasts about an hour. For 5 to 10 minutes, the teacher conducts a mini-lesson on procedures (e.g., where to get materials, how to confer with a classmate), explains a writer's process (e.g., how to organize a piece of writing, how to use a word-processing feature), or models qualities of good writing (e.g., a skill in the CCSS, how to revise or edit). Students spend the next 35 to 45 minutes writing, researching, conferring, revising, editing, and polishing a piece for publication. Then they spend the last 10 to 20 minutes sharing their writing with classmates.

For students to complete the kinds and amounts of writing in grades 3–5 expected by the CCSS, we must create classrooms in which students are not afraid to take risks and work with peers. Scheduling a regular Writing Workshop time during the school day can help establish the type of environment in which students have time to write and are willing to produce writing.

Assessment for Writing Development

ASSESSMENT FOR STUDENTS' WRITING DEVELOPMENT SHOULD HAVE THE purpose of helping them become better writers. One way to assess student writing in the Common Core classroom is to compare them with student samples from Appendix C of the CCSS (NGA & CCSSO, 2010b). After comparing our students' opinion, informative/explanatory, and narrative writing against these samples, we can provide feedback and help decide what type of instruction individual students may need. (Be aware that these samples may change as more student work becomes available.).

Another way we can assess students' writing is to use rubrics that have been created for CCSS writing. As the CCSS initiative has unfolded, school districts have developed writing rubrics for the text types identified in the Standards. The K–5 writing rubrics created by the Jefferson County Public Schools Elementary Literacy Team (2011–2012), of Louisville, Kentucky, provide excellent examples of CCSS rubrics. (These rubrics are available online—see URL in References).

Most importantly, the classrooms should be "a culture of feedback and analysis" (Kentucky Department of Education, 2010). Writers develop when they receive helpful feedback. When students expect feedback from their teacher and classmates and learn to analyze their own writing, they develop strong writing skills. The goal is for our classrooms to become communities of learning, in which peers can give valuable feedback, as well as the teacher.

Thinking about Writing in Grades 3–5

TO MEET THE CCSS WRITING STANDARDS, OUR CLASSROOMS should be welcoming places in which students have opportunities to plan writing, time to research and write, and encouragement to collaborate with peers to revise and edit. If visitors were to peek into our Common Core classrooms, they would see us conferencing with students and providing clear feedback on their writing progress. Students would be writing to learn in every content area and writing to respond to texts of all kinds. The use of technology for planning, drafting, revising, editing, and publishing would be a normal part of students' writing activities. Most of all, visitors would notice that we are not only teachers of writers but also teachers of readers and learners.

REFERENCES

Assaf, L., & Garza, R. (2007). Making magazine covers that visually count: Learning to summarize with technology. *The Reading Teacher, 60*(7), 678–684.

Cunningham, J. W. (1982). Generating interactions between schemata and text. In J.A. Niles & L.A. Harris (Eds.), *New inquiries in reading: Research and instruction. Thirty-first yearbook of the National Reading Conference* (pp. 42–47). Newark, DE: International Reading Association.

Duke, N. K., & Pearson, P. D. (2002). Effective practices for developing reading comprehension. In A. E. Farstrup & S. J. Samuels (Eds.), *What research has to say about reading instruction* (3rd ed., pp. 205–242). Newark, DE: International Reading Association.

Education Northwest. (2013). 6+1 trait™ rubrics (aka scoring guides). *Education Northwest.* Retrieved from http://educationnorthwest.org/resource/464.

Engel, T., & Streich, R. (2006). Yes, there *is* room for soup in the curriculum: Achieving accountability in a collaboratively planned writing program. *The Reading Teacher, 59*(7), 660–679.

Essley, R. (2008). *Visual tools for differentiating reading & writing instruction: Strategies to help students make abstract ideas concrete & accessible.* New York, NY: Scholastic.

Fletcher, R., & Portalupi, J. (2001). *Writing workshop: The essential guide.* Portsmouth, NH: Heinemann.

Fowler, G. L. (1982). Developing comprehension skills in primary students through the use of story frames. *The Reading Teacher, 36,* 176–179.

Garner, R.; Alexander, P.; Slater, W.; Hare, V. C.; Smith, T.; Reis, R. (1986). Children's knowledge of structural properties of expository text. *Journal of Educational Psychology, 78*(6), 411–416.

Graham, S., & Hebert, M. (2010). *Writing to read: Evidence for how writing can improve reading. A Carnegie Corporation Time to Act Report.* Washington, DC: Alliance for Excellent Education.

Harvey, S. (1998). *Nonfiction matters: Reading, writing, and research in grades 3–8.* Portland, ME: Stenhouse.

Hillocks, G. (2011). *Teaching argument writing, grades 6–12: Supporting claims with relevant evidence and clear reasoning.* Portsmouth, NH: Heinemann.

Hoyt, L. (2002). *Make it real: Strategies for success with informational texts.* Portsmouth, NH: Heinemann.

International Reading Association (IRA). (2012a). Guided comprehension: Summarizing using the QuIP strategy. *ReadWriteThink.* Retrieved from http://www.readwritethink.org.

International Reading Association (IRA). (2012b). Persuasive writing strategy guide. *ReadWriteThink.* Retrieved from http://www.readwritethink.org.

Jefferson County Public Schools (JCPS) Elementary Literacy Team. (2011–2012). *JCPS Elementary KCAS Writing Scoring Rubrics.* Retrieved from http://www.jefferson.kyschools.us/Departments/Gheens/LiteracyCloset/Writing%20Workshop%20Instructional%20Materials.html.

Kentucky Department of Education. (2010, May). The Kentucky Writing Program: Creating a culture of feedback and analysis. Retrieved from http://education.ky.gov/curriculum/ELA/Documents/Creating a Culture of Feedback and Analysis 6-1-10.doc.

Lattimer, H. (2003). *Thinking through genre: Units of study in reading and writing workshops 4-12.* Portland, ME: Stenhouse.

Macon, J. M., Bewell, D., & Vogt, M. (1991). *Responses to literature.* Newark, DE: International Reading Association.

McLaughlin, M., & Allen, M. B. (2002). *Guided comprehension: A teaching model for grades 3–8.* Newark, DE: International Reading Association.

National Commission on Writing. (2003). *The neglected "R": The need for a writing revolution.* Retrieved from http://www.nwp.org/cs/public/print/resource/2523

National Governors Association Center for Best Practices & Council of Chief State School Officers (NGA & CCSSO). (2010a). *Common Core State Standards: English language arts and literacy in history/social studies, science, and technical subjects.* Washington, DC: Authors. Retrieved from http://www.corestandards.org/assets/CCSSI_ELA%20Standards.pdf.

National Governors Association Center for Best Practices & Council of Chief State School Officers (NGA & CCSSO). (2010b). Appendix C: Samples of student writing. In *Common Core State Standards.* Washington, DC: Authors. Retrieved from http://corestandards.org/assets/Appendix_C.pdf.

Nichols, J. N. (1980). Using paragraph frames to help remedial high school students with writing assignments. *Journal of Reading, 24,* 228–231.

Tennessee Curriculum Center. (n.d.) *OREO–Persuasive writing. Tennessee Curriculum Center: English Language Arts.* Retrieved from http://www.tncurriculumcenter.org/resource/1886/go.

Vermont Writing Collaborative. (2013). *In common: Effective writing for all students.* Retrieved from http://www.achievethecore.org/page/507/in-common-effective-writing-for-all-students.

Vermont Writing Collaborative. (n.d.). What is the "painted essay"? *Vermont Writing Collaborative.* Retrieved from http://vermontwritingcollaborative.org/Essay.html.

LITERATURE CITED

Macceca, M. L. (2008). *The world of plants. Big Universe Learning.* Retrieved from http://www.biguniverse.com/readkidsbooks/1563/the-world-of-plants.

Weekly Reader Corporation. (2007). All split up? Are all-girls and all-boys classes a good idea? Concepts of Comprehension: Drawing Conclusions 4th Grade Unit. *ReadWorks.org.* http://www.readworks.org/search/apachesolr_search.

Speaking and Listening

ONE OF THE EXCITING THINGS ABOUT THE COMMON Core State Standards (CCSS) for Speaking and Listening is that they pave the way for a collaborative and discussion-based classroom—one in which students express opinions and learn through engaging in academic conversations. In years past, standards for speaking and listening (when they have existed at all) have rarely focused so intently on meaning making and inquiry.

Leslie Montgomery

In a CCSS classroom for grades 3–5, students are involved in whole-class discussions, small-group working conversations, and communication with partners about texts and topics. Students ask and answer questions about text, and they discuss interpretations of the author's message to enhance comprehension. They listen attentively to a speaker or a text read aloud to comprehend the main idea, as well as themes and key details; to respond to media presentations; and to prepare their own media presentations for sharing the results of their research. Accountable talk (Fisher, Frey, & Rothenberg, 2008) fills the school day. As teachers, we need to help our students develop the skills of speaking and listening and to plan opportunities for them to be engaged in many different types of academic conversations.

Talking to Learn

RESEARCH ABOUT CLASSROOM CONVERSATIONS SUGGESTS THAT WHEN STUDENTS participate in discussions about academic topics and texts, they learn. Academic discussion promotes the development of oral language skills and vocabulary concepts and helps students understand texts in a deeper way (Mills, 2009). As students talk about books and concepts across the curriculum, they hear the thinking of their peers and explore their own thinking as well. Discussions that immerse students in literacy, which can be called "grand conversations" (Eeds & Well, 1989), increase students' comprehension.

According to Spiegel (2005), a true discussion is open ended, recursive, collaborative, and constructive. Classroom conversations of this nature serve the following purposes:

- allow students to make meaning through social interaction
- lead to students' richer and deeper understanding of meaning
- promote students' higher-level thinking
- increase students' engagement with and ownership of ideas
- allow all students to participate, regardless of literacy level

Situations that foster academic talk, such as creating small-group, collaborative posters about a text, can help English language learners develop school language (Fisher et al., 2008). In fact, the Center for Research on Diversity, Education, and Excellence (CREDE, n.d.) has identified developing language and literacy across the curriculum through academic conversation as a key element for helping diverse students achieve.

Instructional Conversations

One way we can foster classroom discussion in which students learn is by planning instructional conversations (Tharp & Gallimore, 1988; 1991). To plan an instructional conversation, we first carefully read the text and decide the concepts students should know by the end of a discussion. We think through how students might react to the text, identifying possible points of confusion, ideas that might be developed, and vocabulary that might be challenging. After independent reading (or the teacher reading aloud the text), we facilitate a student-led conversation based on the ideas in the text. As students discuss, our role is to insert appropriate background knowledge, questions, and comments into the student conversation to take the exchange to a higher level of thinking. Students do almost all of the talking, with the teacher providing strategic support only as needed.

In a classroom in which academic discussion is valued and encouraged, students develop oral language, express new ideas, and learn new content. The value of productive classroom talk cannot be overemphasized.

Listening to Learn

THE ABILITY TO LISTEN EFFECTIVELY IS ANOTHER CCSS expectation for students in grades 3–5. We often forget that there is a difference between *hearing* and *listening*. For example, we can *hear* a song playing in the background while we engage in other activities, but only when we slow down and actively *listen* to the words and music can we learn things, such as the beauty (or ridiculousness) of the lyrics or the line of the bass guitar. Hearing is passive. Listening is active. Listening is an art that must be developed (Hancock, 2007). Students need to learn to listen in ways that will help them learn.

Learning to listen can lead to learning across the curriculum. Our students need to develop the following five types of listening (Opitz & Zbaracki, 2004):

1. **Discriminative listening** in young students is the ability to distinguish among sounds, syllables, and rhymes. In older students, discriminative listening can focus on interpreting a speaker's message through his or her vocal tone and pitch and his or her actions, such as body posture, eye contact, head movement, and facial expression (Hancock, 2007). Discriminative listening allows students to interpret the nuances of what a speaker is saying, whether that speaker is a peer, the teacher, a more formal guest speaker, or someone in a video or TV program.

2. **Efferent listening** can be defined as "listening for details." This type of listening focuses on gaining information and comprehending the speaker's message. Students need to be active listeners to follow oral directions and to take notes to remember what a speaker is saying. Introducing graphic organizers for notetaking is often effective to guide students in listening for details.

3. **Aesthetic listening** is sometimes called *appreciative listening*. Appreciative listening takes place in a relaxed atmosphere for the purposes of enjoyment and personal fulfillment. We listen appreciatively to six different types of sounds: the way a speaker presents material; environmental sounds; oral reading of literature; radio, television, and film; live theater; and music (Cohen & Cowen, 2008). An example of appreciative listening is a literature read-aloud. When we read aloud solely for students to relish the text and the sound and rhythm of language, we are reading for enjoyment (Fisher et al., 2004).

4. **Strategic listening** can be defined as "listening for understanding." When students listen for understanding, they must synthesize and determine the "big picture." This type of listening involves the use of comprehension strategies, such as visualizing, summarizing, comparing and contrasting, and making logical inferences. An interactive read-aloud—in which students listen to a text read aloud and interact

with the text to apply comprehension strategies—is a good format to teach listening for understanding.

5. **Critical listening** means listening to analyze a speaker's message. We engage in this kind of listening when we hear a persuasive speaker present an argument. We evaluate the argument to see if the speaker actually supported his or her points with reasons and evidence. We should be critical listeners when we listen to media presentations, such as evaluating the difference between what is "news" and what is "opinion" (Cohen & Cowen, 2008 p. 333).

The Speaking and Listening Standards

THE SPEAKING AND LISTENING STANDARDS FOR GRADES 3–5 are divided into two clusters or categories:

1. Comprehension and Collaboration
2. Presentation of Knowledge and Ideas

The cluster entitled Comprehension and Collaboration includes expectations for academic discussions about texts and topics. The cluster entitled Presentation of Knowledge and Ideas states expectations for sharing information through speaking, such as retelling a story, sharing an opinion about a book, and presenting the results of research. Table 6.1 presents the Speaking and Listening Standards for third-, fourth-, and fifth-graders.

To meet the CCSS in Speaking and Listening for grades 3–5, the topics for instruction and assessment are as follows:

- engaging in collaborative discussions
- listening and responding to read-alouds and media presentations
- listening and responding to speakers
- speaking for an audience
- differentiating ways of speaking

Engaging in Collaborative Discussions

In a discussion-based classroom, students engage in regular collaborative discussions about texts and topics. Speaking and Listening Standard 1 describes expectations and criteria for students to engage in effective collaborative conversations.

Collaborative Discussion and Comprehension   Comprehension is fostered by talk. When we discuss a text, we not only learn from others but we also engage more deeply in thinking about the text. Collaborative discussions can be planned to enhance comprehension throughout the day. When we simply ask students to "turn and talk" or "think-write-pair-share" with a partner about an idea in social studies or a concept in science, we help them increase their knowledge about the idea or concept.

TABLE 6.1 ● *Standards for Speaking and Listening, Grades 3–5*

Grade 3 students:	Grade 4 students:	Grade 5 students:
Comprehension and Collaboration		
1. Engage effectively in a range of collaborative discussions (one-on-one, in groups, and teacher-led) with diverse partners on *grade 3 topics and texts,* building on others' ideas and expressing their own clearly.	1. Engage effectively in a range of collaborative discussions (one-on-one, in groups, and teacher-led) with diverse partners on *grade 4 topics and texts,* building on others' ideas and expressing their own clearly.	1. Engage effectively in a range of collaborative discussions (one-on-one, in groups, and teacher-led) with diverse partners on *grade 5 topics and texts,* building on others' ideas and expressing their own clearly.
a. Come to discussions prepared, having read or studied required material; explicitly draw on that preparation and other information known about the topic to explore ideas under discussion.	a. Come to discussions prepared, having read or studied required material; explicitly draw on that preparation and other information known about the topic to explore ideas under discussion.	a. Come to discussions prepared, having read or studied required material; explicitly draw on that preparation and other information known about the topic to explore ideas under discussion.
b. Follow agreed-upon rules for discussions (e.g., gaining the floor in respectful ways, listening to others with care, speaking one at a time about the topics and texts under discussion).	b. Follow agreed-upon rules for discussions and carry out assigned roles.	b. Follow agreed-upon rules for discussions and carry out assigned roles.
c. Ask questions to check understanding of information presented, stay on topic, and link their comments to the remarks of others.	c. Pose and respond to specific questions to clarify or follow up on information, and make comments that contribute to the discussion and link to the remarks of others.	c. Pose and respond to specific questions by making comments that contribute to the discussion and elaborate on the remarks of others.
d. Explain their own ideas and understanding in light of the discussion.	d. Review the key ideas expressed and explain their own ideas and understanding in light of the discussion.	d. Review the key ideas expressed and draw conclusions in light of information and knowledge gained from the discussions.
2. Determine the main ideas and supporting details of a text read aloud or information presented in diverse media and formats, including visually, quantitatively, and orally.	2. Paraphrase portions of a text read aloud or information presented in diverse media and formats, including visually, quantitatively, and orally.	2. Summarize a written text read aloud or information presented in diverse media and formats, including visually, quantitatively, and orally.

(continued)

TABLE 6.1 • *(continued)*

Grade 3 students:	Grade 4 students:	Grade 5 students:
Comprehension and Collaboration		
3. Ask and answer questions about information from a speaker, offering appropriate elaboration and detail.	3. Identify the reasons and evidence a speaker provides to support particular points.	3. Summarize the points a speaker makes and explain how each claim is supported by reasons and evidence.
Presentation of Knowledge and Ideas		
4. Report on a topic or text, tell a story, or recount an experience with appropriate facts and relevant, descriptive details, speaking clearly at an understandable pace.	4. Report on a topic or text, tell a story, or recount an experience in an organized manner, using appropriate facts and relevant, descriptive details to support main ideas or themes; speak clearly at an understandable pace.	4. Report on a topic or text or present an opinion, sequencing ideas logically and using appropriate facts and relevant, descriptive details to support main ideas or themes; speak clearly at an understandable pace.
5. Create engaging audio recordings of stories or poems that demonstrate fluid reading at an understandable pace; add visual displays when appropriate to emphasize or enhance certain facts or details.	5. Add audio recordings and visual displays to presentations when appropriate to enhance the development of main ideas or themes.	5. Include multimedia components (e.g., graphics, sound) and visual displays in presentations when appropriate to enhance the development of main ideas or themes.
6. Speak in complete sentences when appropriate to task and situation in order to provide requested detail or clarification. (See grade 3 Language standards 1 and 3 on pages 28–29 for specific expectations.)	6. Differentiate between contexts that call for formal English (e.g., presenting ideas) and situations where informal discourse is appropriate (e.g., small-group discussion); use formal English when appropriate to task and situation. (See grade 4 Language standards 1 on pages 28 and 29 for specific expectations.)	6. Adapt speech to a variety of contexts and tasks, using formal English when appropriate to task and situation. (See grade 5 Language standards 1 and 3 on pages 28 and 29 for specific expectations.)

Source: NGA & CCSSO (2010).

In the Common Core Classroom

Adapting the Meeting of the Minds Strategy to Promote Discussion about Text

Melissa teaches third grade at a suburban school. She has been working on ways for her students to engage in speaking and listening to improve comprehension and has decided to employ a strategy called Meeting of the Minds (McLaughlin & Allen, 2002).

In this strategy, students work together to compare and contrast two texts through discussion.

Melissa's students had already completed an English language arts unit about character traits, the central message, and other story elements. With guidance from Melissa, students had read and written several pieces of text in exploring these topics. Melissa felt the current lesson would be a great time for students to apply what they have learned while continuing to work on higher-level comprehension through discussion.

Melissa found directions for the Meeting of the Minds strategy, including a graphic organizer, on the website ReadWriteThink (www.readwritethink.org). The graphic organizer is a three-column chart in which the left-hand column is labeled "Questions," the middle column is labeled "Character Response #1," and the right-hand column is labeled "Character Response #2." In the Meeting of the Minds, students take on the perspectives of characters in two versions of the same story, brainstorm questions an interviewer would ask, and answer the questions as they think the characters would answer.

Melissa thought using this strategy would provide an excellent opportunity for her students to practice asking their own questions and getting into the minds of the characters or individuals in a text. However, after some thought about her students and their needs, she decided to adapt the activity to scaffold her students' learning and help them practice Reading Standard 9, the focus standard her team had chosen to address. Reading Literature Standard 9 for third grade is "Compare and contrast the themes, settings, and plots of stories written by the same author about the same or similar characters (e.g., in books from a series)" (NGA & CCSSO, 2010a, p. 12). Earlier in the school year, Melissa's students had difficulty with open-ended tasks, and she wanted to guarantee that their discussions now were more focused. She decided that if her students engaged in a more structured activity, she could gradually transition them to more open-ended evaluative thinking activities.

Melissa gathered sets of books by the same author for students to compare and contrast. She planned for students to work in pairs or groups of three during two consecutive Reading Workshop times. Doing this would encourage students to think deeper through conversation. Melissa arranged the graphic organizer into three parts labeled "Questions," "Responses: Book 1," and "Responses: Book 2." She also provided the questions for the first column:

- Describe the setting of each book.
- What is the theme or central message of each book?
- List the main events that make up the plot of each book.

To begin, Melissa taught a brief mini-lesson demonstrating how to use the graphic organizer and reviewing setting, theme/central message, and plot. The students wrote key words in the boxes with questions to remind them of what they were looking for. During the class discussion about how to use the organizer, one student reminded the class that the setting includes when and not just where the book took place.

Melissa explained students' task for the day, and together, she and the students came up with a list of student directions. Melissa wrote the directions on the board so students could refer to them during work time:

1. Read two books.
2. Fill out the chart about both books.
3. Write a paragraph or create a Venn diagram comparing and contrasting the books.

During Work Time, students read the books together in pairs or groups of three. They were very excited about the books they selected from the sets Melissa had put together. She had chosen many picture books that would be of interest to her third-graders, with characters such as Arthur, Curious George, and Fancy Nancy, among others. Students were familiar with some of the characters (or the series that featured them), and other characters were new to them. One student who was reading two Henry and Mudge books was very excited that he could compare them to another Henry book he had read previously. The student shared the events in the book he had already read and told his partner that the theme of the book was similar to the themes in the books they were currently reading. Another student even made a connection to what the class had been learning in science.

When reading the books, the student groups discussed how to complete their graphic organizers. Individual students completed their own charts based on discussions with their group members. During the mini-lesson, students had planned that they would read both of their books and then do the graphic organizers. However, as students were working, many of them realized it would be better to fill in the organizer for each book as they read it. Working this way kept students from confusing the books, which were very similar. While students were reading the second books and charting the characteristics, many of them spontaneously initiated conversations about the similarities and differences between the two.

While students worked, Melissa circulated through the classroom to informally assess their understanding. She engaged in conversations with student groups to help them think through the questions on the graphic organizer. After observing some misunderstanding about the nature of setting, Melissa stopped the class during Work Time to clarify, which she calls "Catch and Release." Some students thought the setting had to be a specific date or year. At this point, one student shared how this made sense to her. The student was struggling to find a date in her book but realized from looking at the pictures that the story took place in the summer. The class ended up concluding that *when* can include the date, time, year, or season.

Melissa also observed that many students simply listed each book's setting on the graphic organizer when the question asked them to *describe* the setting. Melissa discussed with several student groups that they were supposed to describe, or paint a picture with words. Melissa further observed some students using text clues to help describe the setting. For example, the story took place on Mother's Day, so they did some research on when Mother's Day is celebrated to help describe the setting.

Melissa took in what her students were learning by listening to their conversations. She was gratified to hear an in-depth discussion about theme, which occurred when one of her students told his partner that he noticed the theme was usually emphasized toward the end of a story. He showed his partner an example of this in the first book they were reading.

FIGURE 6.1 ● Student's Completed Graphic Organizer for Comparing and Contrasting Books

Name Lilee

Date 10-17-12

With a partner, read 2 books by the same author with similar characters. Fill out the chart below about the theme, setting, and plot of each book.

Questions	Responses Book 1: Amelia Bedelia rocket scientist	Amelia bedelia, Book 2: a Mayor
Describe the setting of each book. Where and when.	Science fair day time summer—attum	Out side Attum day time the town the Mayors office the rover's house
What is the theme or central message of each book? What the athur is trying to tell you.	if you believe in your self you can be what ever you want	all ways keep your promises
List the main events that make up the plot of each book.	•Went to science fair .met Dr. Dinglebot . looks at kid's science projects .adds too much baking pourder to volcano .blows Dr.dinglebot hair off .eats pie	•makes lakes .running to the office .running for Mayor •has a debate .catches a dog .stops running debate • frence toast

You and your partner have looked at the theme, setting, and plot of each book. Now think about how the books are alike or different. In your notebook write a paragraph or draw a Venn diagram to compare and contrast the books.

The student read a passage from the book and explained what he thought was the central message. He went into detail about it, basing his analysis on this passage of the book. Then, in reading the second book, the student and his partner looked for the possible theme as they neared the end. Other student groups realized a book could have multiple settings or messages. Melissa heard several great conversations that led students to focus on the most prominent setting or theme. Some groups decided to list them all but put a star next to the main one. Other students decided to list only the one that stood out the most in the book. Figure 6.1 shows one student's completed graphic organizer.

After completing their graphic organizers, individual students had a choice of writing a paragraph or creating a Venn diagram. All of the students decided to create Venn diagrams in their notebooks to compare and contrast the two books. The act of creating the Venn diagram took their thinking out of the graphic organizer and into looking at the similarities and differences of the books. Melissa encouraged students to go beyond the elements of setting, theme/central message, and plot in creating their Venn diagrams.

During Share Time, Melissa facilitated a class discussion of students' learning about setting, theme, and plot. She encouraged her students to be active participants and practice both their speaking and listening skills. Students discussed specific comparisons they had made between their two books.

One way Melissa assessed this lesson was through observation. She took anecdotal notes as she circulated and engaged in conversations with students, which allowed her to assess how students were meeting the Speaking and Listening Standards, as well as Reading Standard 9. She was also able to assess students' comprehension on the texts they read by listening to their conversations. In addition, she collected students' graphic organizers and Venn diagrams and added more notes about individual students' understanding. Doing this showed her each student's ability to determine the central message, setting, and plot. Melissa also took note that her students were more comfortable comparing books by creating a Venn diagram than by writing a paragraph. She decided that the next step would be to teach students to talk about making comparisons as a scaffold to writing comparative paragraphs.

Comprehension Strategies That Include Talking   A number of comprehension strategies involve partner or small-group discussion. For example, Say Something (Short, Harste, & Burke, 1996) is a comprehension strategy in which students read with partners. At a designated stopping point (i.e., after reading a page or paragraph), partners turn to each other and "say something" about what they just read. Partners can predict, clarify, or summarize, as well as express an opinion, ask a question, or make a comment. After each student says something, the partners read the next section and repeat the process.

In the strategy Paired Questioning (McLaughlin & Allen, 2009), student partners read to a designated stopping point and then ask each other questions about the text. At the end of the text, each partner discusses what he or she thought was the most important idea and explains his or her reasoning. Partners can agree or disagree with each other but must support their thinking.

The Discussion Web (Alvermann, 1991; McLaughlin & Allen, 2009) is a strategy to provide a structure for a conversation about a topic. The teacher selects a topic that has two opposing perspectives and presents the topic or a guiding question. Students work with partners to read a text presenting both sides of the argument. The partners use a graphic organizer to list reasons from the text to be pro or con about the issue. After the partners have completed reading and filling in the graphic organizer, they come to a conclusion about what they think as a pair and justify their thinking. Students write their conclusion and their rationale at the bottom of the graphic organizer. After completing these tasks, they are prepared for a whole-group discussion about the issue.

Any number of strategies for improving comprehension use discussion. We should be deliberate in planning for our students to engage in activities that include talking to enhance comprehension.

In the Common Core Classroom

Discussion Webs about Saving Polar Bears

Lonydea teaches third grade at an urban elementary school. She decided to engage her students in a Discussion Web to help them learn to think more deeply about texts. For this activity, Lonydea invited her students to respond to an article entitled "Polar Bears in Trouble" (Debnam, 2007), which the class had read previously in guided reading groups. She planned to introduce the Discussion Web strategy to the whole group as a scaffold for students working as partners.

To begin this lesson, Lonydea explained the Discussion Web to students. They discussed the rules for having a proper discussion and debate, based on Speaking and Listening Standard 1. Lonydea wrote a model of the Discussion Web graphic organizer on the dry-erase board and had students copy it in their notebooks. After students reread the article independently, Lonydea facilitated a class discussion about the article.

After reading the article and participating in the first part of the class discussion, the students knew how the author used facts to show that polar bears are in trouble. Specifically, their icy habitat is disappearing, putting them at risk. Lonydea told students that she wanted to challenge their thinking and asked them to think about the other side of the issue: Why would some people say that polar bears are *not* in trouble? Lonydea then continued to facilitate a whole-group discussion in which students thought of reasons for the other side. Students recorded their thinking in their reading-response journals.

Lonydea observed that at first, students found it hard to discuss the other side of the issue. The informational article contained only facts about why polar bears are in trouble. Students struggled for a while to come up with a counterargument for the issue, but they were enthusiastic and enjoyed thinking this way. After the discussion, students recorded their own responses in the boxes on the web they had copied from the board.

Londyea's informal assessment of her students showed that they were respectful during the discussion and most of them participated. As she circulated around the room while students were working and then reviewed the Discussion Webs in students' notebooks, she observed that most had copied the web template and then completed it in response to the class discussion. Figure 6.2 shows the Discussion Web completed by one of Londyea's students.

FIGURE 6.2 ● Student's Completed Discussion Web

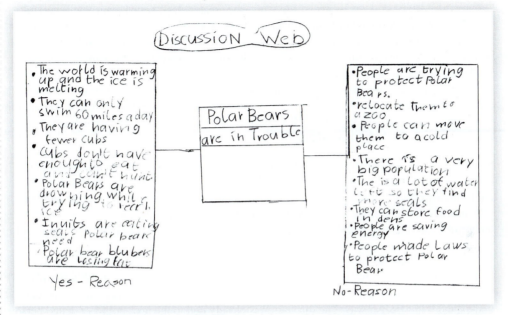

The next week, students in a guided reading group read an online article entitled "Debate! Do Kids Need Their Own Cell Phones?" (TIME for Kids, 2012). The students were intrigued and asked if they could make a Discussion Web for this article. Delighted, Lonydea encouraged them to work in pairs to create webs and then plan a discussion. The partners created their own Discussion Webs, discussed the pros and cons of the issue, and then wrote a paragraph at the bottom of the graphic organizer. The class then engaged in an informal debate about whether students should or should not have cell phones. Enthusiasm was high as students read, discussed, and debated!

Tips for the Teacher

"STUDENTS ARE NOT ASKED TO THINK OUTSIDE OF the box enough. Once we got into peer discussion, my students showed me they could do it. When I did this activity a second time with another text, I did not have to do a lot of teacher-led discussion. They were able to lead the discussion themselves and I sat back and listened. They did an awesome job!"

—Lonydea, grade 3 teacher

Comprehension Routines That Include Collaborative Discussions   A *comprehension routine* is a set of strategies that work together to enhance comprehension. The following two comprehension routines may have the potential to help students build comprehension strategies and meet a number of English Language Arts (ELA) Standards.

Reciprocal Teaching One of the most effective comprehension routines, backed by considerable research, is reciprocal teaching (Palincsar & Brown, 1984). In reciprocal teaching, students learn to use the strategies of predicting, clarifying, questioning, and summarizing to discuss a text.

The original reciprocal teaching routine was based on the teacher modeling the strategies and then turning the teaching over to a student. Oczkus (2010) adapted the routine to capture elementary students' sense of fun when she created Peter (or Madam) the Powerful Predictor, Quincy the Quizzical Questioner, Clara the Careful Clarifier, and Sammy the Super Summarizer (the "Fab Four"). In this approach to reciprocal teaching, students discuss the text in a collaborative discussion by taking on the roles of the characters or by using reciprocal teaching bookmarks as reminders.

Reciprocal teaching has been expanded to produce many different variations, but the basic routine remains the same. Oczkus (2010) suggests several ways to use reciprocal teaching in the elementary classroom in Chapter 2 of her book, which is available online (www.reading.org/Libraries/Inspire/03-507_Chapter02.pdf).

Questioning the Author (QtA) Questioning the Author (QtA) is a whole-class questioning and discussion procedure (Beck et al., 1997; McKeown, Beck, & Worthy, 1993). It is considered a highly effective comprehension routine that focuses on the author's message and craft. QtA was developed in response to research showing that students viewed textbooks as absolute authorities, not realizing that these books merely represent people's ideas that have been written down.

In QtA, the teacher explains that a given textbook was written by an ordinary person and that students can question the way the author wrote the text as they try to understand his or her ideas. Students learn to critique how an author writes as they grapple with the text and understand it in a deeper way. The discussion is closely tied to the text, not to students' personal experiences.

In this comprehension routine, we pose a series of queries as students read through the text, such as "What is the author trying to say?" "Why do you think the author used that word or phrase?" and "What is the author telling us about this topic?" In QtA, students are taught to continually explore the author's meaning by asking questions designed to help them comprehend the text as they read it in sections. As we facilitate discussions using text-dependent questions, QtA has the potential to help students meet the standards for understanding more complex literary and informational texts. A QtA strategy guide can be found on the ReadWriteThink website (www.readwritethink.org).

Students discuss a passage in a text

Cassaundra L. Watkins

Student-Led Literacy Discussions

Student-led collaborative discussions can help students explore ideas in deeper ways. For example, when students engage in Literature Circles to discuss stories, poems, or novels (Daniels, 2002) or Inquiry Circles to discuss informational texts (Harvey & Daniels, 2009), they read, prepare for discussion, and follow agreed on rules for discussion in small groups. As students discuss, they delve into the ideas in the text, ask and answer questions, and draw conclusions based on what they have learned from the discussion. When we focus student-led discussion groups on comprehension strategies, we can ensure that students will apply these strategies to text (Berne & Clark, 2008).

A program that is often associated with the concept of collaborative discussion is Junior Great Books. Junior Great Books uses a method called *Shared Inquiry* to engage students in discussions of classic stories that can be interpreted in multiple ways (Great Books Foundation, n.d.). At the third- and fourth-grade levels, many of the selections in the program are folktales. Students generate questions, prepare for discussion, and engage in student-led conversation using critical-thinking skills to analyze and interpret the text as a group.

Listening and Responding to Read-Alouds and Media Presentations

A wealth of research documents the value of teacher read-alouds with students for developing vocabulary, modeling reading strategies, determining patterns and structures of written language, developing ideas, exploring varied genres, and developing oral language (Fisher et al., 2004; Rasinski, 2003). In addition, the use of read-alouds can lead to improvements in language expression with students who are English language learners (Fisher et al., 2004). Motivation to read is an issue for many students, and teacher read-alouds have been found to increase motivation with students in the intermediate grades (Gambrell, Palmer, & Codling, 1993).

Appendix A to the CCSS (NGA & CCSSO, 2010b) makes this statement about the link between teacher read-alouds and development of reading, speaking, and listening skills:

> Because . . . children's listening comprehension likely outpaces reading comprehension until the middle school years, it is particularly important that students in the earliest grades build knowledge through being read to as well as through reading, with the balance gradually shifting to reading independently. By reading a story or nonfiction selection aloud, teachers allow children to experience written language without the burden of decoding, granting them access to content that they may not be able to read and understand by themselves. Children are then free to focus their mental energy on the words and ideas presented in the text, and they will eventually be better prepared to tackle rich written content on their own. Whereas most titles selected for kindergarten and grade 1 will need to be read aloud exclusively, some titles selected for grades 2–5 may be appropriate for read-alouds as well as for reading independently. Reading aloud to students in the upper grades should not, however, be used as a substitute for independent reading by students; read-alouds at this level should supplement and enrich what students are able to read by themselves. (p. 27)

According to the writers of the CCSS, teacher read-alouds are appropriate and support students as they work on learning to read complex texts independently.

Students in grades 3–5 also begin to develop skills in viewing and listening to media presentations. Today's students are surrounded by media and technology, and media outlets often blur the line between fact and opinion. We need to teach students active and critical ways to listen to and view presentations and develop ways for them to respond so they are accountable for learning.

Responding to Read-Alouds and Media Presentations Speaking and Listening Standard 2 states the expectation that students will determine the main idea and supporting details (grade 3), paraphrase (grade 4), and summarize (grade 5) text read aloud or information presented in diverse media and formats (NGA & CCSSO, 2010a, p. 24). (Ideas for writing summaries are included in Chapter 5 of this book.) However, to respond to oral formats of text, students must first be able to listen in different ways.

To respond to a teacher read-aloud, students must be able to listen for details and understanding, as well as with appreciation for the language and message of the text. To respond to information presented in diverse media and formats, students must be able to listen for details and understanding, listen critically to evaluate the speaker and his or her intent, and practice discriminative listening by interpreting the speaker's body movements, facial expressions, and tone and expression.

More creative types of summarizing may help scaffold students to be able to respond to read-alouds of text. Students can dramatize a read-aloud, writing and acting out a script that includes the elements of a storyline or the main ideas and key details of a historical event or scientific process. Students can create artwork that illustrates the description of a character or setting and then use the artwork as the basis for a written summary. Another engaging idea is to use a three-dimensional cube to summarize a text that has been read aloud. This interactive student activity, called Cube Creator, is described on the ReadWriteThink website (www .readwritethink.org). Students can then use these any of these products as a structure to write a paraphrase or summary of the text.

Listening and Responding to Speakers

Whether listening to a guest speaker or another student in the class, students need to be active listeners. Speaking and Listening Standard 3 includes an expectation for ways students should interact with a speaker.

Listening to a Speaker For students to respond interactively to a speaker, we need to provide opportunities for them to do so. Students should have numerous opportunities to listen to the ideas and opinions of others, whether the speaker is present in the class or entering through some sort of media format. Students should also recognize their classmates as speakers, even when sitting at the same table discussing a text.

SLANT We can teach students to be active listeners when listening to a speaker in the class-room. The SLANT strategy for participation is one way that students can practice active listening. (Ellis, 1991). The acronym SLANT is used as a mnemonic strategy to remember these guidelines for active listening:

S	Sit up.
L	Lean forward.
A	Activate your thinking (or Ask and answer questions).
N	Name key information (or Nod head slightly).
T	Track the talker.

When we expect students to apply SLANT while they are listening, they learn how to actively listen to a speaker—a skill that will pay off in many situations.

Intermediate students can begin to take notes by writing down key words and questions. We can model how to capture key words when a speaker is talking and plan for students to practice this skill regularly. When students also write a brief summary of what the speaker said, they better remember the main points.

Debate   Intermediate students enjoy a good debate! Randomly assign students to teams and give the teams a topic to debate. Team members work together to prepare a position for the side of the issue to which they were assigned, regardless of how they personally feel about the topic. Students research facts and simple statistics to help support their positions. Topics appropriate for elementary students should be noncontroversial but interesting to students, such as the following:

- Should junk food be allowed at school?
- Are sports as important as academics?
- Homework should be banned.

Debate can also be included in science and social studies classes about varied topics. For instance, inviting students to prepare and engage in a simple debate between the American colonists and British soldiers will help ensure they understand the causes of the American Revolution. When students listen to their peers debate and evaluate how they supported their points, they are working toward meeting the Speaking and Listening Standards.

Speaking for an Audience

In grades 3–5, students learn skills that lay the foundation for presenting ideas to an audience. At grades 3 and 4, students are expected to report on a topic or text, tell a story, or recount an experience to an audience. Fifth-graders should also be able to prepare and present a well-supported opinion.

Retelling and Summarizing for an Audience   Retelling and summarizing are both critical for developing comprehension. When students recount (i.e., retell) so we know they have understood the text (Reading Standard 2 for grade 3), we teach them to follow a storyline or logical order and to speak clearly and loudly enough for others to hear. When students present a summary of a text or their opinion on a topic, we teach them to use a logical order. (This skill relates to Writing Standard 1 for grade 5, which states the expectation to provide logically ordered reasons for opinions [NGA & CCSSO, 2010a, p. 20].) We also guide students to speak clearly and project their voices, make eye contact with the audience, and use appropriate posture.

Fifth-graders debate a topic in social studies

Leslie Montgomery

Using Multimedia   Speaking and Listening Standard 5 states that students in grades 3 and 4 should be able to incorporate audio recordings and visual displays in

their presentations to help support their topics and that students in grade 5 should include these and additional multimedia components, such as graphics and sound. Also, when students conduct research (Writing Standards 7 and 8), they need to share the results of their research. In addition to writing answers to questions they have generated, students can share information by preparing and recording radio shows and podcasts, creating digital stories, and preparing presentations with multimedia elements.

Some teachers worry that they don't know enough about technology to guide students. As it happens, students are often much more tech savvy than their teachers. Sometimes, just introducing an idea will spark a few students to learn the nuances of using multimedia, and they in turn can teach the others. In any case, to be college and career ready, students should have opportunities to become skilled in twenty-first century media presentations as a way to help them better learn content.

Giving Speeches   Intermediate students can learn the basics of giving a speech on an opinion about an issue. Teachers can find many resources online for helping students develop these skills. For instance, step-by-step directions for how to write and deliver a speech are available on the Scholastic Speechwriting website (for example, see "Scholastic speech workshop"). Also, a lesson plan for developing, writing, and evaluating persuasive speeches for students in grades 4 and 5 can be found on the ReadWriteThink website (www .readwritethink.org).

In fact, writing and giving speeches can be included in various thematic units across the curriculum—anywhere an opinion can be expressed.

Differentiating Ways of Speaking

Speaking and Listening Standard 6 refers to students' ability to use formal English and to adjust their speech to different tasks and situations. Part of this standard is about the concept of *code switching,* a term used in linguistics to mean moving back and forth between two languages.

Students come to us with different language backgrounds and abilities. Even so, they need to know when it is appropriate to talk informally, using slang or their native language or dialect, and when it is more appropriate to use formal English. Speaking and Listening Standard 6 includes a reference to Language Standard 1, which states the expectation to demonstrate command of the conventions of standard English grammar and usage, and Language Standard 3, which focuses on knowledge of language and its conventions.

Assessing Speaking and Listening

THE BEST WAY WE CAN ASSESS SPEAKING AND listening in our classrooms is to be good listeners and observers ourselves. For this to occur on a regular basis, we must be intentional in planning the type of classroom environment in which purposeful and accountable talk is expected and valued. There, we can observe students, take anecdotal notes, and confer with students about their goals to be better speakers and listeners.

Students can help us create checklists and rubrics for speaking and listening behaviors in the classroom and establish guidelines for literary discussions. We can use these guidelines and rubrics on a regular basis to chart students' progress.

Thinking about Speaking and Listening in Grades 3–5

AS DESCRIBED BY EDUCATOR JAMES BRITTON, "Reading and writing float on a sea of talk" (1970; cited in Mills, 2009). The ELA Standards clearly require students to use talk to improve their learning and literacy. Our classrooms need to buzz with productive conversation and excitement about learning.

We can use a multitude of approaches to get students talking about texts and topics, including those outlined in this chapter for improving speaking and listening in grades 3, 4, and 5. Strategies and experiences that rely on collaborative conversations are the keys to developing comprehension and learning at higher levels in the Common Core classroom. The classroom should be a sea of productive talk as our students learn.

REFERENCES

Almasi, J. F. (1996). A new view of discussion. In L. B. Gambrell & J. F. Almasi (Eds.), *Lively discussions! Fostering engaged reading* (pp. 2–24). Newark, DE: International Reading Association.

Alvermann, D. (1991). The discussion web: A graphic aid for learning across the curriculum. *The Reading Teacher, 45,* 92–99.

Beck, I. L., McKeown, M. G., Hamilton, R. L., & Kucan, L. (1997). *Questioning the author: An approach for enhancing student engagement with text.* Newark, DE: International Reading Association.

Berne, J. I., & Clark, K. F. (2008). Focusing literature discussion groups on comprehension strategies. *The Reading Teacher, 62*(1), 74–79.

Center for Research in Education, Diversity, and Excellence (CREDE). (n.d.). Language development: Developing language and literacy across the curriculum. *CREDE.* Retrieved from http://crede.berkeley.edu/research/crede/lang_dev.html.

Cohen, V. L., & Cowen, J. E. (2008). *Literacy for children in an information age: Teaching reading, writing, and thinking.* Belmont, CA: Thomson Wadsworth.

Daniels, H. (2002). *Literature circles: Voice and choice in book clubs and reading groups.* Portland, ME: Stenhouse.

Eeds, M., & Wells, G. (1989). Grand conversations: An exploration of meaning construction in literature study groups. *Research in the Teaching of English, 23*(1), 4–29.

Ellis, D. (1991). *SLANT: A starter strategy for participation.* Lawrence, KS: Edge Enterprises.

Fisher, D., Flood, J., Lapp, D., & Frey, N. (2004). Interactive read-alouds: Is there a common set of practices? *The Reading Teacher, 58*(1), 8–17.

Fisher, D., Frey, N., & Rothenberg, C. (2008). *Content-area conversations: How to plan discussion-based lessons for diverse language learners.* Alexandria, VA: Association for Supervision and Curriculum Development.

Gambrell, L. B., Palmer, B. M., & Codling, R. M. (1993). *Motivation to read.* Washington, DC: Office of Educational Research and Improvement.

Goldenberg, C. (1991). *Instructional conversations and their classroom application* (Educational Practice Report 2). Santa Cruz, CA: National Center for Research on Cultural Diversity and Second Language Learning.

Great Books Foundation. (n.d.). Professional learning: What is Shared Inquiry? Great Books Foundation. Retrieved from http://www.greatbooks.org/?id=1264.

Hahn, M. L. (2002). *Reconsidering read-aloud.* Portland, ME: Stenhouse.

Hancock, M. R. (2007). *Language arts: Extending the possibilities.* Upper Saddle River, NJ: Pearson.

Harvey, S., & Daniels. H. (2009). *Comprehension and collaboration: Inquiry circles in action.* Portsmouth, NH: Heinemann.

Keene, E. (2012). *Talk about understanding: Rethinking classroom talk to enhance comprehension.* Portsmouth, NH: Heinemann.

McKeown, M. G., Beck, I. L., & Worthy, M. J. (1993). Grappling with text ideas: Questioning the author. *The Reading Teacher, 46*(7), 560–566.

McLaughlin, M., & Allen, M. B. (2009). *Guided comprehension in grades 3–8.* Newark, DE: International Reading Association.

Mills, K. A. (2009). Floating on a sea of talk: Reading comprehension through speaking and listening. *The Reading Teacher, 63*(4), 325–329.

National Governors Association Center for Best Practices & Council of Chief State School Officers (NGA & CCSSO). (2010a). *Common Core State Standards: English language arts and literacy in history/social studies, science, and technical subjects.* Washington, DC: Authors. Retrieved from http://www.corestandards.org/assets/CCSSI_ELA%20Standards.pdf.

National Governors Association Center for Best Practices & Council of Chief State School Officers (NGA & CCSSO). (2010b). Appendix A: Research supporting key elements of the standards and glossary of key terms. *Common Core State Standards.* Washington, DC: Authors. Retrieved from http://www.corestandards.org/assets/Appendix_A.pdf.

Oczkus, L. D. (2010). *Reciprocal teaching at work: Powerful strategies and lessons for improving reading comprehension.* Newark, DE: International Reading Association.

Ontario Ministry of Education. (2011). Grand conversations in the junior classroom. Capacity Building Series, Special Edition 23. Retrieved from http://www.edu.gov.on.ca/eng/literacynumeracy/inspire/research/CBS_Grand_Conversations_Junor.pdf.

Opitz, M. F., & Zbaracki, M. D. (2004). *Listen hear! Twenty-five effective listening comprehension activities.* Portsmann, NH: Heinemann.

Palincsar, A. S., & Brown, A. L. (1984). Reciprocal teaching of comprehension-fostering and comprehension-monitoring activities. *Cognition and Instruction, 2,* 117–175.

Rasinski, T. (2003). *The fluent reader: Oral reading strategies for building word recognition, fluency, and comprehension.* New York, NY: Scholastic Professional Books.

Short, K. G., Harste, J., & Burke, C. (1996). *Creating classrooms for authors and inquirers* (2nd ed.). Portsmouth, NH: Heinemann.

Speigel, D. L. (2005). *Classroom discussion: Strategies for engaging all students, building higher-level thinking skills, and strengthening reading and writing across the curriculum.* New York, NY: Scholastic.

Tharp, R. G., & Gallimore, R. (1988). Rousing schools to life. *American Educator, 13*(2), 20–25, 46–52.

Tharp, R. G., & Gallimore, R. (1991). *The instructional conversation: Teaching and learning in social activity* (Research Report 2). Santa Cruz, CA: National Center for Research on Cultural Diversity and Second Language Learning.

Wells, G. (2007). Semiotic mediation, dialogue, and the construction of knowledge. *Human Development, 50,* 244–274.

Zwiers, J., & Crawford, M. (2011). *Academic conversations: Classroom talk that fosters critical thinking and content understandings.* Portland, ME: Stenhouse.

LITERATURE CITED

Debnam, B. (2007). *Icy habitat disappearing: Polar bears in trouble.* Kansas City, MO: Universal Press Syndicate.

TIME for Kids. (2012, Sept. 12). Debate! Do kids need their own cell phones? *TIME for kids.* Retrieved from http://www.timeforkids.com/news/debate/47056.

chapter 7

Curriculum Implications

PLANNING TO TEACH STUDENTS USING THE ENGLISH LANGUAGE Arts (ELA) Common Core State Standards (CCSS) might seem like a Herculean task (a phrase in the CCSS that intermediate teachers may want to use often!). There are so many things to consider: how to plan engaging instruction that will motivate students to want to learn, how to select materials that meet the rigor of the CCSS yet align with the content or theme, how to schedule the day to meet a variety of expectations, how to meet the needs of diverse learners in our classrooms, and so on.

Leslie Montgomery

Tips for the Teacher

"IN ORDER TO PREPARE STUDENTS FOR THE NEXT level, we have to challenge them to stretch as readers and writers. I am finding that I, as a teacher and lifelong learner, am stretching as a reader and writer more than ever before. At the end of the day, I am comforted and encouraged knowing that teachers everywhere are experiencing similar challenges with the new standards and confident we are doing what is best for our kids."

—Taylor, grade 4 teacher

To begin, it helps if we are highly prepared. Just like surgeons who must learn a new surgical technique or lawyers who must get ready for a difficult case, we must study and contemplate new curriculum implications as we plan for a CCSS-based classroom. To teach students using the ELA Standards, teachers can plan together in the following ways:

1. Study the Standards, including the appendixes.
2. Consider the products and guidelines of national organizations.
3. Discuss how to integrate the Standards into instruction.
4. Plan standards-based thematic units.
5. Plan standards-based lessons.
6. Design a daily schedule that embraces CCSS instruction and assessment.

Putting these guidelines into practice is the focus of the rest of this chapter.

Study the Standards, Including the Appendixes

THERE IS NO SUBSTITUTE FOR STUDYING THE CCSS with your colleagues (NGA & CCSSO, 2010a). It is important that we come to a common understanding with the other teachers in our schools or on our teams about what the standards mean for instruction and assessment at our grade levels. By studying the CCSS vertically as a faculty, teachers at grades 3–5 review the standards for previous grades to plan assessment that will identify the learning gaps of their third-, fourth-, and fifth-graders. Teachers at grades 3–5 must also look ahead to the expectations at grade 6 to determine how to prepare their students for those upcoming demands and how to meet the needs of their gifted readers and writers. By studying the CCSS horizontally as a team, we can better understand what is expected by the end of each grade for reading, writing, speaking and listening, and language.

Studying Appendix A of the CCSS (NGA & CCSSO, 2010b) will help us understand some of the major research philosophies that underlie the Standards and their expectations for students. Appendix A includes research that supports the key elements of the standards and a glossary of key terms. The appendix is divided into these sections and addresses these topics:

- Reading, with an extensive discussion of text complexity
- Foundational Skills for Reading, including phoneme-grapheme correspondences, phonological awareness, and orthography
- Writing, with discussions of the three text types addressed in the Standards: argument, informational/explanatory writing, and narrative writing
- Speaking and Listening, addressing the importance of this skill area for K–5 students
- Language, including the conventions and knowledge of language and vocabulary

Appendix B (NGA & CCSSO, 2010c) provides text exemplars and sample performance tasks for reading. Studying Appendix B for grades 2–3 and 4–5 will give us an idea of the levels of text complexity that students are expected to meet in the CCSS. According to the writers of the Standards, the texts listed in this appendix are not meant as mandates but rather as texts that "primarily serve to exemplify the level of complexity and quality that the Standards require all students in a given grade band to engage with….They expressly do not represent a partial or complete reading list" (NGA & CCSSO, 2010c, p. 2). We should use the titles in Appendix B as models to gauge the complexity of the texts we use in our classrooms. The grades 2–3 text exemplars include stories, poems, read-aloud stories, read-aloud poems, informational texts, and read-aloud informational texts, as well as sample performance tasks for stories, poems, and informational texts. The grades 4–5 text exemplars include stories, poems, and informational texts, plus sample performance tasks for stories, poetry, and informational texts.

Appendix C (NGA & CCSSO, 2010d) provides samples of student writing at each grade level. For grade 3, there are samples of an informative/explanatory piece and a narrative piece. For grade 4, there are samples of an argument (opinion) piece and a narrative piece. For grade 5, there are samples of an informative/explanatory piece and a narrative piece. Each piece includes a number of annotations explaining why it meets the standards for that grade.

Reading the ELA Standards and its appendixes closely several times and discussing them with our colleagues will help us grasp the expectations set for our students.

Consider Products and Guidelines of National Organizations

AS WE PLAN, WE SHOULD CONSIDER A RANGE of other information about the ELA Standards and their implementation. The following information can provide a solid base for further planning:

- products of national assessment consortia that may affect guidelines and mandates in our own states

- recommendations of the *Revised Publishers' Criteria for the Common Core State Standards in English Language Arts and Literacy, Grades 3–12* (Coleman & Pimentel, 2012) to ensure alignment

- recommendations of the International Reading Association about how to address the learning needs of students in a CCSS-based classroom by clarifying research-based literacy concepts

- recommendations from the writers of the CCSS about how to create text-dependent questions and conduct close reading lessons

- components of the universal design for learning (UDL) framework to help meet the needs of diverse students

- ideas about planning for CCSS-based instructional units and lessons that have been suggested by teachers and other literacy leaders in the EQuIP (Educators Evaluating the Quality of Instructional Products) Project (Achieve, 2013)

The following sections review these sources of information and what they recommend about planning a CCSS-based curriculum for grades 3–5. More information about each source can also be found online (see the URL provided for each source).

Assessment Consortia

Two national consortia have designed assessments for English Language Arts and Mathematics Common Core State Standards for grades 3–8 and high school, with implementation set for the school year 2014–2015 (ETS, 2013). The two consortia are the Partnership for Assessment of Readiness for College and Careers (PARCC) (www.parcconline.org) and the Smarter Balanced Assessment Consortium (Smarter Balanced) (www.smarterbalanced.org). Many states that have adopted the CCSS are part of one or the other (and sometimes both) consortia.

Both PARCC and Smarter Balanced have designed assessments to be administered at various times during the school year to gauge students' mastery of the CCSS. PARCC has also created a digital library of resources, including released items, formative assessments, model content frameworks, instructional informative tools and resources, student and educator tutorials and practice tests, scoring training modules, professional development materials, and an interactive report generation system. Similarly, Smarter Balanced offers a digital library of formative tools, processes, and exemplars; released items and tasks; model curriculum units; educator training; professional development tools and resources; scorer training modules; and teacher collaboration tools (ETS, 2013). As we plan for curriculum, instruction, and assessment, we keep in mind that our state likely belongs to one of these national consortia and that the expectations of these assessments should therefore be a key to our planning. Updated information about the consortia, their progress, and assessment prototypes can be found at their respective websites.

Two alternate assessment consortia are Dynamic Learning Maps (DLM) (http://dynamiclearningmaps.org) and the National Center and State Collaborative (NCSC) (www.ncscpartners.org). Both consortia have designed assessments based on the CCSS for students with serious cognitive disabilities, who are unable to participate in general state assessments even with appropriate accommodations. In addition, an English language proficiency assessment consortium called Assessment Services Supporting ELs Through Technology Systems (ASSETS) (http://assets.wceruw.org) has developed a next-generation, technology-based language assessment system for students in grades K–12 who are learning English.

More information about these consortia can be found at the website K–12 Center at ETS (www.k12center.org.)

Publishers' Criteria

Two of the lead authors of the CCSS have provided criteria to guide publishers as they design materials for implementation of the ELA Standards. Although the *Revised Publishers' Criteria for the Common Core State Standards in English Language Arts and Literacy, Grades 3–12* (Coleman & Pimentel, 2012) was written for publishers and curriculum developers, many teachers also find the information in this publication helpful as they contemplate teaching students to meet the standards. The *Publishers' Criteria* includes what qualities to consider in text selection, how to develop questions and tasks, how to approach academic vocabulary, and how to design instruction that requires students in grades 3–12 to write to sources and conduct research. (A separate publication provides guidelines for grades K–2.) This publication also includes additional key criteria for students' reading, writing, listening, and speaking. (The *Publishers' Criteria* can be found online at www.corestandards.org/assets/Publishers_Criteria_for_K-2.pdf.)

Literacy Implementation Guidelines

The International Reading Association (IRA, 2012) has published *Literacy Implementation Guidance for the ELA Common Core State Standards*. This document describes common literacy obstacles when implementing the ELA Standards and provides guidance in meeting these obstacles from experts in the field of literacy. The authors clarify the use of challenging texts, foundational skills and beginning reading, the role of comprehension skills and strategies, vocabulary development, writing, literacy in the disciplines, and how to teach diverse learners in a Common Core classroom. (This IRA document is available online at www.reading.org.)

Creating Text-Dependent Questions and Close Reading Model Lessons

Assessment of students' reading, writing, and thinking about complex texts generally begins in third grade and is expected of all students. To meet this expectation, we need to create text-dependent questions and facilitate close reading lessons that engage students in rigorous text-based conversations about complex texts. Professional development materials and examples of text-dependent questions and close reading model lessons for grades 3–5 can be found on the website Achieve the Core (www.achievethecore.org) in the section "Featured Lessons."

Universal Design for Learning

The writers of the CCSS state explicitly that the Standards do not describe how to address students with disabilities, English language learners, or students who are advanced (NGA & CCSSO, 2010a, p. 6). However, there are brief additions to the CCSS that describe their application to students with disabilities (NGA & CCSSO, 2010e) and to students who are English language learners (NGA & CCSSO, 2010f). (See the References for the URLs of these documents, or go to www.corestandards.org/the-standards/download-the-standards.)

The document "Application to Students with Disabilities" (NGA & CCSSO, 2010e) includes a reference to the principles of universal design for learning (UDL). Actually, UDL is a framework for designing curriculum for *all* students, including students with disabilities, English language learners, struggling readers and writers, and gifted students to reduce barriers that prohibit learning (CAST, 2012). The overarching idea of UDL is that because every student learns differently, the curriculum should be designed to accommodate the needs of diverse learners, rather than designed for average learners and adapted for other learners after the fact. Within the UDL framework, students gain knowledge, skills and strategies, and enthusiasm for learning. Instruction should provide students with multiple means of representation (i.e., presenting information and content in different ways), multiple means of action and expression (i.e., differentiating the ways that students can express what they know), and multiple means of engagement (i.e., stimulating students' interest and motivation for learning).

Although UDL was created to assist in curriculum design for diverse learners, teachers find it helpful when planning units and lessons in Common Core classrooms. All students are expected to master the CCSS, which means we must plan instruction to meet the needs of individual students.

More information about UDL can be found at the website of the National Center on Universal Design for Learning (www.udlcenter.org).

EQuIP Rubric

Educators from Massachusetts, New York, and Rhode Island (facilitated by Achieve, Inc.) collaborated to create rubrics to evaluate ELA CCSS lessons and units to ensure rigor and alignment to the Standards. The EQuIP (Educators Evaluating the Quality of Instructional Products) rubric can also be used to design instruction and for evaluation.

The "CCSS-Based Thematic Unit Checklist" and the "CCSS-Based Lesson Checklist" that appear at the end of this chapter were both adapted from the EQuIP rubric. (Achieve, 2013). The most recent version of the rubric can be found on the Achieve website (www.achieve.org/EQuIP).

Integrate the ELA Standards in Instruction

THE ELA STANDARDS WERE BUILT ON AN INTEGRATED model of literacy and designed to be connected and interwoven. The ELA CCSS document states, "Although the Standards are divided into Reading, Writing, Speaking and Listening, and Language strands for conceptual clarity, the processes of communication are closely connected, as reflected throughout this document" (NGA & CCSSO, 2010a, p. 4). The expectation is that the CCSS should not be taught in isolation; rather, they should be integrated when planning instruction and assessment. In fact, the writers of the CCSS state unambiguously, "While the Standards delineate specific expectations in reading, writing, speaking, listening, and language, each standard need not be a separate focus for instruction and assessment. Often, several standards can be addressed by a single rich task" (NGA & CCSSO, 2010a, p. 5).

When planning for instruction, we should look for the obvious connections between and among standards to create such rich instructional tasks. For example, suppose we are planning a reading task in which fifth-grade students will read an informational text. We can address several Reading Standards for Informational Text at the same time by considering these standards for fifth grade:

- **RI.5.1:** Quote accurately from a text when explaining what the text says explicitly and when drawing inferences from the text.

- **RI.5.2:** Determine two or more main ideas of a text and explain how they are supported by key details; summarize the text.

- **RI.5.8:** Explain how an author uses reasons and evidence to support particular points in a text, identifying which reasons and evidence support which point(s). (NGA & CCSSO, 2010)

When we facilitate a discussion of the text and ask students to share their opinions, we can integrate these standards for Speaking and Listening within the task:

- **SL.5.1:** Engage effectively in a range of collaborative discussions (one-on-one, in groups, and teacher-led) with diverse partners on *grade 5 topics and texts,* building on others' ideas and expressing their own clearly.

- **SL.5.4:** Report on a topic or text or present an opinion, sequencing ideas logically and using appropriate facts and relevant, descriptive details to support main ideas or themes; speak clearly at an understandable pace. (NGA & CCSSO, 2010)

If we ask students to respond to the reading by writing an opinion about the text, then we can add appropriate Writing standards to the task:

- **W.5.1:** Write opinion pieces on topics or texts, supporting a point of view with reasons and information.

  a. Introduce a topic or text clearly, state an opinion, and create an organizational structure in which ideas are logically grouped to support the writer's purpose.
  b. Provide logically ordered reasons that are supported by facts and details.
  c. Link opinions and reasons using words, phrases, and clauses (e.g., *consequently, specifically*).
  d. Provide a concluding statement or section related to the opinion presented.

- **W.5.9:** Draw evidence from literary or informational texts to support analysis, reflection, and research. (NGA & CCSSO, 2010)

The Language standards can also be integrated within the task through writing and speaking activities:

- **L.5.1:** Demonstrate command of the conventions of standard English grammar and usage when writing or speaking.

- **L.5.2:** Demonstrate command of the conventions of standard English capitalization, punctuation, and spelling when writing.

- **L.5.6:** Acquire and use accurately grade-appropriate general academic and domain-specific words and phrases, including those that signal contrast, addition, and other logical relationships (e.g., *however, although, nevertheless, similarly, moreover, in addition*). (NGA & CCSSO, 2010)

When we plan to integrate the Standards, our students get a much richer experience and a better understanding of how reading, writing, speaking and listening, language, and vocabulary are interrelated. And we address several standards at the same time!

Planning CCSS-Based Thematic Units

To teach in a way that integrates the CCSS and content, meets the needs of all learners, and engages and motivates students, we may want to plan integrated thematic instruction. Planning an integrated CCSS-based thematic unit means examining the curriculum and looking for ways to connect language arts and other content areas, such as science, social studies, the arts, and mathematics. It means taking into account the needs of the particular students in our classes and designing engaging instruction in which students have choices. It also means providing a variety of assessments for a variety of purposes.

As we plan a standards-based thematic unit, we consider these questions:

What should be the focus of a CCSS-based thematic unit?   A CCSS-based instructional unit should target a specific set of ELA/Literacy standards. These are the standards we will use to assess students throughout the unit. The unit should include a clear and explicit purpose for instruction, and it should be planned to build both students' content knowledge and their understanding of reading and writing in the content areas (i.e., social studies, the arts, science, or technical subjects) through the coherent selection of appropriate texts. Finally, the thematic unit should clearly address instructional expectations and be easy to understand and use.

How should I select texts for the unit?   At the elementary level, provide a balance of 50% informational texts and 50% literary texts for instruction. When planning a unit focused on a literary topic, we include informational texts about components of the topic. For example, if we are planning a unit on poetry, we include informational texts about the life and writing style of the poet, historical events that may have influenced the poem, or scientific information about the topic of the poem. When planning a unit on content, such as the Underground Railroad, we include both informational texts on the topic and literature (e.g., stories, plays, poems, songs) related to the content. This will enrich students' thinking and help them understand how people try to survive, as well as what it took to escape such gruesome conditions.

The CCSS state expectations for students to read complex texts closely and discuss text-dependent questions as they analyze a text. Complex texts to be read closely should be selected within the grade-level text complexity band that presents vocabulary, syntax, text structures, levels of meaning/purpose, and other qualitative characteristics similar to the CCSS grade-level exemplars presented in Appendix A (NGA & CCSSO, 2010b) and Appendix B (NGA & CCSSO, 2010c). At grade 3, texts should be selected from the high end of the text complexity band for grades 2–3. Texts for grades 4 should be from the low end of text complexity band for grades 4–5 and from the high end of the band but with scaffolding provided. Texts for grade 5 should be from the high end of the grades 4–5 text complexity band.

In addition, a variety of levels of texts about the unit topic and related topics should be available in the classroom for research and self-selected reading at independent levels.

What should be the focus of instruction?   A CCSS-based instructional unit should be planned to integrate reading, writing, speaking and listening, and language so that students apply and synthesize their developing literacy skills. Motivation is a key part of learning, and learning experiences should be planned that cultivate students' interest and engagement in reading, writing, and speaking about texts as well as application of literacy skills. Opportunities should be provided for authentic learning, in which students have choices and purposes for activities, and time should be provided for student-directed inquiry, analysis, evaluation, and reflection.

The unit should be planned to show a progression of learning, recognizing how concepts and skills advance and deepen over time. The lessons in the unit should be sequenced to provide scaffolding as necessary but gradually remove supports, requiring students to demonstrate their independent capacities. Unit lessons should also integrate targeted instruction in such areas as grammar and conventions, writing strategies, discussion roles, and all of the foundational aspects of reading for grades 3–5.

What are key considerations for each strand of the ELA Standards?   In Reading, the central focus of instruction in the unit should include learning experiences in which students are required to read texts closely, examine textual evidence, and discern the meaning. There should also be a focus on comprehending challenging sections of text and engaging students in a productive struggle to understand such text through the use of discussion questions and other supports that build toward independence. The unit should include learning experiences that invite students to read a progression of complex texts from the appropriate grade-level band. The unit should provide opportunities for students to build knowledge about a topic or subject through analysis of a coherent selection of strategically sequenced, discipline-specific texts. Students should also have opportunities for independent reading based on their choices and interests to build stamina, confidence, and motivation. However, a plan should be in place to ensure student accountability for independent reading.

In Writing, the unit should include learning experiences that expect students to draw evidence from texts to produce clear and coherent writing that informs, explains, or expresses an opinion supported by reasons and evidence in various forms (e.g., notes, summaries, short responses, informal essays). The unit should include a balance of on-demand and process writing (e.g., multiple drafts and revisions over time) in short, focused research projects, incorporating digital texts when appropriate.

In Speaking and Listening, the unit should include learning experiences that engage students in rich and rigorous evidence-based discussions. Such discussions can be initiated by asking a sequence of specific thought-provoking and text-dependent questions, including, when applicable, illustrations, charts, diagrams, audio/video, and media.

In Language, the unit should include learning experiences that focus on building students' academic vocabulary in context throughout instruction.

The unit should also use technology and media to deepen students' learning and draw attention to evidence in texts as appropriate.

How can I be responsive to the needs of varied learners?   A thematic unit should provide *all* students with multiple opportunities to read texts of appropriate complexity for the grade level and include appropriate scaffolding so that students correctly experience the complexity of the text. The unit should integrate appropriate supports in reading, writing, listening, and speaking for students who are English language learners, have disabilities, or read well below the grade-level text band. The unit should also provide extensions and/or more advanced texts for students who read well above the grade-level text band.

How should I plan assessments?   Varied modes of assessments should be used in the unit, including a range of pre-, formative, summative, and self-assessment measures. Assessments should elicit direct, observable evidence of the degree to which a student independently demonstrates achievement of the targeted grade level standards with an appropriately complex text. The assessments in the unit should assess students' proficiency using methods that are unbiased and accessible to all students. Assessments should involve CCSS-aligned rubrics or guidelines that provide sufficient information for interpreting student performance.

An example of a checklist for CCSS-based lesson planning is provided at the end of this chapter. An example of a CCSS-based integrated thematic unit at the intermediate level is provided in Chapter 8 of this book.

Plan a Daily Schedule

PLANNING A DAILY SCHEDULE FOR A COMMON CORE classroom can be tricky. Students in grades 3, 4, and 5 still need substantial instruction in reading and writing, and they are grappling with the higher expectations of the CCSS. We need to plan the day in a way that will meet the needs of all students in the classroom plus provide instruction and experiences that will help students master the Standards at their particular grade levels.

Figure 7.1 shows a sample daily schedule for a grades 3–5 CCSS-based classroom. Of course, no class schedule is this neat and tidy! On any given day, there will be assemblies, fire drills, and classroom emergencies. Also, different schools have different schedules for special areas of instruction (e.g., art, music), and some schools have recess while others do not.

Regardless, the figure presents a basic schedule that can be adapted to help students meet the requirements of the CCSS. Explanations of the literacy elements of the sample schedule follow.

FIGURE 7.1 ● Sample Daily Schedule for CCSS-Based Classroom, Grades 3–5

8:30 – 8:50	Read-Aloud
8:50 – 9:15	Standards-Based Reading or Writing Skill Lesson
9:15 – 10:15	Reading/Writing Workshop with guided reading: ● Reading ● Writing ● Research ● Teacher meets with guided reading groups as needed
10:15 – 10:25	Break
10:25 – 11:15	Standards-Based Mathematics
11:15 – 11:45	Lunch
11:45 – 12:15	Special Area (art, computer, music, PE, etc.)
12:15 – 1:00	Reading Lesson of literature, science, social studies, or technical text (same lesson can continue more than one day)
1:00 – 1:30	Vocabulary
1:30 – 1:40	Break
1:40 – 2:20	Science
2:20 – 3:00	Social Studies
3:00 – 3:30	Novel Study/Collaborative Discussion

Read-Aloud

The teacher begins the day with a read-aloud of a brief, complex text that relates to the instructional unit. It can be a story, scene from a drama, poem, song lyrics, essay, nonfiction text, or website page. Students should be able to see the text as the teacher reads aloud expressively and with appropriate enthusiasm to model fluent reading. After the read-aloud, students should engage in an interactive, text-based discussion and be encouraged to state their opinions about the text while including reasons and evidence for those opinions. Students may be asked to respond to the text in some way.

Standards-Based Reading or Writing Skill Lesson

Students will engage in whole-class instruction on standards-based reading and writing skills, such as how to find the main idea and supporting details or how to write an opinion piece. After the lesson, students will complete an assignment that asks them to apply what they have learned (e.g., analyze text for the main idea and supporting details or write an opinion piece). This writing can extend into Reading/Writing Workshop.

Reading/Writing Workshop with Guided Reading Groups

Students need time to read texts they have chosen, engage in the kind of writing required in the CCSS, and conduct research on authentic questions and projects related to social studies, science, and technical subjects. While students work, the teacher will meet with small, guided reading groups based on students' needs. When not working with guided reading groups, the teacher will conference with small groups and individual students about their reading and writing. The teacher will also do individual informal assessments to gauge students' understanding.

Standards-Based Mathematics

Although the bulk of this time block is for hands-on mathematics, teachers need to provide instruction that helps students understand how to read math texts and how to write to demonstrate their understanding of math. Teachers should plan to teach students how to read and write about mathematics as part of their math development.

Reading Lesson

The time on the schedule for the reading lesson is reserved for two types of instruction. Every other week, students engage in whole-class, close, attentive reading of an unfamiliar complex text in literature, science, or social studies or a technical text. Students will read closely, engage in rich discussion, ask and answer text-dependent questions, participate in a visualization activity, and develop a written analysis of the text (e.g., an opinion or explanatory paragraph).

When students are not working on close reading, they are engaged in comprehension instruction and assessment that helps them learn how to comprehend different types of text. This instruction is focused on metacognitive strategies, such as monitoring comprehension, making inferences, asking questions, and so on. Instruction should also include attention to text structures and features, including the visual elements of physical and digital texts. As the year progresses, these two types of instruction should naturally merge as students become more skilled in reading challenging texts.

Interactive Vocabulary

Third- through fifth-graders are developing an academic vocabulary that they will use throughout the rest of their academic careers. This time period on the schedule is reserved for engaging students in interactive vocabulary instruction that builds their knowledge about words in content areas and that they will find across texts. Vocabulary instruction should focus on building word relationships, determining the meanings of words in context, figurative language, word nuances, and domain-specific words and phrases. Students should also learn to use reference materials and engage in practice with morphology.

Science and Social Studies

Students need to learn how to read and write in science and social studies. The Reading Lesson time block on the schedule should include reading of science and social studies texts. Students need practice applying reading strategies when engaged in content area instruction.

Novel Study or Collaborative Discussion

Students engage in the study of a chapter book or novel that aligns with a thematic focus or a literary discussion of a text the group has chosen.

Thinking about Curriculum Implications for Grades 3–5

Planning to implement the CCSS in the classroom is not easy. Even so, teachers at every grade level must accept responsibility for their part in the bigger mosaic of CCSS implementation. To be ready to teach in a Common Core classroom, we must study the Standards, read and discuss information from organizations involved in implementation, learn how to integrate the Standards across the curriculum, and design standards-based thematic units, lessons, and daily schedules. Our students deserve our best thinking to ensure that every student is college and career ready.

REFERENCES

Achieve, Inc. (2013). *EQuIP rubric for lessons and units: ELA/Literacy (grades 3–5) and ELA (grades 6–12).* Retrieved from http://www.achieve.org/files/EQuIP-ELArubric-06-24-13-FINAL.pdf.

CAST. (2012). About UDL. *National Center on Universal Design for Learning, at CAST.* Retrieved from http://www.udlcenter.org/aboutudl/whatisudl.

Coleman, D., & Pimentel, S. (2012). *Revised publishers' criteria for the Common Core State Standards in English language arts and literacy, grades 3–12.* Washington, DC: National Governors Association, Council of Chief State School Officers, Achieve, Council of Great City Schools, and National Association of State Boards of Education. Retrieved from http://www.corestandards.org/assets/Publishers_Criteria_for_3-12.pdf.

Educational Testing Service (ETS). (2013, June). *Coming together to raise student achievement: New assessments for the Common Core State Standards.* Center for K–12 Assessment and Performance Management at ETS. Retrieved from http://k12center.org/rsc/pdf/Coming_Together_June_2013.pdf

International Reading Association (IRA). (2012). *Literacy implementation guidance for the ELA Common Core State Standards.* Common Core State Standards (CCSS) Committee. Retrieved from http://www.reading.org/Libraries/association-documents/ira_ccss_guidelines.pdf.

National Governors Association Center for Best Practices & Council of Chief State School Officers (NGA & CCSSO). (2010a). *Common Core State Standards: English language arts and literacy in history/social studies, science, and technical subjects.* Washington, DC: Authors. Retrieved from http://www.corestandards.org/assets/CCSSI_ELA%20Standards.pdf.

National Governors Association Center for Best Practices & Council of Chief State School Officers (NGA & CCSSO). (2010b). Appendix A: Research supporting key elements of the standards and glossary of key terms. *Common Core State Standards.* Washington, DC: Authors. Retrieved from http://www.corestandards.org/assets/Appendix_A.pdf.

National Governors Association Center for Best Practices & Council of Chief State School Officers (NGA & CCSSO). (2010c). Appendix B: Text exemplars and sample performance tasks. *Common Core State Standards.* Washington, DC: Authors. Retrieved from http://www.corestandards.org/assets/Appendix_B.pdf.

National Governors Association Center for Best Practices & Council of Chief State School Officers (NGA & CCSSO). (2010d). Appendix C: Samples of student writing. *Common Core State Standards.* Washington, DC: Authors. Retrieved from http://corestandards.org/assets/Appendix_C.pdf.

National Governors Association Center for Best Practices & Council of Chief State School Officers (NGA & CCSSO). (2010e). Application to students with disabilities. *Common Core State Standards.* Washington, DC: Authors. Retrieved from http://www.corestandards.org/assets/application-to-students-with-disabilities.pdf.

National Governors Association Center for Best Practices & Council of Chief State School Officers (NGA & CCSSO). (2010f). Application of Common Core State Standards for English language learners. *Common*

Core State Standards. Washington, DC: Authors. Retrieved from http://www.corestandards.org/assets/
application-for-english-learners.pdf.

New York State Department of Education. (2011). Common Core instructional shifts. *EngageNY.* Retrieved from
http://engageny.org/resource/common-core-shifts/.

CCSS-Based Thematic Unit Checklist
GRADES 3–5

ALIGNMENT TO THE RIGOR OF THE CCSS

Focus of Unit

Y   N   1. Does the unit target a set of grades 3–5 CCSS ELA/Literacy standards?

Y   N   2. Does the unit include a clear and explicit purpose for instruction?

Y   N   3. Is the unit planned to build both students' content knowledge and their understanding of reading and writing in social studies, the arts, and science or technical subjects?

Y   N   4. Does the unit address instructional expectations, and is it easy to understand and use?

Text Selection

Y   N   5. Does the unit include texts within the grade-level text complexity band that present vocabulary, syntax, text structures, levels of meaning/purpose, and other qualitative characteristics similar to those of the CCSS grade-level exemplars in Appendixes A and B? (Grade 3 is the high end of the text complexity band for grades 2–3. Grade 4 is the low end of the grades 4–5 text complexity band with scaffolding provided. Grade 5 is the high end of the grades 4–5 text complexity band.)

Y   N   6. Does the unit include a balance of 50% informational and 50% literary texts, as stipulated in the CCSS at the elementary level?

INSTRUCTIONAL FOCUS

Y   N   7. Is the unit planned to integrate reading, writing, and speaking and listening so that students apply and synthesize their advancing literacy skills?

Y   N   8. Is the unit planned to cultivate students' interest and engagement in reading, writing, and speaking about texts?

Y   N   9. Is the unit planned to provide for authentic learning, application of literacy skills, and student-directed inquiry, analysis, evaluation, and reflection?

Y   N   10. Is the unit planned to include a progression of learning in which concepts and skills advance and deepen over time?

Y   N   11. Do unit lessons gradually remove supports, requiring students to demonstrate their independent capacities?

Y   N   12. Do unit lessons integrate targeted instruction in such areas as grammar and conventions, writing strategies, discussion roles, and all foundational aspects of reading for grades 3–5?

KEY AREAS FOR INSTRUCTION

Reading

Y   N   13. Does the unit include learning experiences that require students to read text(s) closely, examine textual evidence, and discern the meaning as a central focus of instruction?

Y   N   14. Does the unit focus on comprehending challenging sections of text(s) and engage students in a productive struggle to understand them through the use of discussion questions and other supports that build toward independence?

Y   N   15. Does the unit include learning experiences that have students read a progression of complex texts drawn from the appropriate grade-level band? Does it provide text-centered learning experiences that are sequenced, scaffolded, and supported to advance students toward independent reading of complex texts at the college- and career-readiness level?

Y   N   16. Does the unit provide opportunities for students to build knowledge about a topic or subject through analysis of a coherent selection of strategically sequenced, discipline-specific texts?

Y   N   17. Does the unit include independent reading based on students' choices and interests to build stamina, confidence, and motivation? Does it indicate how students are accountable for independent reading?

Writing

Y   N   18. Does the unit include learning experiences that expect students to draw evidence from texts to produce clear and coherent writing that informs, explains, or expresses an opinion supported by reasons and evidence in various forms (e.g., notes, summaries, short responses, formal essays)?

Y   N   19. Does the unit include a balance of on-demand and process writing (e.g., multiple drafts and revisions over time) and short, focused research projects, incorporating digital texts when appropriate?

Speaking and Listening

Y   N   20. Does the unit include learning experiences that engage students in rich and rigorous evidence-based discussions through a sequence of specific thought-provoking and text-dependent questions (including, when applicable, illustrations, charts, diagrams, audio/video, and media)?

Language

Y   N   21. Does the unit include learning experiences that focus on building students' academic vocabulary in context throughout instruction?

Technology

Y   N   22. Does the unit use technology and media to deepen students' learning and draw attention to evidence in texts as appropriate?

RESPONSIVENESS TO VARIED STUDENT NEEDS

Y   N   23. Does the unit provide *all* students with multiple opportunities to engage with texts of appropriate complexity for the grade level and include appropriate scaffolding so that students correctly experience the complexity of the texts?

Y   N   24. Does the unit integrate appropriate supports in reading, writing, listening, and speaking for students who are English language learners, have disabilities, or read well below the grade-level text band?

Y   N   25. Does the unit provide extensions and/or more advanced texts for students who read well above the grade-level text band?

ASSESSMENTS

Y   N   26. Do assessments in the unit elicit direct, observable evidence of the degree to which a student can independently demonstrate the major targeted grade-level CCSS standards with appropriately complex texts?

Y   N   27. Do assessments in the unit assess student proficiency using methods that are unbiased and accessible to all students?

Y   N   28. Do assessments in the unit include aligned rubrics or assessment guidelines that provide sufficient guidance for interpreting student performance?

Y   N   29. Do assessments in the unit use varied modes, including a range of pre-, formative, summative, and self-assessment measures?

Note: Adapted from *EQuIP rubric for lessons and units: ELA/Literacy (grades 3–5) and ELA (grades 6–12)* (Achieve, 2013).

CCSS-Based Lesson Checklist
GRADES 3–5

ALIGNMENT TO THE RIGOR OF THE CCSS

Focus of Lesson

Y   N   1. Does the lesson target a set of grades 3–5 CCSS ELA/Literacy standards?

Y   N   2. Does the lesson include a clear and explicit purpose for instruction?

Y   N   3. Is the lesson planned to build both students' content knowledge and their understanding of reading and writing in social studies, the arts, and science or technical subjects?

Text Selection

Y   N   4. Does the lesson include a text within the grade-level text complexity band that presents vocabulary, syntax, text structures, levels of meaning/purpose, and other qualitative characteristics similar to those of the CCSS grade-level exemplars in Appendixes A and B? (Grade 3 is the high end of the text complexity band for grades 2–3. Grade 4 is the low end of the grades 4–5 text complexity band with scaffolding provided. Grade 5 is the high end of the grades 4–5 text complexity band.)

INSTRUCTIONAL FOCUS

Y N 5. Is the lesson planned to integrate two or more standards so that students apply and synthesize their advancing literacy skills?

Y N 6. Is the lesson planned to cultivate students' interest and engagement in reading, writing, or speaking about texts?

Y N 7. Is the lesson planned to provide for authentic learning, application of literacy skills, and student-directed inquiry, analysis, evaluation, and reflection?

Y N 8. Does the lesson provide supports where necessary but gradually remove them, requiring students to demonstrate their independent capacities?

KEY AREAS FOR INSTRUCTION

Does the lesson focus on at least *one* of these key areas of instruction in the ELA CCSS?

Y N 9. Does the lesson focus on reading text closely, examining textual evidence, and discerning deep meaning?

Y N 10. Does the lesson focus on facilitating a rich and rigorous evidence-based discussion through a sequence of specific, thought-provoking, and text-dependent questions (including, when applicable, illustrations, charts, diagrams, audio/video, and media)?

Y N 11. Does the lesson focus on students drawing evidence from the text to produce clear and coherent writing that informs, explains, or supports an opinion in various written forms (e.g., notes, summaries, short responses, formal essays)?

Y N 12. Does the lesson focus on building students' academic vocabulary in context?

RESPONSIVENESS TO VARIED STUDENT LEARNING NEEDS

Y N 13. Does the lesson provide *all* students with multiple opportunities to engage with texts of appropriate complexity for the grade level and include appropriate scaffolding so that students correctly experience the complexity of the texts?

Y N 14. Does the lesson integrate appropriate supports in reading, writing, and/or listening and speaking for students who are English language learners, have disabilities, or read well below the grade-level text band?

Y N 15. Does the lesson provide extensions and/or more advanced text for students who read well above the grade-level text band?

ASSESSMENTS

Y N 16. Do assessments align with the purpose of the lesson (pre-, formative, summative, or self-assessment)?

Y N 17. Do assessments in the lesson assess student proficiency using methods that are unbiased and accessible to all students?

Y N 18. Do assessments in the lesson include aligned rubrics or assessment guidelines that provide sufficient guidance for interpreting student performance?

Y N 19. Do assessments in the lesson elicit direct, observable evidence of the degree to which a student can independently demonstrate the major targeted grade-level CCSS standards with appropriately complex texts?

Note: Adapted from *EQuIP rubric for lessons and units: ELA/Literacy (grades 3–5) and ELA (grades 6–12)* (Achieve, 2013).

Integrating the Language Arts/Literacy Standards in the Content Areas

WE DON'T NEED 100 EYES LIKE ARGOS, the mythical Greek giant, to see that knowledge of myths and mythology is an important part of the Literature Standards at grades 3, 4, and 5. In particular, Reading Literature Standard 4 for fourth grade states, "Determine the meaning of words and phrases as they are used in a text, including those that allude to significant characters found in mythology (e.g., Herculean)" (NGA & CCSSO, 2010, p. 12). Because of these specific

Kelly Sraj Toms

expectations for knowledge of mythology at fourth grade, this chapter contains a sample thematic unit of study on the topic. The unit "Rock Stars of the Sky!" is based on the topic of Greek and Roman mythology, and it integrates related concepts from intermediate science and social studies. Integration of concepts across the content areas helps students build knowledge.

Building Knowledge Through Thematic Instruction

GIVING STUDENTS ACCESS TO A COLLECTION OF RESOURCES on one topic helps them meet the English Language Arts (ELA) Common Core State Standards (CCSS) and build knowledge, as stated in the standards document:

> Building knowledge systematically in English language arts is like giving children various pieces of a puzzle in each grade that, over time, will form one big picture. At a curricular or instructional level, texts—within and across grade levels—need to be selected around topics or themes that systematically develop the knowledge base of students. Within a grade level, there should be an adequate number of titles on a single topic that would allow children to study that topic for a sustained period. (NGA & CCSSO, 2010, p. 33)

To look for resources on Greek mythology is to get lost in an array of riches, and gathering resources for this unit is no exception. A number of websites and books are dedicated to teachers who plan to teach mythology—for instance, the website Mythology Teacher.com (www.mythologyteacher.com)—and many others are intended for children who are studying Greek and Roman mythology. The Bibliography section at the end of the unit provides an extensive list of resources for this theme, and only materials applicable for grades 3–5 have been included. Many more resources are available, as well.

The language arts concepts in this unit can be taught across the daily curriculum, or teachers can choose to connect only two or more subject areas. Detailed descriptions or examples of the teaching strategies mentioned have been provided in previous chapters of this book.

Integrating the CCSS

THE UNIT "ROCK STARS OF THE SKY!" CAN be adapted for students in grades 3–5, but in terms of the ELA Standards, the focus in this chapter is on the fourth grade. All of the strands of the ELA Standards are included in this unit: Reading Literature, Reading Informational Text, Reading Foundational Skills, Writing, Speaking and Listening, and Language. In addition, the unit is integrated with a basic exploration of astronomy and its relationship to the names of planets and constellations, which will prepare students for more in-depth study of earth and space science. Many of the names from Roman mythology are modern names for planets and constellations. Similarly, a number of words we use every day are from mythology. In this unit, there is a special focus on vocabulary words that are derived from Greek and Roman mythology. The unit is also integrated with social studies, addressing how myths were created by ancient Greeks to explain the world around them and how the Romans adopted the myths but renamed the major characters.

To motivate students to learn about Greek myths, we begin with read-alouds of two humorous picture books about the gods and goddesses of Olympus: *Z Is for Zeus* (Wilbur, 2008) and *Mount Olympus Basketball* (O'Malley, 2003). Students love humor, and these books introduce the Greek gods and goddesses in a light-hearted way.

For intermediate students, the unit then moves to the novel *The Lightning Thief* (Percy Jackson and the Olympians Series 1) (Riordan, 2005). This novel has a Lexile level of 740L, putting it in the middle of the current Lexile band for grades 4–5, and at the low end of the "stretch" Lexile band for the same grades. However, when we consider the reader and the task—another component of text complexity—*The Lightning Thief* may not be appropriate for a particular group of students unless we provide support. Providing a combination of read-alouds and independent student reading with appropriate learning supports (e.g., collaborative discussions, technology, art, and drama) should help all students enjoy the story and learn the references to Greek myths. To differentiate for reading level and interest, consider two other books: *It's All Greek to Me* (Time Warp Trio) (Scieszka, 1999), which is in the grades 2–3 text complexity band and has a Lexile level of 530L, and *Pandora Gets Jealous* (Hennesy, 2008), which is geared for girls in the grades 4–5 text complexity band and has a Lexile level of 840L.

Teaching about Greek myths and their influence on modern life in a fun and exciting way opens a world of possibilities for students' vocabulary development, reading comprehension, knowledge about astronomy and democracy, and future academic endeavors. As Jerome Bruner, renowned cognitive psychologist once said, "Any subject can be taught effectively in some intellectually honest form to any child at any stage of development" (Bruner, 1960, p. 33). Please take from this unit what is appropriate for your students, and have fun learning together!

Rock Stars of the Sky!

TOPIC: Greek mythology in literature

GRADE LEVEL: Intermediate

DURATION: 3–4 weeks

CROSS-CURRICULAR SUBJECTS: Science, History/Social Studies

ENDURING UNDERSTANDING: Mythology has had a lasting influence on many aspects of human life.

ESSENTIAL UNDERSTANDINGS

1. The Ancient Greeks created myths to explain concepts in the world they didn't understand.
2. The Ancient Romans adopted Greek myths but often changed the names of characters and places.
3. Greek mythology has influenced the English language and modern life.
4. References to Greek and Roman myths can be found when studying about the universe in earth and space science.

GUIDING QUESTIONS

1. How did ancient humans use myths to understand the world around them?
2. How have Greek and Roman myths influenced the English language?
3. How are Greek and Roman myths connected to earth and space science?

ELA STANDARDS NGA & CCSSO (2010)

After completing this unit, students will be able to do the following:

Reading: Literature

RL.4.1:   Refer to details and examples in a text when explaining what the text says explicitly and when drawing inferences from the text.

RL.4.2:   Determine a theme of a story, drama, or poem from details in the text; summarize the text.

RL.4.4:   Determine the meaning of words and phrases as they are used in a text, including those that allude to significant characters found in mythology (e.g., Herculean).

RL.4.9:   Compare and contrast the treatment of similar themes and topics (e.g., opposition of good and evil) and patterns of events (e.g., the quest) in stories, myths, and traditional literature from different cultures.

Reading: Informational Text

RI.4.1:   Refer to details and examples in a text when explaining what the text says explicitly and when drawing inferences from the text.

RI.4.2:   Determine the main idea of a text and explain how it is supported by key details; summarize the text.

RI.4.4:   Determine the meaning of general academic and domain-specific words or phrases in a text relevant to a *grade 4 topic or subject area*.

RI.4.7:   Interpret information presented visually, orally, or quantitatively (e.g., in charts, graphs, diagrams, time lines, animations, or interactive elements on Web pages) and explain how the information contributes to an understanding of the text in which it appears.

Reading: Foundational Skills

RF.4.4b: Read on-level prose and poetry orally with accuracy, appropriate rate, and expression on successive readings.

Writing

W.4.2:   Write informative/explanatory texts to examine a topic and convey ideas and information clearly.

W.4.7:   Conduct short research projects that build knowledge through investigation of different aspects of a topic.

W.4.8:   Recall relevant information from experiences or gather relevant information from print and digital sources; take notes and categorize information, and provide a list of sources.

W.4.9:   Draw evidence from literary or informational texts to support analysis, reflection, and research.

Speaking and Listening

SL.4.1:   Engage effectively in a range of collaborative discussions (one-on-one, in groups, and teacher-led) with diverse partners on *grade 4 topics and texts,* building on others' ideas and expressing their own clearly.

SL.4.2:   Paraphrase portions of a text read aloud or information presented in diverse media and formats, including visually, quantitatively, and orally.

SL.4.4:   Report on a topic or text, tell a story, or recount an experience in an organized manner, using appropriate facts and relevant, descriptive details to support main ideas or themes; speak clearly at an understandable pace.

SL.4.5:   Add audio recordings and visual displays to presentations when appropriate to enhance the development of main ideas or themes.

Language

L.4.1:   Demonstrate command of the conventions of standard English grammar and usage when writing or speaking.

L.4.2:   Demonstrate command of the conventions of standard English capitalization, punctuation, and spelling when writing.

L.4.4c: Consult reference materials (e.g., dictionaries, glossaries, thesauruses), both print and digital, to find the pronunciation and determine or clarify the precise meaning of key words and phrases.

L.4.6:   Acquire and use accurately grade-appropriate general academic and domain-specific words and phrases, including those that signal precise actions, emotions, or states of being (e.g., *quizzed, whined, stammered*) and that are basic to a particular topic (e.g., *wildlife, conservation,* and *endangered* when discussing animal preservation).

SCIENCE CONNECTIONS

Next Generation Science Standards Framework

The Next Generation Science Standards were developed to provide a set of standards arranged in a coherent manner across disciplines and grades to provide all students an internationally-benchmarked science education (NGSS, 2013). Disciplinary Core Ideas entitled "The Universe and Its Stars" and "Earth and the Solar System" are currently placed at the fifth-grade level in the Next Generation Science Standards. The related science experiences in this fourth-grade unit are meant to enhance students' curiosity about Greek and Roman mythology, help students understand connections among concepts, and build knowledge to pique interest and prepare students for more in-depth study of earth and space science.

SOCIAL STUDIES CONNECTIONS

NCSS Curriculum Standards for Social Studies

The National Council for the Social Studies (NCSS) has issued the National Curriculum Standards for Social Studies (2010). Considered a framework for teaching, learning, and assessment, the NCSS Standards are based on 10 themes. The social studies experiences in this unit align with two of those themes:

1. **Culture:** Social studies programs should include experiences that provide for the study of culture and cultural diversity. Students should learn that human beings create, learn, and adapt to culture, and that cultures are dynamic and change over time.

2. **Time, Continuity, and Change:** Social studies programs should include experiences that provide for the study of the past and its legacy. Students should learn that studying the past makes it possible for us to understand the human story across time and the ways in which human beings have viewed themselves, their societies, and the wider world at different periods in time. (NCSS, 2010)

UNIT SCHEDULE

The following unit schedule follows the suggested classroom schedule introduced in Chapter 7. The schedule describes activities in which teachers can engage students to meet the listed standards. Teachers should use professional judgment about which activities to choose and how often to plan for these activities in the classroom.

Week 1
Days 1–2: Unit Introduction (CCSS SL.4.2, RL.3.1, RL.4.9)
The teacher will read aloud *Z Is for Zeus* (Wilbur, 2008) and *Mount Olympus Basketball* (O'Malley 2003) to create interest about Greek gods and goddesses. Students will generate questions about Greek myths, gods, and goddesses.   As a follow-up, encourage students to use the Trading Card Creator, an interactive tool on the website ReadWriteThink (http://www.readwritethink.org). Students create trading cards of their favorite gods and goddesses and can compare and contrast the information on the cards.
Days 3–5: Read-Aloud (CCSS SL.4.1, SL.4.2)
Using *The Treasury of Greek Mythology: Classic Stories of Gods, Goddesses, Heroes, and Monsters* (Napoli, 2011) or another collection (see Bibliography), the teacher will read aloud major Greek myths (especially those about the 12 main gods and goddesses) and identify words that relate to the planets and major constellations. Students will discuss the story by expressing opinions and supporting them with information from the story.
Writing Skill Lessons (CCSS R.4.9, W.4.2)
The teacher will demonstrate how to write an informative/explanatory paragraph using the Paragraph Hamburger graphic organizer. Information about using this strategy and templates of the graphic organizer are available on the Reading Rockets website (www.readingrockets.org/strategies/paragraph_hamburger).   Students will begin a "Mythology Rock Stars!" notebook (physical or electronic). Each student will describe a selected myth or mythological character in a written informational paragraph and provide a sketch, as well.
Reading Lessons (CCSS RL.3.1, RL.4.2, RL.4.4, SL.4.1 SL.4.2)
Students will read Greek myths (especially those about the 12 main gods and goddesses) and review words that relate to the planets and major constellations. The teacher will demonstrate how to approach a complex text by thinking aloud (Davey, 1983). Students will practice thinking aloud.

Week 1 (continued)

Students will participate in the Paired Questioning strategy (McLaughlin & Allen, 2009) by working with partners. Each student will read to a designated stopping place and then ask his or her partner a question about the passage.

Vocabulary (CCSS RL.4.4, L.4.4c)

The teacher will demonstrate how to search for the meaning of a word that comes from Greek or Roman mythology (see list of words at end of unit) by using text features (e.g., the table of contents, index, hyperlinks) and reference materials (e.g., dictionaries, glossaries, and thesauruses). Students will practice searching for words related to the unit.

Science Connections (CCSS RI.4.7, W.4.7, W.4.8)

Using the informational book *13 Planets: The Latest View of the Solar System* (Aguilar, 2011), students will learn facts about one planet per day throughout the unit. Students will take virtual field trips to explore planets and constellations using websites recommended for children by the National Aeronautics and Space Administration (NASA) and a virtual telescope (see list of websites in Bibliography).

Students will take notes to collect information and then write paragraph summaries of their findings.

Social Studies Connections (CCSS RI.4.2, SL.4.1, SL.4.2)

The teacher will introduce an informational text appropriate for intermediate students on ancient Greece (see Bibliography). Students will read selected brief passages about the how the ancient Greeks lived, with a special emphasis on the Greeks' belief in gods and goddesses. Students will determine the main idea and key details of each paragraph.

Students will create artwork for a classroom art show that illustrates how the ancient Greeks used myths to explain the world. Each student's artwork should explore this question: How did myths influence the culture of the ancient Greeks?

Novel Study/Collaborative Discussion (CCSS R.L.4.1, SL.4.1)

The teacher will introduce *The Lightning Thief* (Riordan, 2005) by having students participate in a five-minute Reader's Theater based on the first chapter (available online at http://www.rickriordan.com).

Throughout the unit, students will read chapters and participate in whole-class collaborative discussions and Literature Circle discussions (Daniels, 1994) about Percy Jackson's adventures with the characters of Greek mythology. More educational activities related to *The Lightning Thief* are available on Rick Riordan's website (www.rickriordan.com).

Week 2

Read-Aloud (CCSS RL.4.2, RL.4.4, SL.4.1, SL.4.2)

Using *The Treasury of Greek Mythology: Classic Stories of Gods, Goddesses, Heroes, and Monsters* (Napoli, 2011) or another collection (see Bibliography), the teacher will continue to read aloud major Greek myths (especially those about the 12 main gods and goddesses) and identify words that relate to the planets and major constellations. Students will participate in collaborative discussions about the myths.

Week 2 (continued)

Writing (CCSS W.4.2, W.4.4, W.4.5, W.4.6)

The teacher will instruct students in how to write an essay using the Painted Essay strategy for elementary students described by the Vermont Writing Collaborative (http://vtwritingcollaborative.org/Essay.html). Each student should follow a writing process to produce an essay ready for publication.

Students will continue writing in their "Mythology Rock Stars!" notebooks. Each student will describe a selected myth or character in a written informational paragraph and provide a sketch, as well.

Reading Lesson (CCSS RL.4.1, W.4.2, W.4.9)

Students will do a close reading of a Greek myth. After discussing text-dependent questions, students will dramatize the myth to visualize it. Each student will write a paragraph analyzing the myth.

Vocabulary (CCSS RI.4, L.4.4c)

Each student will choose a word or phrase that comes from Greek or Roman mythology (see list of words at end of unit). Using books in the classroom, as well as websites and reference materials, each will research his or her word to determine its origin.

Science Connections (CCSS RI.4.7)

Using *13 Planets: The Latest View of the Solar System* (Aguilar, 2011), students will continue to learn facts about one planet per day. Each student will begin an "Electronic Alphabet Book" (McLaughlin & Allen, 2009) to document facts related to the topic of planets.

Social Studies Connections (CCSS RI.4.7, W.4.7, W.4.8, W.4.9)

Students will work in small groups to participate in a WebQuest about life in ancient Greece. Guidelines for conducting a WebQuest on this topic are available on the website Mythology Teacher. com (http://www.mythologyteacher.com/Ancient-Greece-Webquest.php).

At the end of the WebQuest, students will compare and contrast ways that life in ancient Greece is similar to and different from modern life in the United States (e.g., "Girls go to school today in the U.S.; girls did not go to school in ancient Greece"). Students should record their ideas on the interactive Venn diagram that is available at the website ReadWriteThink (http://www.readwritethink.org).

Independent Reading/Collaborative Discussion (CCSS R.L.4.1, SL.4.1)

The class will continue reading and discussing *The Lightning Thief* (Riordan, 2005).

Weeks 3 and 4

Read-Aloud (CCSS RL.4.2, RL.4.4, SL.4.1, SL.4.2)

Using *Treasury of Greek Mythology: Classic Stories of Gods, Goddesses, Heroes, and Monsters* (Napoli, 2011) or another collection (see Bibliography at the end of this unit), the teacher will continue to read aloud major Greek myths (especially those about the 12 main gods and goddesses) and review words that relate to the planets and major constellations.

Writing (CCSS RL.4.9, W.4.2, W.4.4, W.4.5, W.4.6)

Each student will write a Painted Essay to compare and contrast the themes in two myths. To plan these essays, students will use the Compare and Contrast Map student interactive on the website ReadWriteThink (www.readwritethink.org).

Students will continue their "Mythology Rock Stars!" notebooks. Each student will describe a selected myth or character in a written paragraph and draw a sketch, as well.

Week 3 and 4 (continued)

Reading Lessons (CCSS RL.4.2, RL.4.4, RF.4.4b, SL.4.1, SL.4.2)

Students will prepare and participate in a Reader's Theater production of a Greek myth using *Greek Myth Plays, Grades 3–5: 10 Readers Theater Scripts Based on Favorite Greek Myths That Students Can Read and Reread to Develop Their Fluency* (Pugliano-Martin, 2008). Students will work on reading fluently and with expression.

Vocabulary (CCSS RL.4.4, W.4.7, SL.4.4, SL.4.5, L.4.6)

The teacher will demonstrate how to make a PowerPoint Portrayal (Overturf, Montgomery, & Smith, 2013). Then each student will create a PowerPoint Portrayal of his or her chosen vocabulary word and present it to the class. Choosing a word that originates from a Greek or Roman myth, the student will describe the word's relationships to other words (e.g., synonyms, antonyms, connections), draw a picture that somehow represents the word, and write a summary of the myth the word comes from. For example, a presentation about the word *cereal* would include a slide showing the word, a slide providing the explanation (*Ceres* = Roman goddess of grain), a slide containing a drawing of a related Greek name (*Demeter* = Greek goddess of the harvest), a slide containing a few lines about the myth of Ceres, and a slide showing pictures of grain or cereal.

Science Connections (CCSS RI.4.2, W.4.7, W.4.8)

In small groups, students will create models of the solar system based on what they have learned, presenting the sun, eight planets, and dwarf planet in the correct order and at the appropriate relative sizes. Students will also create a label for each planet that summarizes the most important information.

Social Studies Connections (CCSS RI.4.1, W.4.2)

Students will participate in a close reading on a passage about the history of the Olympic Games. After discussing text-dependent questions, students will dramatize an event from the reading.

Students will then use the Paragraph Hamburger graphic organizer to write informative paragraphs about what they learned about the history of the Olympic Games from the reading.

Independent Reading/Collaborative Discussion (CCSS R.L.4.1, SL.4.1)

The class will continue reading and discussing *The Lightning Thief* (Riordan, 2005).

ASSESSMENT AND EVALUATION

Both formal and informal assessments should be used throughout the unit of study. Examples of formal assessments include analyzing students' projects and presentations, formal writings, research-related products, and quiz scores. Examples of informal or formative assessment include observations of student participation (e.g., contributions and questions in discussions about texts) and informal analyses of student writing (through conferencing), completed strategy applications, artworks, and so on.

Culminating Assessment

The culminating assessment for the unit of study should require students to develop answers to the guiding questions posed at the beginning of the unit:

1. How did ancient humans use myths to understand the world around them?

2. How have Greek and Roman myths influenced the English language?

3. How are Greek and Roman myths connected to space science?

Each student will use his or her "Mythology Rock Stars!" notebook and other resources to demonstrate his or her learning from the unit of study by writing an organized paragraph in response to each question. Each paragraph should include a sentence that introduces the question, several sentences that provide facts (evidence), and a closing sentence. A polished paragraph will include expressive language when appropriate and accurate spelling, punctuation, grammar, and usage.

Needs of particular students should be taken into account in this culminating assessment. Students should be allowed to demonstrate their learning in other ways, if desirable.

POSSIBLE EXTENSION ACTIVITIES

- Use the Greek alphabet to write a friendly letter in code. (See the resources available on Mr. Donn's Social Studies Site: http://greece.mrdonn.org/alphabet.html.)
- Write your own Greek myth.
- Create a Greek monster. Make a model and create a museum display.
- Write and perform an original Reader's Theater script based on a Greek myth.
- Do some of the extension activities on the NASA websites—for instance, calculate what you would weigh on a different planet or construct a spacecraft. (See the list of websites in the unit Bibliography.)
- Create a model of a Greek city.
- Use an animation program and animate an event from the original Olympic Games. (Make sure the athletes wear clothes!)
- Use an online comic creation program to create a comic about a Greek myth. (See the student interactive lesson Comic Creator on the ReadWriteThink website: www .readwritethink.org.)

CULMINATING ACTIVITY

Students invite family and friends to a "Rock Stars of the Sky!" event. Students should make invitations and help plan the event. At the event, students can do the following:

- Perform a Reader's Theater version of a Greek myth. (Another option is to digitally record the drama at an earlier time and then show it at the event.)
- Present PowerPoint Portrayals of vocabulary words.
- Ask family members to attend the classroom art show.
- Display "Mythology Rock Stars!" notebooks.
- Present the "Electronic Alphabet Books" via a projector that scrolls continually through the students' books.
- Display the models of the solar system.
- Share writing projects, such as the paragraphs comparing and contrasting two myths.
- Display the culminating assessment paragraphs.
- Share extension projects.

At the event, serve theme-related refreshments, including Planet Pies (pizza), ambrosia (ice cream), and nectar (juice). If the event is held at night, have a local astronomy buff set up a telescope outside. Invite guests to observe the night sky and have students share their knowledge about the sky and where planets and constellations got their names.

Most of all, have fun! Students need to become college and career-ready, and they should also learn the joy of learning.

BIBLIOGRAPHY

Greek Mythology

Alexander, H. (2011). *A child's introduction to Greek mythology: The story of the gods, goddesses, heroes, monsters, and other mythical creatures.* New York, NY: Black Dog & Leventhal.

Aliki. (1997). *The gods and goddesses of Olympus.* New York, NY: HarperCollins.

Bryant, M. E. (2009). *Oh my gods! A look-it-up guide to the gods of mythology (Mythlopedia).* Danbury, CT: Franklin Watts.

Bryant, M. E. (2009). *She's all that! A look-it-up guide to the goddesses of mythology (Mythlopedia).* Danbury, CT: Franklin Watts.

Byrd, R. (2005). *The hero and the minotaur: The fantastic adventures of Theseus.* New York, NY: Dutton Children's Books.

Craft, C. (1999). *King Midas and the golden touch.* New York, NY: Morrow Junior Books.

D'Aulaire, I., & D'Aulaire, E .P. (1962). *Book of Greek myths.* New York, NY: Delacorte Press.

Freeman, P. (2012). *Oh my gods: A modern retelling of Greek and Roman myths.* New York, NY: Simon & Schuster.

Hoena, B. A. (2003). *Athena.* Mankato, MN: Capstone Press.

Hoena, B. A. (2003). *Zeus.* Mankato, MN: Capstone Press.

Kelly, S. (2009). *What a beast! A look-it-up guide to the monsters and mutants of mythology (Mythlopedia).* Danbury, CT: Franklin Watts.

Kimmel, E. A. (2008). *The McElderry book of Greek myths.* New York, NY: Margaret K. McElderry Books.

Lattimore, D. N. (2000). *Medusa.* New York, NY: Joanna Cotler Books.

Napoli, D. J. (2011). *The treasury of Greek mythology: Classic stories of gods, goddesses, heroes & monsters.* Washington, DC: National Geographic Society.

Nardo, D. (2012). *The heroes and mortals of Greek mythology.* Mankato, MN: Compass Point Books.

Nardo, D., & Steffans, B. (2005). *Monsters: Cyclops.* Farmington Hills, MI: Kidhaven Press.

Otfinoski, S. (2009). *All in the family: A look-it-up guide to the in-laws, outlaws, and offspring of mythology (Mythlopedia).* Danbury, CT: Franklin Watts.

Ancient Greece

Chrisp, P. (2003). *Ancient Greece revealed.* New York, NY: Dorling Kindersley.

Hynson, C. (2009). *How people lived in ancient Greece.* New York, NY: Rosen Group.

McGee, M. (2007). *National Geographic investigates ancient Greece: Archaeology unlocks the secrets of Greece's past.* Washington, DC: National Geographic Society.

Peppas, L. (2005). *Life in ancient Greece.* New York, NY: Crabtree.

Steele, P. (2011). *Ancient Greece.* New York, NY: Kingfisher.

Tames, R. (2009). *Passport to the past: Ancient Greece.* New York, NY: Rosen Group.

Related Resources

Florian, D. (2007). *Comets, stars, the moon, and Mars: Space poems and paintings.* Orlando, FL: HMH Books for Young Readers.

Gamewright. (2006). *Zeus on the loose: A card game of mythic proportions, ages 8 and up.* Newton, MA: Author.

Hennesy, C. (2008). *Pandora gets jealous.* New York, NY: Bloomsburg Books.

Hoffman, M., & Ray, J. (1998). *Sun, moon, and stars.* New York, NY: Dutton Children's Books.

O'Malley, K. (2003). *Mount Olympus basketball.* New York, NY: Walker.

Pugliano-Martin, C. (2008). *Greek myth plays, grades 3–5: 10 readers theater scripts based on favorite Greek myths that students can read and reread to develop their fluency.* New York, NY: Scholastic Teaching Resources.

Reynolds, S. (2006). *The first marathon: The legend of Pheidippides.* Morton Grove, IL: Albert Whitman.

Richardson, A.D. (2003). *Hercules.* Mankato, MN: Capstone Press.

Riordan, R. (2005). *The lightning thief* (Percy Jackson and the Olympians Series 1). New York, NY: Hyperion.

Scieszka, J. (1999). *It's all Greek to me* (Time Warp Trio). New York, NY: Puffin Books.

Sis, P. (2000). *Starry Messenger: Galileo Galilei.* New York, NY: Square Fish.

Wilbur, H. L. (2008). *Z Is for Zeus: A Greek Mythology Alphabet.* Ann Arbor, MI: Sleeping Bear Press.

Worth-Baker, M. (2005). *Greek mythology activities, grades 5 and up.* New York, NY: Scholastic.

Space Science (Focus on the Solar System and Constellations)

Aguilar, D. A. (2011). *Super stars: The biggest, hottest, brightest, most explosive stars in the Milky Way (plus black holes, brown dwarfs, constellations, and more).* Washington, DC: National Geographic Society.

Aguilar, D. A. (2011). *13 planets: The latest view of the solar system.* Washington, DC: National Geographic Society.

Apfel, N. H. (1995). *Orion, the hunter.* New York, NY: Clarion Books.

Banqueri, E. (2007). *Field guides: The night sky.* New York, NY: Enchanted Lion Books.

Carson, M. K. (2011). *Far-out guide to Jupiter.* Berkeley Heights, NJ: Bailey Books.

Driscoli, M. (2004). *A child's introduction to the night sky: The story of the stars, planets, and constellations-and how you can find them in the sky.* New York, NY: Black Dog & Leventhal.

Halpern, P. (2004). *Faraway worlds: Planets beyond our solar system.* Watertown, MA: Charlesbridge.

Jefferis, D. (2009). *Star spotters: Telescopes and observatories.* New York, NY: Crabtree.

Kerrod, R. (1998). *Astronomy: A fascinating fact file and learn-it-yourself project book.* Milwaukee, WI: Gareth Stevens.

Leedy, L., & Schuerger, A. (2006). *Messages from Mars.* New York, NY: Holiday House.

Rusch, E. (2012). *The mighty Mars Rover: The incredible adventures of Spirit and Opportunity.* Boston, MA: Houghton Mifflin Books for Children.

Simon, S. (2000). *Destination: Mars.* New York, NY: HarperCollins.

Magazines

Each magazine website provides a means of subscribing, plus free online versions of some content.

Kids Discover (www.kidsdiscover.com)

National Geographic Explorer (http://ngexplorer.cengage.com/pathfinder)—Search the archives for articles about space, ancient Greece, and so on.

TIME for Kids (www.timeforkids.com)—Search the online magazine for articles about space, Greece, and mythology.

Websites

Ancient Greece and Mythology

Kidipede: History for Kids—Ancient Greece for Kids (www.historyforkids.org/learn/greeks/index.htm (articles print without ads)

MythMania (www.mythman.com)—Myths told with a modern flare; the "Homework Help" section is particularly helpful.

Mythweb (www.mythweb.com/gods/index.html)

National Geographic Kids—Quiz Your Noodle: Greek Myths (http://kids.nationalgeographic.com/kids/
games/puzzlesquizzes/quizyournoodle-greek-myths/)—A quiz on the Greek characters in the
Percy Jackson story.

Starfall: Greek Myths (www.starfall.com/n/level-c/greek-myths/load.htm?)—A collection of easy-to-
read myths.

Storynory (http://www.storynory.com/category/educational-and-entertaining-stories/greek-myths)—
Greek myths read aloud.

Theoi Greek Mythology (www.theoi.com/greek-mythology/olympian-gods.html)—Classical literature
and artwork about mythology.

Stars and Constellations

Astronomy for Kids (www.frontiernet.net/~kidpower/astronomy.html)

NASA: Solar System Exploration (http://solarsystem.nasa.gov/kids/index.cfm)

NASA: Star Child (http://starchild.gsfc.nasa.gov/docs/StarChild/StarChild.html)

NASA: Star Finder (http://spaceplace.nasa.gov/starfinder/redirected)

neoK12: Solar System (www.neok12.com/Solar-System.htm)

Oracle ThinkQuest: Constellations—Virtual Telescope (http://library.thinkquest.org/3645/
constellations.html)

VOCABULARY: Familiar Words and Phrases with Greek and Roman Origins

Achilles' heel

amazon

atlas

cereal

chaos

chronological

echo

fates

Herculean

hypnosis

Midas touch

museum

nemesis

Nike

Olympics

Pandora's box

promethean

tantalize

titanic

volcano

Other lists of words derived from Greek and Roman mythology are available at these websites:

Your Dictionary: Greek Language: Roots of English Words in Greek Mythology (http://reference.
yourdictionary.com/resources/roots-english-words-greek-mythology.html)

An Etymological Dictionary of Classical Mythology (http://library.oakland.edu/information/people/
personal/kraemer/edcm/index.html)

REFERENCES

Bruner, J. (1960). *The process of education.* Cambridge, MA: Harvard University Press.

Committee on a Conceptual Framework for New K–12 Science Education Standards, Board on Science Education, Division of Behavioral and Social Sciences and Education, National Research Council. (2012). *A framework for K–12 science education: Practices, crosscutting concepts, and core ideas.* Washington, DC: National Academies Press. Retrieved from http://www.nap.edu/openbook.php?record_id=13165.

Daniels, H. (1994). *Literature circles: Voice and choice in the student-centered classroom.* York, ME: Stenhouse.

Davey, B. (1983). Think aloud: Modeling the cognitive processes of reading comprehension. *Journal of Reading, 27*(1), 44–47.

McLaughlin, M., & Allen, M. (2009). *Guided comprehension in grades 3–8* (comb. 2nd ed.). Newark, DE: International Reading Association.

National Council for the Social Studies (NCSS). (2010). *National curriculum standards for social studies.* Washington, DC: Author. Retrieved from http://www.socialstudies.org/standards/strands.

National Governors Association Center for Best Practices & Council of Chief State School Officers (NGA & CCSSO). (2010). *Common Core State Standards: English language arts and literacy in history/social studies, science, and technical subjects.* Washington, DC: Authors. Retrieved from http://www.corestandards.org/assets/CCSSI_ELA%20Standards.pdf.

Overturf, B. J., Montgomery, L., & Smith, M. H. (2013). *Word nerds: Teaching all students to learn and love vocabulary.* Portland, ME: Stenhouse.

Index

Credits

Introduction Chapter: Pearson Education; **p. 16 (bulleted list):** Based on Double Jeopardy: How Third-Grade Reading Skills and Poverty Influence High School Graduation. 2012. The Annie E. Casey Foundation; **p. 23 (Tips):** Reprinted with permission from Leslie Montgomery; **p. 23 (photo):** Leslie Montgomery Leslie Montgomery; **p. 35 (Figure 2.1):** Hasbrouck, Jan and Tindal, Gerald (2013). Fluency Norms Chart. WETA; **p. 38 (Tips):** Reprinted with permission from Melissa Durham; **p. 38 (photo):** Leslie Montgomery; **pp. 46, 52, 74, 98, 122, 126, 150, 156, 158, 160, 184, 186, 188 (www.readwritethink .org URLs):** Reprinted with permission by International Reading Association, Delaware. © 2014 IRA/ NCTE. All rights reserved; **p. 48 (Figure 2.4):** Kucan, Linda (2007). *The Reading Teacher,* 60(6). International Reading Association (IRA); **p. 51 (wordle.net URL):** Wordle; **p. 55 (block quotation):** Leahy, Siobhan et al., (2013.). *Educational Leadership,* 63 (3). Association for Supervision and Curriculum Development (ASCD); **p. 62 (Tips):** Reprinted with permission from Margot Smith; **p. 62 (photo):** Leslie Montgomery; **p. 66 (cdl.org URL):** Center for Developmental Learning; **p. 68: (shakespeare-online.com URL):** Shakespeare Online; **p. 79 (freerice.com URL):** © 2007–2013 World Food Programme. All Rights Reserved; **p. 79 (vocabulary.co.il URLs):** Copyright © 2013 www.vocabulary.co.il; **p. 79 (simplek12 .com URL):** Copyright © 2000–2013 InfoSource, Inc.; **p. 79 (eduscapes.com URL):** © 2003–2011 Annette Lamb; **pp. 84–85 (numbered list):** Reprinted with permission from Elfrieda H. Hiebert; **pp. 85, 86 (lexile.com URL):** © 2013 MetaMetrics. All rights reserved; **p. 86 (renlearn.com URL):** **Renaissance** Learning, Inc.; **p. 86 (readingmaturity.com URL):** Pearson Education; **p. 86 (questarai URL):** © 2013 Questar Assessment, Inc. All Rights Reserved; **pp. 89–93 (Figures 4.2–4.3):** Achieve the Core; **p. 94 (ksde.org URL):** Copyright June 19, 2008 © KSDE; **p. 99 (Figure 4.6):** Reprinted with permission by International Reading Association, Delaware; **p. 100 (guysread.com URL):** Guys Read. All Rights Reserved; **p. 102 (Tips):** Reprinted with permission from Leslie Montgomery; **p. 102 (photo):** Cassaundra L. Watkins; **pp. 104–105 (Figure 4.8):** Achieve the Core; **p. 114 (Figure 5.1):** Reprinted with permission by Carnegie Corporation of New York; **p. 115 (Tips):** Reprinted with permission from Cassaundra L. Watkins; **p. 115 (photo):** Kelly Sraj Toms; **p. 123 (readworks.org URL):** © 2013 ReadWorks; **p. 126 (uen.org URL):** State of Utah Office of Education; **p. 126 (webenglishteacher.com URL):**webenglishteacher.com; **p. 135 (fablevisionlearning.com URL):** Copyright © 2014 FableVision Learning, LLC; **p. 135 (animoto.com URL):** Animoto Inc.; **p. 135 (goanimate4schools.com URL):** Go Animate 4 school; **p. 135: (Microsoft.com URL):** Microsoft Office; **p. 135 (storybird.com URL):** storybird.com; **p. 155 (Tips):** Reprinted with permission from Lonydea Todd; **pp. 156, 167 (reading.org URL):** © 1996–2013 International Reading Association. All rights reserved; **p. 164 (Tips):** Reprinted with permission from Taylor C. Haydock; **p. 164 (photo):** Leslie Montgomery; **p. 165 (bulleted list):** Reprinted with permission from International Reading Association; **p. 166 (k12center.org URL):** Educational Testing Service (ETS); **pp. 166–167 (corestandards.org URLs):** © Copyright 2010. National Governors Association Center for Best Practices and Council of Chief State School Officers. All rights reserved; **p. 167 (udlcenter.org URL):** © Copyright CAST, Inc. 2012; **p. 168 (achieve.org URL):** © 2013 Achieve, Inc. All rights reserved; **pp. 175–177 (checklist):** Adapted From Tri-State Quality Review Rubric for Lessons & Units: ELA/Literacy (Grades3–5) and ELA (Grades 6–12) Version 4. 2012. Achieve, Inc. **pp. 177–178 (checklist):** Adapted from Tri-State Quality Review Rubric for Lessons & Units: ELA/Literacy (Grades 3–5) and ELA (Grades 6–12) Version 4.1; **pp. 180, 186 (mythologyteacher .com URL):** Mythology Teacher; **pp. 183–184: (NCSS Standards):** National Council for the Social Studies; **p. 184 (readingrockets.org URL):** © Copyright 2013 WETA Washington, D.C.; **p. 185 (rickriordan.com URLs):** Rick Riordan; **p. 186 (vtwritingcollaborative.org URLs):** The Vermont Writing Collaborative; **p. 188 (greece.mrdonn.org URL):** Ancient Greece for Kids.